MICHEL REMERY

HOW TO
GROW IN FAITH

POWERED BY

Appeal for donations

If you can and wish to contribute financially to the initiatives *Tweeting with GOD* and *Online with Saints* we would be very grateful. You can transfer your donation via the website www.tweetingwithgod.com/donate or directly to the following bank account:

Bank: ING Bank
Account holder: JP2 Stichting Leiden
Mention: "Tweeting with GOD"
IBAN: NL31 INGB 0005717224
BIC/SWIFT: INGBNL2A

Address of the bank:
ING Bank NV Foreign Operations
P.O. Box 1800
NL-1000 BV Amsterdam
The Netherlands

The JP2 Foundation, based in Leiden, The Netherlands, was set up to cover the financial and contractual aspects of our projects. For its income, this nonprofit organisation depends entirely on the help of sponsors. All donations are used for funding our projects only. If you send us your address, you will receive a confirmation of your donation.

We thank you in advance for your generosity!

www.tweetingwithgod.com/donate

HOW TO
GROW IN FAITH

www.howtogrowinfaith.com

Nihil obstat: Rev Gerard Diamond MA (Oxon), LSS, D.Theol, diocesan censor
Imprimatur: Very Rev Joseph Caddy AM Lic.Soc.Sci VG, vicar general
Archdiocese of Melbourne, 13 July 2020

Developed by the makers of *Tweeting with GOD* and *Online with Saints*
www.tweetingwithgod.com | www.onlinewithsaints.com

Graphic design: G. Huguenin.

© 2020 Michel Remery & JP2 Stichting, Leiden. All rights reserved.
Published 2021 in the United States of America by Our Sunday Visitor
ISBN 978-1-68192-771-8

www.howtogrowinfaith.com

Preface

To grow in faith is the most important thing people can do in life. It means growing in a personal relationship with their God of love. And this growth has great and beautiful consequences, as I have experienced myself!

Tweeting with GOD and *Online with Saints* have given me the opportunity to visit many places and cultures across the whole world. In spite of the many obvious differences, I continue to be surprised how the world truly is a global village. Although the globalization supported by the economic, technical, and social media developments of recent years definitively contributes to bringing people together, I believe the main reason I experience the world as a global village is a completely different one.

Wherever I go, I am received by local people who let me be part of their lives for a few days. I share their joys, sorrows, worries, and hopes. Whatever their culture, language, and ethnic origin, they are in the first place children of the same Father in heaven. That is the sense in which I experience the world to be a global village, a village where everyone is connected by family ties. What brings us so close in the first place is our faith in the same God of love.

Therefore, to grow in faith means to grow in understanding of our family ties with God and with other people simultaneously. "No one lives for themselves," Saint Paul wrote (Rom 14:7). This course is intended as a joint adventure for people who are searching, questioning, doubting … and above all desiring to grow. They can be completely new to the faith or have many years of experience in their relationship with God. They can be seasoned teachers or beginning leaders. What they all have in common is the desire to grow in faith and help others to do so.

This book came into being thanks to the request of people from around the world who are using *Tweeting with GOD* and *Online with Saints* for faith formation in schools, parishes, communities, and many more circumstances. Some of them have been mentioned on the credits page, others preferred to remain quietly in the background. During the writing process of this book, I could always count on their feedback. Therefore, I would like to express a sincere a word of thanks to all who contributed to this book in any way!

The reader will see that this book has two parts. The first pages called "Getting started" (GS) introduce the approach, the course schedule, and give tips for moderating the meetings. The second part of the book describes how to go about the different meetings. May this book assist you in helping others to grow in faith – and advance in your personal relationship with God on the way.

Father Michel Remery

Table of Contents

Appendices

GS1 About this course

What if growing in faith were just as easy, natural, and contemporary as interacting on social media? *How to grow in faith* shows that it is just that! This course aims to provide participants with an opportunity to ask questions, search for answers together, and discover how God loves each of them very deeply. Every meeting begins with a question which helps the participants to explore their personal faith. This results in a very interactive program that challenges the participants to truly participate while searching together for answers that will reveal the truth about life, love and faith. It can be used for people of all ages and backgrounds (SEE GS2)

This is a detailed handbook for helping people to grow in faith. It covers all stages of the course: from the first meeting with the participants (and even their parents or spouses), to the detailed layout of every course meeting. The course is based on the content of the *Tweeting with GOD* book (#TwGOD), and the connected online resources, videos, mobile apps and social media (SEE GS4). A double page gives an overview of the meeting, followed by the detailed procedure and worksheets presenting interactive activities. Free downloads make the course complete (SEE GS4).

Flexibility

No need to have a Twitter account or other social media if you want to start *Tweeting with GOD*: you can be online with God anytime anywhere. The most important thing is to communicate with him and grow into a relationship. To speak about God, *Tweeting with GOD* employs a language which can be understood today. For this reason, it is used throughout the world for finding answers, faith formation and preparing for sacraments like Confirmation, Baptism, First Holy Communion, or Matrimony. *Online with Saints* adds to this the example of the saints, who are great companions on life's journey with God.

The very concept of *Tweeting with GOD* is flexibility: readers are not expected to read the book from cover to cover but can go directly to the question of their interest. The same is true for *How to grow in faith*. Feel free to adapt the proposed program to the needs of your group. Participants will be much more motivated if their own questions are addressed first. Do not hesi-

Working with this book

- The introductory pages called "Getting started" give an overview of the course and tips for moderation.
- References to Questions in the *Tweeting with GOD* book are indicated with "#TwGOD".
- The box "To prepare" on the "Procedure" page indicates what is needed for that particular meeting.
- Available downloads for the moderator are indicated with (DL).
- The appendices contain useful extra material for the moderator with tips for giving a testimony, interactive methods, praying with the Bible, other prayers, and content for extra meetings.

tate to leave the prepared theme until later in order to discuss some question raised by the participants. Several meetings are dedicated exclusively to their questions (SEE GS10).

Centrality of the participants

How to grow in faith is about engaging with the participants where they are at. They, not the course, are the central focus, and not even God in a doctrinal sense. The program seeks to help them on their life journey, starting with their experiences and their questions at this moment. Discovering the closeness of God and his desire to enter into a relationship with each of the participants will hopefully develop into a more intimate knowledge of God which is the basis for all personal faith!

No one can believe alone. Faith is all about a relationship with God and with others. The course will probably start off with individuals who do not know each other well. To offer them a safe environment to express their thoughts even when these are not yet fully developed, they will need to become a group, a community if you like. The questions and answers formulated by each of the participants are given due attention, together with peer-to-peer dialogue. Exercises that help the participants to relate in the group are part of every meeting, just as ways to support their asking or reflecting.

Dialogue and moderation

Dialogue within the group is an important element of this course's approach. During an open and free dialogue, participants will look for answers together. This is not a course in the traditional sense of the word, where the teacher is talking, and the students are listening. Rather is it the opposite: the participants are speaking, and the leader is merely moderating the discussion. Thus we speak consequently of the "moderator," who is not so much the teacher who knows everything, but the facilitator who accompanies the process. Ideally moderation is done by a team (SEE GS8).

GS2 Who is this for?

This course is designed for teenagers, young people and adults of all generations: those who are searching or doubting, those who do not know what to think, and those who have a certain relationship with God. Exploring and questioning the faith can start at any moment in life.

The course can be used by schools as a program for religious education, by communities as a catechetical program to grow in faith, or by parishes to support those preparing for the Sacraments of Confirmation or First Holy Communion, catechumens seeking Baptism (RCIA), or couples preparing for Marriage (SEE BOX). Think also of the personal development of teachers, health workers, social workers ... or as follow-up after introductory courses like the Alpha Course. *How to grow in faith* can be used in all these circumstances.

The beginning leader

Beginning leaders may experience some fear or doubt when having to lead a group. No worries! In this book, every exercise is explained in detail. All that is needed for the meeting is listed in a box, and suggestions are made as to what you could say at every point. Reading through the proposed material, together with the related pages in the *Tweeting with GOD* book, will equip the leader(s) to moderate the meeting and even to answer most questions about the theme. Everyone can be a great moderator with the help of the procedures of *How to grow in faith* and the guidance of the Holy Spirit!

....

Use it for Schools, Confirmation, RCIA, Marriage, Faith discussion ...

- **Religious Education at schools:** You can use the program during a semester or a term, optionally spreading the content of each meeting over two sessions of 50 to 60 minutes.

- **Confirmation program:** You can opt for a two-year course of one meeting a month, a more intensive course of one year, or even a three-year course adding some questions. Confirmation can take place after meeting 14, for example.

- **First Holy Communion, initiation of adults to the faith (RCIA), or Marriage preparation:** You can have regular meetings over a shorter period of time, following the content of the meetings for a full preparation course. Depending on the moment the sacrament(s) are received during the course program, there will be enough material for continuing after the sacrament (in RCIA the period of mystagogy).

- **Faith discussion group or faith formation:** You can opt for a term program, or spread the contents of the meetings over multiple years, possibly adding other questions from *Tweeting with GOD*. You can adapt the order of the meetings to comply with the needs of your group.

The seasoned teacher

Most seasoned teachers, professionals and catechists will not need the breakdown of every exercise and every question in detail: they know how to get a group to speak about a given topic. Therefore, every double introductory page to a meeting contains a box with the main questions of that particular meeting: "The gist of it." The seasoned teacher can take this framework and decide how to work towards the learning goal of the day, choosing whatever they deem best suited for their group from among activities and exercises.

Adults or teenagers?

Working with teenagers may seem daunting for some moderators who prefer to work with adults. But remember that the teens will be even more insecure. How often is a teenager seriously asked for their opinion, and how often is the one asking really interested in the answer? Teens simply are not (yet) used to being listened to! A teenager – even more than an adult – looks at the world from his or her own perspective. Life often seems to be a fight. As a result, the world is about themselves in the first place, and only then about themselves in relation to others. Paradoxically, teens are very concerned about others' opinions of them.

Although most adults will not admit it, most of this is true also for them! Whatever the age of the group, it is important to create a safe environment, and help everyone to understand that judgemental reactions to each other are not acceptable. Everyone should be able to voice any serious opinion – always presented in a way that avoids hurting others. Another key rule is that whatever is said during the meetings will not be spoken about elsewhere (SEE GS4).

GS3 Five keys for growing in faith

How to grow in faith seeks to help participants to find answers and develop a desire to be part of the life and mission of the Church community. The meetings intend to provide a space for the participants to not just ask questions, reflect and learn about the faith, but also pray, act with charity – and celebrate together:

1. **RELATE:** Yes, you can think about God and pray all by yourself. But your faith is not complete without sharing it with the brothers and sisters that God gave you. This also applies to our meetings. These are not just classes, but a place for each participant to grow in relationship with others and God. In every meeting special attention will be given to relating within the group.

2. **THINK:** Thinking and asking are fundamental for our lives. When you like someone, you want to know more about them. The more you love them, the more you want to know. Searching for answers to questions about God, life, and faith is not just an intellectual activity. It is an important step in growing in relationship with him. Let the discoveries become part of your life and see how they call you to action in various ways.

3. **PRAY:** Give the answers you have found a firm basis in your personal life through a direct relationship with God. Prayer is part of every meeting, and participants are invited to pray also individually between the meetings. Several meetings will be dedicated to prayer alone (SEE MEETING 4 & 14). Prayer is the most intensive way in which the relationship with God is experienced.

4. **ACT:** Bring your faith into practice, so that you realize it is not an intellectual or theoretical exercise, but part of real life. Every meeting will help participants question themselves about the importance of what they learned. The "dual challenge" (SEE GS6) offers a way to implement what was discussed at home, both intellectually and practically. A special meeting will be dedicated to acting charitably towards others (SEE MEETING 7).

5. **CELEBRATE:** Enjoy your successes together, celebrate with God in the liturgy, and with others at a party. The last meeting will be dedicated to this theme (SEE MEETING 18). Obviously, celebrating together brings us back to the first key.

Q&A

The *Rite of Christian Initiation of Adults* (RCIA) speaks of the importance of the "inquiry on the part of the candidates" (RCIA, NO. 7). The candidates' questions are considered essential in their quest to discover their personal relationship with God. This is true for everyone, whatever stage they have reached on their faith journey. The central focal point of this course are the questions of the participants themselves. The course is based on the conviction that the initial answers will lead to new and deeper questions, so that ideally the inquiry will continue throughout life!

Relationship

The five keys together will help the participants grow in faith, love and hope together. Bonding of the group will greatly enhance their capacity to dialogue, which is important as one of the main assets of this course is dialogue among the participants. "No one lives for themselves," Saint Paul wrote (ROM 14:7). Our faith is all about relationship. Often a relationship with God starts through a relationship with people who speak about him. Wherever someone loves another being, they share in the love of God. Even when they do not (yet) know God (1 JN 4:8). Jesus died and lived again out of love, to make it possible for us to love, to relate to God (SEE #TWGOD 1.26). We are destined to live forever with him in love (SEE #TWGOD 1.45). *How to grow in faith* wants to help people advance on their journey with God in this way.

Head, heart, hands

This journey is aimed at the person as a whole, with their head, heart, and hands. Just thinking with your head is not enough; it is essential that participants internalize in their heart what was discussed so that the fruits become part of daily life. As participants discover God's love, we hope that they will start to seek him in prayer and respond to his love with small gestures of love. That they will place their hands and feet at the service of God, so to say. From time to time, participants can be invited to reflect on how they have practised charity over the past few weeks. And ... when people get to know God better, they will also want to speak about his love to others, which is the origin of mission. This course equips people with an understanding of their relationship with God in such a way that they can also share their faith with those around them.

Do not judge

Jesus' words "Do not judge!" (LK 6:37) are very important for creating an atmosphere of trust, where participants feel free to share. Help them experience that there is no such thing as stupid questions. People are often afraid to be considered a bad Catholic or not faithful enough, and as a consequence do not dare to ask questions. It is therefore crucial that they feel free to ask anything and voice any thought without fear of being judged.

GS4 Resources and "rules"

Every participant is invited to join in the conversations on different faith topics. To stimulate the participation of all, it helps to create a welcoming setting where they can share their thoughts without fear of making mistakes, touching on taboos, or saying something wrong. It is only possible to progress on our path towards the truth in complete freedom of spirit. The "rules" of *Tweeting with GOD* (SEE BOX) aim to stimulate the personal search of each participant, and promote this freedom. These basic rules emerged from the experience during the encounters that gave rise to the initiative *Tweeting with GOD* (SEE *TWEETING WITH GOD Manual* A.1-B.1). They are the basis for a fruitful use of the following resources or tools.

Essential resources

- Each participant will need the **book *Tweeting with GOD. Big Bang, prayer, Bible, sex, Crusades, sin...*** (Freedom Publishing Books). The book can be read during and between the meetings: it will provide many answers to personal questions. The "dual challenge" at the end of each meeting indicates the Questions from the *Tweeting with GOD* book that should be read for the next meeting (SEE GS6).
- Participants are asked to download the ***Tweeting with GOD* app** (SEE GS10). The app will be used during the meetings. It can also be used to pray in various ways, and to follow the Order of the Mass in many different languages. Participants are invited to discover the SCAN option for the book and read the short answers in the app.
- Also the ***Online with Saints* app** is needed (SEE GS4). This app, too, will be used during the meetings. At home, participants can explore the "social media profiles" of the saints in the app to get to know them further.
- Participants will need a **Bible with Old and New Testament** (SEE GS1). In this course we prefer to use a hard copy of the Bible to help participants get to now its structure and learn how to find biblical texts.

For purchasing links see www.howtogrowinfaith.com.

Multimedia

This course often uses multimedia resources, available from www.tweetingwithgod.com and www.onlinewithsaints.com. If you consider the use of modern media a challenge, do not worry, but simply ask the participants to help you. Instead of a video arrangement you could simply use a tablet or laptop with an external speaker for smaller groups. Or you can ask the participants to watch videos on their phones. In case the participants do not have a smartphone available, the resources can be used on a shared tablet, laptop or desktop computer.

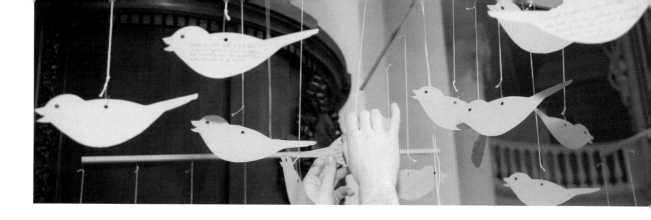

Downloads

- Moderators can download the **material needed during the meetings**. In this handbook, downloads are indicated with (DL) in the "To prepare" boxes. With just some (double-sided) printing and cutting you have all the material for the meetings right at your disposal.
- A **Participant's Guide** to accompany the participants is available for download. This contains brief information pertaining to each meeting, like a reminder to the dual challenge (SEE GS6), and what to bring. It can be printed as an A5 booklet that can be trimmed so that it fits in the *Tweeting with GOD* book. The content can be adapted by the moderator.
- **Short videos** of 1-2 minutes are available through the apps or on YouTube (SEE GS10).

For downloading links see www.howtogrowinfaith.com.

Optional extras

- The **book *Online with Saints. Discover friends and companions on your path to God*** (Our Sunday Visitor Books) can give further ideas, answers to contemporary questions, and information about "Today's hero."
- Further optional inspiration for the moderator can be found in the **Tweeting with GOD Manual: Exploring the Catholic Faith together** (Freedom Publishing Books).
- The **Tweeting with GOD Specials** offer procedures for extra meetings (SEE WWW.TWEETINGWITHGOD.COM/HOWTO).

The "rules" of *Tweeting with GOD*

1. Welcome all questions regarding faith and life, regardless of the position they may represent or the answer they may imply.

2. Listen respectfully to the others in the group and try to understand the reasoning behind their statements.

3. Let the arguments behind the Church's teaching speak for themselves.

4. Do not try too hard to convince; simply testify to your own faith. Remember that only God can convert people's hearts.

5. Be discreet: do not discuss what people say with others outside the group.

GS5 Course program

The proposed course consists of 18 meetings of about two hours, and several meetings on the sacraments. The contents of every meeting can easily be spread over two sessions of 50-60 minutes. If you need more than the proposed meetings, you can add some related questions from the *Tweeting with GOD* book (SEE GS10). The appendix gives some further suggestions for themes (SEE APPENDIX 6). This program can be used in many ways and with very different groups (SEE GS2). The program can be spread over one, two, three, and even more years, with extra material available (SEE APPENDIX 6).

Preparatory meetings: Meeting the participants; meeting parents or spouses (SEE GS7).

Meeting 1: Science & Faith – God, Trinity, Creation and you. See yourself as a child of God – who in the Trinity is relationship in himself: he loves you and he is your Creator.

Meeting 2: Revelation – Scripture, Tradition, and God's voice. Discover that the Bible is more than just a book; it is God's Word, through which – in union with the Tradition transmitted by the Church – God reveals himself to us.

Meeting 3: Scripture – The great stories in the Bible. Learn about major events in the Old Testament, and understand how these are related to Jesus.

Meeting 4: Prayer – The Christian view of prayer. Discover how prayer can bring you closer to God; that various forms and categories of prayer can help you in your life.

Meeting 5: Your group's questions 1. Speak about your group's questions.

Team: Evaluation and team building (SEE GS8).

Meeting 6: Good & Evil – Evil, sin, & grace. Understand that the existence of evil is not in accordance with the plan of God, who created us with a free will and supports us with his grace.

Meeting 7: ACT – Help someone else. Volunteering in a nursing home, in the community, or with a charitable organization, with the purpose of putting what has been learned so far into practice.

Meeting 8: Christmas & Easter – Jesus and God's plan of salvation. Learn about the core of our faith and what God saves us from through the birth, suffering, death, and resurrection of Jesus.

Meeting 9: Pentecost – Your vocation and the Church. Everyone has a vocation; learn how to discover your personal calling in relation to the Church community.

Meeting 10: Your group's questions 2. Speak about your group's questions.

Team: Evaluation and team building (SEE GS8).

Meeting 11 – Retreat. Make time to listen to God in silence and temporary solitude

Meeting 12: Sacraments & Liturgy. Perceive how the seven sacraments and the liturgy are essential in the everyday life of a Christian.

Meeting 13: Sacramental grace – The gift of the sacraments. See how God's sacramental grace – received through the working of the Holy Spirit – confirms the link with Jesus and his Church, and helps us to live as convinced Christians.
13A Baptism
13B Confirmation
13C Eucharist
13D Matrimony
13E Holy Orders & Anointing of the Sick
13F Reconciliation

Meeting 14: PRAY – Prayer & Reconciliation. This is the perfect moment to pray together and to receive the Sacrament of Reconciliation.

[**Celebration of the sacraments.** This is a good moment to receive the Sacraments of Baptism, Confirmation, Eucharist, or Matrimony, if the course is leading up to this].

Team: Evaluation and team building (SEE GS8).

Meeting 15: Your group's questions 3. Speak about the questions of your group.

Meeting 16: Sanctity – Mary, the saints & me. You are not alone: those in heaven accompany us, they pray with us and for us!

Meeting 17: Christian life – Creed & Commandments. Synthesis of all that was discussed and experienced so far on the basis of the Creed, taking the Ten Commandments as a guide for daily life.

Meeting 18: CELEBRATE – Party, Eucharist & thanksgiving. Think about what makes a good Catholic party, the celebration of the Eucharist, and partying in thanksgiving.

Team: Evaluation (SEE GS8).

Follow-up after *How to grow in faith*

GS6 Organization of meetings

How to grow in faith is fundamentally based on group dialogue supported by the five keys: relate, think, pray, act charitably, and celebrate (SEE GS3). The recommendations can be adapted freely according to the age and particular needs of the participants.

For each theme, interactive exercises are alternated with moments of profound dialogue. It is essential to encourage a real, active participation by each participant. If possible, you could have a meal together before starting the meeting. This will help the participants to relate, and therewith to be more open in the following dialogue.

Course program
The full program consists of the following meetings (SEE GS5):
- Regular course meetings
- Course meetings about your group's questions (SEE GS10)
- Special meetings for charity, retreat, prayer or celebration (SEE MEETING 7, 11, 14 & 18)
- Meeting with the team, and the initial meetings with the participants and their family/friends (SEE GS7).

Meetings
Every course meeting follows a set schedule (SEE BOX), which is presented on three kinds of pages:
- A double introductory page gives an overview vision of the meeting, its objectives and additional suggestions.
- The double page of the procedure gives an overview of the entire meeting at a glance, with a detailed step-by-step instruction.
- The worksheet contains the material needed for the various activities and Round Tables.
- The appendices contain further information with interactive methods, prayers, and content for additional meetings.

Procedure
The meetings are scheduled with a duration of about two hours, with the intention to study and consider a topic from several angles. It is perfectly possible to split the meetings in two sessions of 50 to 60 minutes. Simply add a prayer at the end of the first and the beginning of the second session (SEE APPENDIX 5).

> ### Typical program for a session
>
> - Opening prayer (2 min)
> - Relate and initial exchange (5-8 min)
> - Recap of the last meeting (3 min)
> - 2-3 rounds of dialogue (15-25 min each)
>   - Round Tables
>   - Interactive exercises
>   - Multimedia video
>   - Small groups
>   - Testimony of a saint
> - Synthesis and actualization (1-5 min)
> - Closing prayer (10-15 min)
> - Conclusion and explanation of the dual challenge for the next meeting (3 min)

Obviously, you are free to adapt parts or all of the procedure, the most important elements of which are:

- **Opening prayer.** Ideally initiated by a participant, using the proposed prayers or another prayer of their choice.

- **Relate.** Especially at the beginning, activities or games that help to relate are important for the group formation and creating an atmosphere of trust. Then focus briefly on what people took away from the previous meeting, and see how they fared with the proposed "dual challenge" (SEE BELOW). The idea is to create a brief moment for sharing rather than a full debate. Encourage participants who did not do the challenge to become more involved in the upcoming meetings.

- **Think:** The Round Tables are generally conceived of as dialogue in the search for answers. The theme is approached through interactive methods, videos, small group dialogues, group exchanges, testimonies, etc. This is the heart of the meeting; therefore, be sure to encourage the dialogue, the involvement of all participants, and the formulation of questions (SEE GS10).

- **Pray.** We recommend that this take place in a church or chapel if possible. For each meeting, we suggest prayers that can be adapted to the group's situation. This prayer time is aimed at helping participants integrate the new intellectual information into their growing relationship with the Lord.

- **Act: Dual challenge.** To help the participants further internalize the information received, at the end of each meeting two activities are proposed which should be carried out at home. Two double pages from *Tweeting with GOD* are suggested for personal reading, and a practical exercise is proposed. Rather than homework, this should be seen as a way for each participant to progress in their personal relationship with God and their neighbor.

GS7 Meeting the participants and their families or friends

Before beginning the course we suggest that the moderator has a preparatory meeting with the participants. It can be very useful to also organize a meeting with their families, parents, or spouses, although it may be a struggle to get them together. It is important to distinguish between these two meetings.

Meeting the participants

At the first meeting with the participants, explain what they can expect from this preparation course. They will need to get to know the moderator and each other in order to genuinely exchange in trust, freedom, and sincerity. We suggest several interactive methods to stimulate this process (SEE APPENDIX 3.7). You can agree with the participants on attendance expectations and commitment to the program. This first meeting is also the right moment for inviting participants to start asking questions. We offer some suggestions to help formulate these questions (SEE GS10). Do not worry if at the first meeting you do not get a lot of feedback: you are just at the beginning (SEE GS9). It is a good idea to propose a social media channel or other point of contact to send questions, both now and throughout the course. It is up to you to choose at which moment in the course these questions will be addressed (SEE GS10).

Meeting family and friends

If the participants are young, their parents may want to see the moderator to know more about the program with its organizational, financial, and further demands. If the participants are adults, their spouses or others close to them may also have questions. It is a great opportunity to help them connect with the vision of the *How to grow in faith* program, and see how they too are invited to grow in faith. When you explain the course program, these friends and family may realize they have limited knowledge of the faith. Would it not be wonderful if the faith

---

"My child/spouse is following the *How to grow in faith* course. So, what's my role?"

This will not be possible everywhere, but if there is enough interest, one or two meetings could be organized especially for the family and friends of the participants. These meetings could either take the form of a summary introduction to the faith for those who have no knowledge of it, or a brief "refresher course" if they have some basic understanding. This way, they can taste for themselves what their child or loved one is experiencing during the meetings. You could, for example, follow the program of the first two meetings with them. In any event, we suggest that you leave plenty of room for the guests' questions, as you do with the participants during the course.

journey of the participants also became a personal faith journey for their friends and family? The *Tweeting with GOD* book and app can help them find answers. You could even organize one or two meetings especially for them (SEE BOX).

Meeting the community

No one can believe alone. The course aims at helping the participants to become part of the life and mission of the Church. In an ideal situation, the entire Church community will be involved with the journey of *How to grow in faith* through prayer, accompaniment, and especially example. It is important to link the structure of the program to the life of the local community. Jesus instituted the Church community precisely because God is love. Unfortunately, our communities often are far from the perfect love that we are called to (1 JN 4:17). It can be very hard to love the Church unconditionally. But "Christ loved the Church and gave himself up for her" (EPH 5:25). Community is not optional for Christians. We are created as relational beings, and need other people. Together we can share love in friendship. Together we can reach out to God in prayer. Together we can stand up against evil. And together we can search for answers about life and faith. To grow in faith is something we have to do together, as a community.

Meeting the Word and the saints

The aim of faith is not knowledge about Jesus, but (getting) to know him. Meeting Jesus occurs in a growing relationship with him. The starting point in the search for answers will often be the Bible, which plays a central role in divine revelation. This is God's Word, addressed to us at this very moment. Frequently looking up Bible references will help the participants to get acquainted with the Bible, and hopefully stimulate them to read more.

The witness of the saints' lives, with their questions, difficulties and joys in their journey with God can help those seeking a relationship with the Lord. Several saints will accompany the participants in this course. To get to know the saints better, participants are encouraged to read the app or the book *Online with Saints* (SEE GS4). They can entrust their journey of preparation to the prayers of one or more other saints (SEE MEETING 16).

GS8 Moderating is ideally teamwork

When you are getting ready to accompany participants in their journey of growing in faith, it is important to realize that you are not alone: the Lord is working with you. He is the first to reach out to them. You can help them on their path, but only God can change hearts (SEE #TwGOD 4.49-4.50). Growing in faith is the calling of the whole church community, which is invited to accompany the participants and the moderator in prayer. Whether you are alone or work in a team, the five keys for how to grow in faith are important to each of you: you will need to relate, think, pray, act charitably, and celebrate (SEE GS3).

Team and moderation

This course can be used fruitfully by a single leader, teacher, catechist, or pastor. However, if the local situation allows it, it can be very rewarding to bring together a team to assist the group. Ideally, the team includes young people, lay leaders, educators, clergy or religious, married couples. ... Although it may often not be possible to have a priest in the team, it would be great if a member of the clergy could accompany the team. If they can be present for at least some of the course meetings, participants can get to know them and ask specific questions.

For practical reasons, in this course we always speak of the "moderator" in the singular. Depending on the possibilities of the team members, moderation can be done in turn or by several at once. It is important that the division of tasks ensures that each member of the team feels comfortable. There are teams in which everyone does everything. It is also possible to assign roles more permanently: moderation, activities, music, prayer ...

Teamwork ... with God

The team needs a shared vision of accompaniment in the faith and knowledge of the principal methods used. All team members should read the Questions linked to every meeting in the *Tweeting with GOD* book, and discuss difficult topics together. It is equally important that each of the team members continues to deepen their personal relationship with the Lord; he is the center of the course,

Beginning as a team

The first team meeting could take the following shape:
- Begin with a time of prayer and ask the Holy Spirit to inspire and help you in your work together.
- Introduce yourself and answer the question, "Why do I want to be part of this team?" Have a free exchange about your motivations.
- Speak about the question, "What is my vision for this course?" Speak about this freely. It is important that you all share a common vision.
- Plan the implementation of the *How to grow in faith* program, including team roles, venue, time and frequency, integration with existing initiatives, important moments of the liturgical year, promotion ...
- Schedule team meetings and evaluation structures.
- Conclude with a time of prayer, in a chapel or church if possible.

just as of their own lives. The team's collaboration is only possible with the grace that God wants to give to everyone who has a relationship with him. Personal prayer, receiving the Eucharist, Reconciliation, and the other sacraments, and daily living of a Christian life are an important foundation for each moderator and team member. After all, they are a role model for the participants and can help them a lot through their life testimony.

Evaluation and team building

We recommend that the team regularly meets apart from the course meetings for evaluation and team building. Given their importance, some moments have been indicated in the course program as a suggestion (SEE GS5). You could share a meal and engage in an informal exchange on the progress of the participants and the course. You can also take time for prayer, praise, or Eucharistic adoration together, to place the Lord at the center of your activity once more. Do not forget to have fun and celebrate together at times. All of this will affect not only the quality of the preparation but will also help each of the team members to advance further in their personal faith.

Team prayer

A team that prays together can grow in faith together. Prayer is essential to the success of your work and should be part of each meeting. Ask the Holy Spirit to be present and help you to communicate not only intellectual facts, but above all your passion for Christ.

An array of prayers is accessible on the *Tweeting with GOD* app, which could support the team to expand their ways of praying (SEE #TWGOD APP > 🙏 > 🙏). It is good to pray regularly for each of the participants, and for the other team members.

GS9 Moderating: Do not be afraid

Moderators need to prepare themselves for the meeting by reading the course material. Reading also the suggested Questions from the *Tweeting with GOD* book will provide them with the knowledge and basic arguments to lead the conversation and raise questions when necessary to stimulate the dialogue (SEE GS9).

The course accompanies the participants in their life of faith. If the participants are mature enough to start searching seriously for God's Will for their lives, it would be good to help them find a personal spiritual director (SEE MEETING 9). Such spiritual accompaniment goes beyond the task of the moderator.

Difficult questions

Note that the moderator's role is not to know everything but conduct the dialogue towards a fruitful exchange. Do not be afraid of difficult questions! It is perfectly normal sometimes to reply: "I do not know," or "Let me find out, we will talk about it next time." In most cases, the answer can be found in the *Tweeting with GOD* book. As the meetings are based on the participants' questions and answers, the sessions will be different every time and will also help the moderators to grow continually in their faith. Depending on their experience and creativity, moderators can come up with new methods and reorganize the order of the topics.

Do not be afraid

Often, group moderators have a double fear. The first is: "What will I do if there are no questions and no answers, if I am the only one talking?" (SEE GS8). And the second is: "What if the tone rises during discussion and a 'war of words' is unleashed?" (SEE GS9). The first answer to both questions is: Do not be afraid! You are not alone! To begin with, you are not doing this for yourself but for the Lord, so he will help you. You only need to do what you are capable of doing and invest yourself fully. Furthermore, there are the other members of the team and – even if you are alone – you can empower the participants and give them a role in the moderation.

On the one hand, it can indeed be terrifying for the moderator when a question is followed by total silence. Don't panic! Silence can be your ally. Silence offers participants an opportunity to reflect for a moment.

Also, an awkward silence may stimulate a participant to find the necessary courage to make the first move. After a first reaction, the dialogue often takes off very quickly. The lack of response may be caused by a too general starting question, in which case you can ask some more specific questions related to the topic (SEE GS10).

When, on the other hand, the discussion gets too heated, and everyone speaks at the same time, it may be a good moment to call for a break. Or you could simply say: "Let's come back to this topic another time," and thenpropose an activity that sets people's mind to a new topic.

Questions in the fridge

Moderation involves making choices (SEE BOX). On the one hand, you want to avoid being too restrictive in moderation, in order not to hinder the good contributions and questions of the participants. On the other hand, to go really deeper into a question, you will have to ensure that the dialogue does not stray too far from the topic at hand, and that you come back to the central point after every digression. Important questions that go beyond the topic at hand can be postponed to one of the meetings about your group's questions. Then you can say something like: "We moved away from the question we were discussing; what else can we say about that topic?"

Speaking too little or too much

- If a usually silent participant speaks for the first time, let them speak a few minutes, even if they go off topic. Then help the participants to return to the theme of the meeting.
- A participant who talks a lot may need to be gently and diplomatically restrained. You could compliment them for their knowledge, and ask their help to give all participants opportunity to speak. You might even consider making them co-moderator.
- Do not be afraid of emotional, provocative, or aggressive questions or answers. These show that at least there is some involvement with the theme!
- It is crucial for participants to have the time and the opportunity to discover the main arguments by themselves so that they can start to see the logic and sense of believing. So be careful not to provide conveniently complete answers too quickly.

GS10 Moderating: Your group's questions

How to grow in faith seeks to encourage participants to ask questions about life and faith. While the content covered in the course provides a clear formation pathway, the overall aim is to engage the participants in searching for answers to their own questions. If they discover that the course deals with their questions, they will be more motivated to invest in their participation.

Integrate questions
It is important to listen to the group's questions from the offset: Most of these questions can be inserted into the meetings schedule, and others discussed during one of the sessions on your group's questions or briefly discussed in private. The meetings about "your group's questions" are integrally part of the course program. You can freely add more meetings like this to your program.

The meeting
The procedure for a meeting on your group's questions can be similar to that of other meetings (SEE GS6). The moderator and participants are jointly responsible for the way the meeting runs. As the participants themselves have asked these questions, they will be particularly interested in seeking answers together. They have already journeyed together for some time and are used to the method. So, they can be asked to help with the preparation of the meeting, the methods, and possibly moderate single sessions.

The final goal remains that of helping participants to progress on their personal journey with the Lord. Prayer is essential for this. You can repeat a prayer method from one of the previous meetings or prepare your own prayer time together with the participants.

Suggestions
- Especially for this meeting, you can ask one or two people to prepare a short presentation on the theme, based on what they read in the *Tweeting with GOD* book.
- A good way to deepen a theme is to invite the participants to talk for some time in small groups (SEE APPENDIX 3.1 & 3.2).
- To find audio-visual material adapted to the theme, visit the *Tweeting with GOD* app, website, or YouTube channel.
- For "Today's hero" visit the *Online with Saints* app, website, or YouTube channel, where you find many saints with their biographies and life experiences.
- You can conclude – before the prayer – with a few questions that help to reflect on what the participants have received during this meeting, and what its importance is for each of them at this moment (SEE APPENDIX 3.6). You can also ask a participant to follow the dialogue from the beginning of the meeting and to present a brief synthesis at the end (SEE E.G. APPENDIX 3.5).

- It is good to maintain the dual challenge at the end (SEE GS6). Indicate two Questions from the *Tweeting with GOD* book that are related to the topic and that should be read before next meeting. And decide together on a brief task to perform home in order to deepen the theme.
- The *Tweeting with GOD Manual* contains further tips on how to run a meeting (SEE GS4).

....

Encouraging participants to ask questions

It can be quite a challenge to get your group to talk and ask questions. Relating within the group is very important in this regard (SEE GS4). At the beginning of each meeting, interactive methods are proposed to break the ice and to start smiling at each other (SEE APPENDIX 3.7).

Asking some direct questions about the topic at hand may help to get a conversation started. A useful trick to get the group involved is by asking: "Who has a question about the faith?" If you are lucky, a few people will raise their hands and you can begin with their questions. However, to get everyone involved you can then ask the following question: "Who does not have any questions about God or the faith?" Now all those who did not respond to the first question should raise their hands, but they will realize that they have not answered truthfully. There you are: you just got your group to start thinking! (SEE ALSO APPENDIX 3.3 & 3.4).

You can also ask the group about a time when someone questioned them about their faith. Or: "Which of you some-times talks about the faith with friends? What do you speak about?" People often experience a clash between their daily lives in society and their faith. Where does this clash occur? Do participants consider themselves to be different from other people in society? If someone says: "My friends do not believe, and I do," you can ask: "How do you deal with that difference?" Sometimes it can help to bring things to the fore. You could, for example, ask the participants: "Do you believe everything the Church teaches?" If they are honest, there will be some reactions here.

GS11 Moderating:
Practical advice for the group leader

Whether or not you have had experience as a group leader in moderating discussions, it is important to keep striving to become a better leader and a better Christian. On these pages we list what we consider the most important dos and don'ts for the moderator, although this list is not exhaustive. We hope this will help you to recognize that it does not take very much to be a good group leader. By following these few tips, you will be well on your way to becoming the best group leader you can be! That way, the sessions will be inspiring for your personal life too.

Dos

1. **Pray!** Ask God to guide you in your preparation and during the meetings. Remember that you do not have to do this alone!
2. **Walk the talk.** Be aware that you function as a role model for your group. Young people in particular are highly impressionable: if you lead the meeting on Friday night, and they see you drunk on Saturday night, you lose credibility.
3. **Prepare well.** Sometimes you can't help having things go wrong, but do your best to make the meetings go smoothly. This includes preparing the questions (and possible answers) and all materials you will need.
4. **Do it together.** Involve the participants in the planning, with the selecting of questions, and also with the inviting, shopping, etc. You may struggle with delegating, and it may take more time than doing things yourself; but your job is to build up the group.
5. **Encourage and thank.** A word of encouragement or thanks goes a long way. Participants may feel insecure and self-conscious and need positive feedback. Compliment those who prepared the meal or snack, thank those who cleaned up, and comfort those who became emotional.

Don'ts

1. **Don't speak all the time.** Sure, you can share your own experiences if doing so is conducive to the conversation, but try to give the floor to the participants and their personal stories and questions.
2. **Don't just share information;** share a vision. Mere information just doesn't appeal. The beauty of our faith is that it involves us in a dynamic relationship with the God who loves us!
3. **Don't put people on the spot,** especially not in the beginning. Not everyone is comfortable praying in public or speaking about his personal opinion. You can always ask for a volunteer. When the group gets to know each other better, you can sometimes gently encourage shy members to speak.
4. **Don't use Church jargon without an explanation.** Words such as Eucharist, grace, and sin are not familiar to all people. *How to grow in faith* is about getting to know the faith, not about feeling excluded if you do not know everything yet.
5. **Don't be discouraged if your group is small.** It's quality not quantity that counts. Your group is a safe place for people to discover the faith step by step, not a factory producing first-class theologians by the dozens.

Be yourself

The most important rule for dealing with a group as a moderator is to be authentic: Be yourself! Be willing to share your personal faith and convictions, without imposing. Be open even about what you do not know (yet). Be careful, however, not to discourage the group in their search for the answers to their questions. Your doubts about certain issues may not be suitable for sharing here; keep them for when you meet your spiritual director (SEE QUESTION 3.4 & 4.6). Try to be positive at all times!

Breaking down the questions

Depending on the background of the participants, a question such as "Was Jesus against women?" (SEE QUESTION 2.16) might need to be broken down to be discussed fruitfully in the group. A good starting question is, "Why do you ask?"

Some of the sub-questions will come to you when you read the text of the Question during your preparation. In the case of Question 2.16, for example, you'll want the participants to think of what they know of Jesus: Did he treat men and women differently? Were there women Apostles? Why not? Are man and woman the same in every respect? What does the Bible say? Do the differences between the sexes matter?

[CF. #TWGOD MANUAL B.5]

TWEETING WITH GOD

Communicating with God is as simple as posting or liking on social media. Whether your favorite tool is Instagram, Facebook, or Twitter, *Tweeting with GOD* helps you to see how simple it is to relate to God, even when you are offline!

Through a close integration between social media, modern technology and printed books, *Tweeting with GOD* aims at helping you discover answers to your questions about the faith. The project was brought to life by young people with many questions, who have been seeking the meaning of their relationship with Jesus in their lives.

Download the free Tweeting with GOD app

Use this interactive tool to learn more about the faith on the go:

- Follow Mass in 15+ languages
- Pray the Rosary and many other Catholic prayers in 15+ languages
- Find a brief answer to 200+ burning questions
- Scan the *Tweeting with GOD* book to find online extras

Available on the
App Store

GET IT ON
Google Play

www.tweetingwithgod.com

Tweeting
with
GOD

Access videos

Turn on the subtitles in YouTube

- via the app: scan an image in the book
- via the app: click on a question, scroll down, play the video
- via the website tweetingwithgod.com
- via the YouTube channel of *Tweeting with GOD*

Follow us: #TwGOD

 /TweetingwithGOD

 @TwGOD_en

 /FatherMichelRemery

 @FrMichelRemery

ONLINE WITH SAINTS

Imagine you could meet and greet a saint, which saint would you choose? *Online with Saints* offers a virtual encounter with 100+ saints from all around the world. Women and men, carpenters and scholars, mothers and popes, princes and paupers: their inspiring life stories are linked to real life modern questions. Be sure to check the social media profiles of the saints in the app!

Anyone can become a saint! Every saint is different, with their own unique personality and destiny. Each of them found their vocation in a different way – demonstrating that God has a special plan and vocation for each individual.

Download the free Online with Saints app

Discover much more information about the saints:

- Social media profiles of the saints
- Animated videos about their lives
- Information on their history
- Pray with the saints & find patron saints

Available on the
App Store

GET IT ON
Google Play

www.onlinewithsaints.com

Access videos

Turn on the subtitles in YouTube

- via the app: scan a saint in the book
- via the app: click on a saint's profile, play the video
- via the website onlinewithsaints.com
- via the YouTube channel of *Online with Saints*

Follow us: #OnlineSaints

  /OnlinewithSaints

 Online With Saints

Meeting 1: Science & Faith – Doesn't science contradict the story of creation?

The purpose of this first meeting is to help the participants see themselves within the whole of creation as a beloved child of God (SEE BOX). God is love (1 JN 4:8), and he created the entire universe out of love for us to live in. He is relationship in himself, love shared between Father, Son, and Spirit. We first speak about the relationship between the Big Bang and the story of creation. This theme was chosen because one can think about it without immediately showing one's deepest feelings. More sensitive topics will be left for later meetings, when everyone should be more confident in the group.

The moderator should read the #TwGOD Questions related to this meeting in advance, in order to be able to animate the session and help find answers to the questions (SEE BOX). Participants are invited – according to their abilities – to read these Questions *after* the meeting, as part of the dual challenge (SEE GS6), so that they can further explore what has been said.

The meeting

It is likely that not everyone knows each other yet. It is therefore important to start with a brief introduction and an activity to relate within the group (SEE GS1). The suggested topics and time schedules can be followed as presented or adapted at will. Do not be afraid if the conversation does not proceed smoothly at first. Everyone needs to get used to the group (SEE GS8). For most participants, this is probably the first time they have formulated their ideas and thoughts about faith out loud. For some, it will take time to learn to think for themselves instead of repeating the opinions they hear around them. It is the role of the moderator to encourage dialogue (SEE GS9).

Prayer

As this is your first time together, briefly explain to the participants the concept of praying together. We offer you some suggestions for praying at the beginning or the end of the meeting (SEE APPENDIX 5). In addition, the *Tweeting with GOD* app offers many more prayers (SEE #TwGOD APP > 🕊 > ⛪).

God, Trinity, Creation and you

Objective of this meeting:
See yourself as a child of God – who in the Trinity is relationship in himself: he loves you and he is your Creator.

Related Questions:
1.1, 1.2, 1.3, 1.5, 1.9, 4.1

Dual challenge:
- Read these questions in the *Tweeting with GOD* book: 1.1 & 1.5.
- Search, borrow or buy a bible (Old and New Testaments together) and bring it along next time.

To help the participants, you can begin by praying the Our Father and Hail Mary together using the app (SEE #TwGOD APP > 🕊 > ⛪ > ⊙ & Ⓐ). Given the importance of these prayers, ask the participants to learn them by heart if they do not know them yet. Explain that this will enable the participants to pray anytime, anywhere, also when they do not know what to say. You can also practice one or two songs that can be repeated at other meetings.

Before closing the meeting, ask the participants to bring a bible for next time. Although they could download a Bible on their smartphone, it is better to have a printed Bible in hand to see its structure and learn how to navigate in it.

Additional suggestions

- There will probably not be enough time to discuss related topics like the story of Adam and Eve or the theory of evolution (SEE #TwGOD 1.2 & 1.3). If the group so wishes, you could dedicate one of the meetings on your group's questions to this theme (SEE GS8).

The gist of it

- **Welcome, pray, relate, recap**
- **Intro: Genesis and science**
- **Round Table 1: Big Bang vs. Creation**
  - Video: Doesn't the Big Bang rule out faith in God? (#TwGOD 1.1)
  - Which two questions are answered by Genesis and the Big Bang theory?
  - Activity: Find the "Wisdom of the Church" in the #TwGOD app

....

- **Round Table 2: A God of relations**
  - Sketch: The Trinity
  - Why did God want to share his love with us in creation?
  - Sketch: Your relationship with God
  - Compare the two sketches: How close is God?
- **Today's hero: Saint Francis of Assisi**
- **Synthesis & actualization**
- **Closing prayer**
  - Thanking God
  - Quiet prayer in silence or aloud
- **Dual challenge**
  - Read the #TwGOD Questions
  - Search, borrow or buy a printed bible for the next meeting

Procedure for Meeting 1

Relate

00.00 Welcome

- Welcome the participants to this first meeting: "In a minute we will get to know each other a little. You are here because you want to know more about life and about God. The title of our course is *How to grow in faith*. Maybe you do not really know what you believe. Maybe you have a strong faith. Maybe you are full of questions about the existence of God. That is perfectly all right. In this course we want to go on a journey with you. Each of you has their own personal life and convictions. We are not going to take these away from you. On the contrary: We hope to help you develop new thoughts and strong convictions based on what we will discuss during the *How to grow in faith* course."
- Explain that you will start every meeting with a prayer: "You may not have much experience with prayer. Do not worry, you are not alone! Just try to join in according to how you feel about this. We'll speak more about prayer at a later stage in the course."

00.03 Opening prayer

- Make the sign of the cross and say a short prayer, for example: "Dear God, we are gathered here to learn more about you. Some of us may feel they are very far from you. Some of us know you already a bit. We ask you to help us all to be open to listen, think, learn and speak about what is important to us. Be with us at this moment, through Christ our Lord. Amen."

00.05 Presentation: Names & statements

- Everyone introduces themselves briefly, for example saying their name, age, or occupation, and color of socks they are wearing today.

- Then follow the indications on Worksheet 1.1.

00.23 *Tweeting with GOD* rules

- Present the *Tweeting with GOD* rules (SEE GS6) as a basis for every dialogue and ask everyone to agree to agree to follow them.

Think

00.25 Introductory dialogue: Genesis and science

- To begin with, a participant reads the first verses of the Bible (AT LEAST GEN 1:1-5.26.31).
- Follow the indications on Worksheet 1.2.

00.35 Round Table 1: Big Bang vs. Creation

- Watch the video of #TwGOD Question 1.1: "Doesn't the Big Bang rule out faith in God?" (SEE GS11).
- Divide the participants into small groups (SEE APPENDIX 3.1 & 3.2). Explain that the Big Bang theory of science and the history of creation of the Bible answer two different questions. Which questions? Can we believe in both the Big Bang and the story of creation? Speak about this in the small groups.
- Then all come together and see what answers the participants have found. In general, the Big Bang theory seeks to explain the *how* of creation (God initiated it) and the Bible reveals the *why* (for love of man to whom God wanted to give a place to live).
- In the *Tweeting with GOD* app, open #TwGOD Question 1.1, scroll down to the "Wisdom of the Church," read together one of the proposed articles and discuss it.
- Say: "Note that Saint John Paul II said that it is contrary to human reason to look only at the consequence (the Big Bang) and never look for the cause (God). What do you think?"

00.55 Break [END FIRST & START SECOND SESSION (SEE GS2)]

01.00 Today's hero: Saint Francis of Assisi

- Explain that there is another aspect to creation, which is its beauty. That beauty is a reflection of the love of God, which led him to create the world for us. Saint Francis recognized God's love for him. In response he tried to live in harmony with God, the people he met, and all creation.
- Watch the video of Saint Francis of Assisi via *Online with Saints* (SEE GS11).
- Ask the participants why they think Saint Francis is the patron saint of animals and creation? What can we learn from the example of Saint Francis? A small detail: the feast of Saint Francis is 4 October, which is why world animal day is celebrated that day.

01.10 Round Table 2: A God of relations

- Follow the indications on Worksheet 1.3.

Pray & Act

01.40 Synthesis & actualization

- Ask: "What touched you most in this meeting?" Exchange thoughts about the answers. The goal is not that all arrive at the same opinion, but that this be the starting point of a personal path with God.
- Conclude with the question: "How can what I have learned nourish my personal faith and relationship with Jesus? How can I put this into action?" Speak briefly about this.

01.45 Closing prayer

- Go (if possible) to a chapel or church, light the candles. (Sing a song).
- Explain that here we are in the presence of God, who is a great listener. Praying means simply spending time with God. Nothing else is important at this moment.
- Invite the participants to think back over the events of the day so far, with special attention for what they are grateful for. As they are in the presence of God, they can tell him what they want in the silence of their heart.
- (After a period of silence, optionally repeat the song).
- Conclude with the Our Father and Hail Mary, possibly with the help of the *Tweeting with GOD* app.

01.58 Conclusion in the meeting room

- Invite the participants to learn the Our Father and Hail Mary by heart using the *Tweeting with GOD* app.
- Remind participants of the date for the next meeting and present the dual challenge:
  - Read these Questions in the *Tweeting with GOD* book: 1.1 & 1.5.
  - Search, borrow or buy a Bible (Old and New Testaments together) and bring it along next time.

TO PREPARE
- Bibles
- Video equipment (internet)
- *Tweeting with GOD* book & app
- *Online with Saints* app
- Sheet names & statements (DL)
- Paper & pencils & pens

Worksheet 1

1.1 Presentation: Names & statements

1. Preparation: on a sheet of paper, list a number of statements about the participants, for example:

I have a dog	I enjoy singing	I have been to three continents	I have been baptized
I hardly ever eat breakfast	I doubt that God exists	I like to buy fair trade products	I do not leave the house without make-up
I want to grow in faith	I sometimes pray to Mary	I have received the Sacrament of Confirmation	I play a musical instrument
I like ice cream	I play sports	I do not drink alcohol	I am an altar server
I have a sister	I speak Spanish	My birthday is in May	I am an aunt/uncle
I like to read comics	I am vegetarian	I have a cat	I like singing

2. Give a copy of this sheet and a pen to each group member. If the group is small, you can delete some items.
3. Explain the rules: "You will receive a list of statements. The goal is to find a different person to match each statement within 10 minutes." Ask them to choose a statement on your list that describes them. Write their name on your list next to the statement they choose. Then move on to another person. Each statement can be used only once.
4. Hand out pens and paper. Have someone watch the time.
5. At the end of the activity, discuss some of the statements. For a given statement, ask a participant to tell whose name they have noted and to tell briefly about their meeting with that person.
6. Are certain participants not mentioned? Ask them to choose a statement that applies to them and say briefly why.
7. (Competition can be stimulating. You can give a small prize to the first person who found names for all the statements).

1.2 Introductory dialogue: Genesis and science

1. Draw an (imaginary) line in the meeting room. All participants stand on the line to begin with. Indicate clearly which side of the line is "true" and which is "false."
2. Explain the rules: "I will read out statements, to which you will respond. You can express yourself by moving around in the room, in silence, so without speaking:
   - 1 big step right means you agree, 2 steps right means you totally agree;
   - 1 big step left means you disagree, 2 steps left means you very much disagree;
   - no steps means you remain neutral or do not know the answer."
3. To practice, you can read a statement like this: "I like Apple more than Android," "I like caramel chocolate ice cream with little pieces of real chocolate," "I have traveled to a country that speaks a language other than English," "I have dark eyes," etc.
4. Now move to faith-related statements like:
   - The story of creation needs to be replaced with the Big Bang theory.
   - The Bible is not old-fashioned, and contains a message for today.
   - A good scientist does not need God, for modern science has all the answers.
   - Our society should rediscover the importance of the Bible.
   - Faith and science are both important.
5. Once the participants have responded to a statement by moving around, you can ask them to share briefly about their response and about the deeper meaning of the statement. The purpose of this question is to help participants think for themselves and not simply follow a hunch or a friend. There are no right or wrong answers for now; any argument will be useful for the group to advance in their search for an answer. The moderator should remain impartial, without revealing their opinion.
6. If necessary, help participants to deepen their position by asking them questions. For example, you can ask: "Do you know who was the first to present the Big Bang theory?" Most will be surprised to learn that it was Georges Lemaître (†1966), a Catholic priest who received several signs of Church recognition for his work in the scientific field.

1.3 Round Table 2: A God of relations

- Distribute paper and pencils. Ask each participant to make a very schematic sketch – in 2 minutes – on the theme: "God one and three. The Trinity of the Father, Son and Holy Spirit." For the moment do not give other explanations. Leave the sketches aside for the moment.
- Explain: "God is relationship in himself (SEE #TWGOD 1.33). There is a relationship of friendship and deep love between Father, Son, and Holy Spirit. God wanted to share this love with us. Therefore he created us, and therefore he sent Jesus to tell us about his love. He hopes that we will love him back, helped by the Holy Spirit. Why is it so important to us that God is relationship?" Speak about this together.
- Then explain: "Because God is relationship in himself, he did not want to keep his love for himself. He wanted to share this love with us. He wants to get in touch with you, that is why he created you! (SEE #TWGOD 1.2). This notion of God's relationship with us is central to our faith. How do you see that?"
- Now, give 2 minutes to make another sketch, this time on the theme: "God and me: how do I imagine my relationship with God?"
- Ask the participants to compare the two sketches. Talk about the differences and similarities.
- Then ask: "Can you say that the first sketch is more technical, while the second is warmer, with God much closer? If so, you have made an essential discovery: God wants to be close to each of you right now! Later we will talk about different ways to get in touch with God. For today it is important to realize that God created the world *for you!*"

Meeting 2: Revelation – How can I know the claims of faith are true?

The objective of this second meeting is that participants realize how the Bible is not just a book like any other. It is one of the two principal ways through which we can know something about God – the second way is the Tradition of the Church. These are ways in which God reveals himself to us people. The objective is also to help participants learn to find their way in the Bible and help them to find particular texts. In doing so, they will gradually discover what the Bible can mean for their own lives. In addition, we want to help them recognize the role of the Church both in their transmission and explanation. The content of the meeting is based on the related #TwGOD Questions (SEE BOX). The moderator will need to read these in preparation. As before, the times that structure this meeting are a suggestion which can be adapted as needed.

The meeting

With the last meeting our course started well. Now we will continue to deepen relationships within the group, together with their desire to learn about the faith.

On the next pages you will find the consecutive steps for this meeting. You can start by asking the participants what touched them most in the previous meeting, and which aspects they have deepened since. The most important thing is that they begin to see their life and existence in the light of God, their Creator and loving Father. It is equally important to come back to the dual challenge proposed at the end of the last meeting (SEE GS6). The aim is not a formal check of "homework," but an encouragement to the participants to perform their dual task, which serves their own Christian lives and their advancement in the faith.

You can watch the video for #TwGOD Question 1.12, using the app, the website or the YouTube channel of *Tweeting with GOD*. Remember to switch on the subtitles (SEE GS10).

Prayer

Today, the participants are invited to pray with a biblical text, which is why we schedule more time for prayer. This may seem audacious for a second meeting, but we hope it will help participants see how the Bible can help them

---

Scripture, Tradition, and God's voice

Objective of this meeting:
Discover that the Bible is more than just a book; it is God's Word, through which – in union with the Tradition transmitted by the Church – God reveals himself to us.

Related Questions:
1.6, 1.10, 1.11, 1.12, 1.15, 1.18

Dual challenge:
- Read these Questions in the *Tweeting with GOD* book: 1.10 & 1.11.
- Pray at least once with the Bible at home (SEE APPENDIX 4 OF THE *TWEETING WITH GOD* BOOK).

in their daily lives. And that prayer brings them closer to God. If you do not have enough time, abbreviate another element of the program, and give priority to praying with the Bible.

Given the importance of the Word of God, all participants are invited to make time for a moment of personal prayer at home with the Bible before the next meeting. The explanation of Appendix 4 in the *Tweeting with GOD* book can help.

Additional suggestions

- Before the prayer, you can conclude the meeting with a few questions that will help to reflect on what was received during this meeting (SEE APPENDIX 3.6).
- If the participants express a desire to read the Bible, you can suggest starting with the Gospel of Saint Mark, which is the shortest and perhaps the easiest text for beginners. It would be great to take this up at a later stage, and to let participants express their experiences and ask questions.
- One or two people can be invited to prepare a short presentation of the theme based on the #TwGOD Questions for the next meeting.

The gist of it

- **Pray, relate, recap**
- **Brief recap**
- **Intro: Navigating in the Bible**
- **Round Table 1: God's Word**
  - Video: Did God write the Bible himself? (#TwGOD 1.12)
  - Small groups: Does the Bible contain God's Word for us today?

....

- **Today's hero: Saint Jerome**
- **Round Table 2: God speaks through the Church**
  - The Bible seems to contradict itself. How do we interpret it correctly?
  - Does God also speak in other ways? What is the Tradition?
  - What is the role of the Church in interpreting God's Revelation?
- **Synthesis and actualization**
- **Closing prayer**
  - Pray with Mt. 6:19-34
- **Dual challenge**
  - Read the #TwGOD Questions
  - Pray at least once with the Bible at home

Procedure for Meeting 2

Relate

00.00 Opening prayer
- Choose a prayer from Appendix 5 or use the *Tweeting with GOD* app.

00.02 Welcome: Sit & share
- Help the group to relate. This is the second time they come together. Follow the indications on Worksheet 2.1.

00.15 The previous meeting
- Recall the *Tweeting with GOD* rules (SEE GS6) and invite everyone to agree.
- Engage in a simple and quick recap: this is not the moment for a long debate. What touched the participants most in the previous meeting? Are there new questions or ideas? How did they fare with the dual challenge?
  - Are there doubts about the Questions in the *Tweeting with GOD* book?
  - Was everyone able to bring a Bible?

Think

00.20 Introductory dialogue: Navigating in the Bible
- For starters, explain that the Bible (also called Scripture) consists of a collection of very different "books": there are historical accounts, poems, prayers, letters, etc., that speak of God and his relationship with people. It is divided into two parts: the Old Testament – 46 books about the time before Jesus – and the New Testament – 27 books about Jesus and beyond. (Note that Protestant Bibles may have fewer books.)
- Continue explaining that finding a specific phrase – a "verse" – is simple: seek first the book, then the chapter, and then the verse in question. Check out Appendix 1 in your *Tweeting with GOD* book for a list of the abbreviations of Bible books. Ask everyone to take their Bibles in their hands, and suggest for example to look up the following verse: John 3:16. Help those who have difficulties.
- Follow the indications on Worksheet 2.2.

00.30 Round Table 1: God speaks to you in the Bible
- Explain that the Bible is not just a collection of ancient books: the text contains a message for us today. That is why for centuries the Bible has been the most read book in the world. In the video we will hear that God inspired the authors who wrote the biblical texts. That is why we say that the Bible is "the Word of God" (SEE #TwGOD 1.10).
- Watch the video of #TwGOD Question 1.12 together: "Did God write the Bible himself?"
- Divide the participants into small groups (SEE APPENDIX 3.1 & 3.2). Ask them to discuss the following questions: "What struck you in the video? Did you ever read the Bible? What do you find difficult? Is there a text or a person in the Bible which specifically inspired you? In what way? Do you have any tips for each other with regard to the Bible?"
- After some 10 minutes, come back together and ask if there are still unanswered questions. Discuss these together.
- Ask: "Why can we say that the Bible contains the Word of God for us today?" Discuss together.

00.55 Break [END FIRST & START SECOND SESSION (SEE GS2)]

01.00 Today's hero: Saint Jerome
- Watch the video of Saint Jerome via *Online with Saints*.
- Ask the participants: "Why is the translation work of Saint Jerome so important? What can we learn from his example?"

01.10 Round Table 2: God speaks to you through the Church

- Have four people in the group search for the following texts, and read these out loud in this order: Deuteronomy 7:2, Deuteronomy 19:21, Matthew 5:38-39, Matthew 5:44 (SEE #TwGOD 1.19). Speak together about what could be the right interpretation of these texts. Which one is correct? Who decides that?
- Ask: "We have just seen that the Bible can be used to preach different messages, so how can you know which is the correct interpretation?"
- Continue explaining that, thankfully, God speaks to us in a second formal way, next to the Bible (SEE #TwGOD 1.11). He does so through the teaching of what we call the Tradition of the Church. The Bible was given to the community of Christians, not to individuals. Only the Church community, led by the successors of the Apostles (the pope and the bishops), can define the teaching of the Bible. As their task has been instituted by Jesus himself (SEE #TwGOD 2.15), we can be sure that the Holy Spirit helps them to interpret the Bible correctly.
- Today we read the Bible in the light of the interpretation that was handed down through the ages. This is how God speaks to us also through the Tradition of the Church. Speak briefly about this together.
- Finally ask: "Why is it important for us here and now that God reveals himself in those two ways?" Speak about this.

Pray & Act

01.25 Synthesis & actualization

- You can say in conclusion that the two formal ways in which God speaks to us are the Bible and the Church's teaching, or Tradition. The Holy Spirit helps those who guide the Church to discern the truth in a definite way when they speak about the Bible, the faith, and moral life. The Holy Spirit also helps individuals to read the Bible in the truth, helped by the formal Church teaching as we personally can get the interpretation wrong.
- Conclude with the question: "How can what I have learned nourish my personal faith and relationship with Jesus? How can I put this into action?" Speak briefly about this.

01.30 Closing prayer: Praying with the Bible

- Read together Appendix 4 in the *Tweeting with GOD* book: "Praying with a text from the Bible." Invite the participants to take their bibles and look up the text of Matthew 6:19-34. Read the text together and briefly talk about difficult passages.
- Follow the indications on Worksheet 2.3.

01.58 Conclusion in the meeting room

- Remind participants of the date for the next meeting and present the dual challenge:
  - Read these Questions in the *Tweeting with GOD* book: 1.1 & 1.11.
  - Pray at least once with the Bible at home (SEE APPENDIX 4 OF THE *TWEETING WITH GOD* BOOK).

TO PREPARE
- Bibles
- Video equipment (internet)
- *Tweeting with GOD* book & app
- *Online with Saints* app
- 1 chair per participant

Worksheet 2

2.1 Welcome: Sit & share

1. Let all participants sit on a chair in a big circle. The moderator has no seat and stands in the middle. possible empty seats taken away.
2. Explain the rules: "Everyone has a chair, apart from me. So I will take the first turn. I will tell you my name and age, and share something simple about myself, for example: 'My name is X, I am 18 years old, and my favorite color is yellow.'"
3. Continue: "Now everyone whose favorite colour is yellow stands up. Go and sit on another chair. I too will quickly take a seat. Beware: you cannot sit on a seat next to you or your own seat."
4. One person will be left standing: they can tell their name and age, and share something about themselves. Those to whom this also applies stand up. If no one stands up, the one in the middle shares something else.

2.2 Introductory dialogue: Navigating in the Bible

Mention a biblical reference, and let everyone search the verse as soon as possible. The first to find it stands up and reads the verse aloud. He or she receives a point and the game continues. Use the following biblical references:

John 3:16	Matthew 6:33
Proverbs 3:5-6	Deuteronomy 31:6
2 Thessalonians 3:3	Philippians 4:19
Isaiah 41:10	Joshua 1:9
Matthew 11:28	Matthew 11:28
Psalm 23:4	Isaiah 40:31
1 Corinthians 10:13	John 16:33
Isaiah 12:2	Psalm 120:1
John 16:3	1 Thessalonians 5:11
Psalm 31:24	Psalm 62:6
Mark 12:30	1 Peter 5:7
Psalm 27:1	Psalm 118:14
Ephesians 6:10	2 Timothy 1:7
Exodus 15:2	Psalm 29:11

Beginning the prayer
- Go (if possible) to the chapel or church. Light the candles and sing a song.
- Say: "You are here in the presence of God. You can choose how you will spend this time with him: sitting, kneeling on the floor. … In a moment of silence, you can ask for a grace: that which you need to get to know him better."

Entering into the scene
- Help participants to visualize and enter into the scene:
- "Jesus is on the mountain with his disciples sitting on the ground around him (Mt 5:1). This is the famous Sermon on the Mount, in which Jesus gives many indications to the disciples. Imagine the scene: you are on a mountain with a beautiful view, sitting on the dry grass. A clear sun is shining, and there is a pleasant breeze. You see the disciples around Jesus. He sits in the middle and looks very serene as he speaks."
- "Go near the group and find yourself a place. You can sit just outside the circle of disciples. Or you can sit down among the Apostles. You could also take the place of Saint Peter, Saint John, or another disciple of your choice. You can also advance even more and sit next to Jesus or at his feet."
- "When you have found your place, trying to feel the warmth of the sun, the freshness of the wind. You can feel the warm earth and dry grass. You see the beautiful view from the mountain, the disciples covered with dust after walking, and especially Jesus in their midst, radiating while he speaks. Now listen to his words …"
- "Pray, for example: 'God, we thank you for this meeting and for this moment of prayer. Through your Holy Spirit, help us to pray with your Word in this moment.'"
- "We will now look calmly at the Bible text. Let the text speak to your heart. It is God who speaks to you through his Word in the Bible."

First point
- Simply say: "Jesus speaks to you at this moment" and read Matthew 6:19-21:
- "It is Jesus who speaks to you now. He warns you not to get attached to material treasures that you can lose. You may have the desire to live more simply, have no attachment to things. This will give you more interior freedom for living in the simple joy of the encounter with Jesus and the people around you. These relationships cannot be stolen or destroyed. They are the true treasure that God wants for you. Only here can you find true joy that does not disappear."
- Spend a few minutes in silence.

Second point

- Simply say: "Jesus speaks to you at this moment" and read Matthew 6:25-26:
- "Do not worry! Jesus knows what you need to live, to eat and drink. Even fashion is not important: Your clothes do not make you a different person. It is you whom God loves, just as you are! With him, you do not need to present yourself in one way or another. You do not need to try to make yourself beautiful. He loves you as you are! You are more important to him than the birds and they are without worry: You can really put all your trust in God."
- Spend a few minutes in silence.

Third point

- Simply say: "Jesus speaks to you at this moment" and read Matthew 6:34:
- "You can be very quiet and leave all concerns here before the Lord. He tells you not to worry about tomorrow. So often we are concerned about what is not yet and what may never be. Jesus invites you to live here and now, with your attention not focused on the future, but on this present moment. If you manage to have such an attitude, everything will be easier. It will change your whole life. Let him act. Do not worry!"
- Spend a few minutes in silence.

Conclusion

- Invite the participants to spend a few minutes in silence to speak directly to Jesus. "He is here and you are here. What would you like to say to him, ask him, praise him ... in the silence of your heart?"
- Conclude by praying the Our Father and the Hail Mary together.

Meeting 3: Scripture – Aren't these Old Testament stories outdated?

The purpose of this meeting is to begin to see how the great stories of the Bible are all related and contain the single message of the nearness of God to his people. The aim is to see the common link between the biblical adventures: not only do these tell of the establishment of the people of Israel, but they also carry a message for us today.

As Christians we are part of this people of God! God's nearness becomes visible and is experienced in the relationship with Jesus: all the great stories of the Old Testament are a preparation for his coming.

The meeting
In preparation, read the #TwGOD Questions and the biblical texts related to this theme (SEE BOX). It will be necessary to adapt to the experience and knowledge of participants. If they followed some catechism classes they may remember the great stories that are presented here. If not, we suggest reading the essential passages together (SEE BELOW). You could also read the summary of the texts in the *Tweeting with GOD* book (SEE #TwGOD 1.22-1.24).

The three major texts discussed in this meeting help to recognise how God always wants to be close to us and seeks a lasting covenant with his people. In Jesus' sacrifice, this covenant became truly definitive: while the Old Testament covenant with God had to be made over and again when the trust had been broken by the sin (SEE #TwGOD 4.13) of the people, Jesus made a covenant with God once and for all through his sacrifice on the cross (SEE MEETING 8).

Prayer
We suggest praying with an Old Testament text, the calling of Abraham. Alternatively, you could use the same text and prayer of Meeting 2 (SEE WORKSHEET 2.3). There are many ways to pray with the Bible: you can follow the model presented in *Tweeting with GOD* (SEE #TwGOD 3.8; MEETING 2) or choose another method.

The important thing is always to try to listen to the Word of God – more than to oneself. Silence and meditating can be a great help to grow in relationship with the Lord.

The great stories in the Bible

Objective of this meeting:
Learn about major events in the Old Testament and understand how these are related to Jesus.

Related Questions:
1.21, 1.22, 1.23, 1.24

Dual challenge:
- Read these Questions in the *Tweeting with GOD* book: 1.21 & 1.23.
- "Interview" someone who reads the Bible on occasions, and ask what is the most important story for them and why?

Additional suggestions

- To further get to know the great biblical events touched upon in this meeting, you can read the following excerpts: Noah (SEE GEN 6:1-22; 7:1-4.23; 8:6-14; 9:8-13; #TwGOD 1.22), Abraham (SEE GEN 12:1-4.10; 13:1-2.8-9.14-16; 15:1-18; #TwGOD 1.23), Moses (SEE WORKSHEET 3.2; #TwGOD 1.24).
- You could repeat the game to find Bible texts as quickly as possible (SEE WORKSHEET 2.2). The texts to be searched are obviously those of #TwGOD Questions 1.22-1.24.
- To encourage participants to read the Bible, you can say that the Word of God has a message for them today, and remind them that it is helpful to pray with biblical texts (SEE MEETING 2).
- Before the prayer, you can ask a few questions that help to reflect on what the participants received during this meeting and what is important to them right now (SEE APPENDIX 3.6).
- One or two people can be invited to prepare a short presentation of the theme based on the #TwGOD Questions for the next meeting.

The gist of it

- Pray, relate, recap
- Intro: God is close
  - Video: Should I believe everything in the Bible? (#TwGOD 1.21)
- **Round Table 1: Noah and God's covenant**
  - Activity: What is the story of Gen 6-9?
  - Why is this covenant important?
- **Round Table 2: Abraham on the road with God**
  - What is the story of Gen 12-15?
  - Why is this covenant important?

....

- **Dialogue: The importance of the Bible**
  - Video: Why is the Bible so important? (#TwGOD 1.10)
- **Round Table 3: Moses and the Exodus**
  - Activity: What is the story of Ex 1-31?
  - Why is this covenant important?
- **Today's hero: Saint Augustine**
- **Synthesis & actualization**
- **Closing prayer**
  - Gen 12:1-4a: Are you ready to go like Abraham?
  - Ask Jesus to help you say "yes" like Abraham
- **Dual challenge**
  - Read the #TwGOD Questions
  - "Interview" someone who reads the Bible occasionally

Procedure for Meeting 3

Relate

00.00 Opening prayer
• Choose a prayer from Appendix 5 or use the *Tweeting with GOD* app.

00.02 Welcome: Scripture charades OT
• Follow the indications on Worksheet 3.1.

00.15 The previous meeting
• Engage in a simple and quick recap. What touched the participants most in the previous meeting? Are there new questions or ideas? How did they fare with the dual challenge?
   – Are there doubts about the Questions in the *Tweeting with GOD* book?
   – What was it like to pray with the Bible at home?
• (The participants who prepared today's Questions can briefly present the theme).

Think

00.20 Introductory dialogue: God is close
• For starters, remind participants of the meeting on the Big Bang and Creation (SEE MEETING 1). Say that at the time of creation, God wanted to share his love with us, his creatures. It is for us that he created the world, nature, animals ... and our brothers and sisters! Now we will see some episodes of the Bible that tell how God continues to be close to his people. God is not a "mechanic" who retires when he finishes making a machine, but a father who loves his children so much!
• Watch the video of #TwGOD Question 1.21: "Should I believe everything in the Bible?"
• Explain that much of the Old Testament was written as a kind of poetry, with a meaning that goes deeper than the simple facts. "There is much symbolic language in the biblical passages we will look at now. Try to look for the deeper message instead of saying beforehand: 'This is impossible.' Rather ask yourself: 'What is the meaning of this?'"

00.30 Round Table 1: Noah and God's covenant
• Follow the indications of Worksheet 3.2.

00.45 Round Table 2: Abraham on the road with God
• Invite the participants to take their Bibles and read together the beginning of the story of Abraham (GEN 12:1-8).
• Ask people to tell the story in their own words.
   – Abraham hears the voice of God and obeys it without hesitation.
   – He leaves his country and everything he knows, placing his trust in God alone.
   – His confidence gains him his name and the promised land (to be called Israel).
   – The most important thing in this story is the relationship of Abraham (and us) with God.
• Explain that because of Abraham's obedience, God made a covenant with him. He was a just man, like Noah (GEN 15). But only Jesus will conclude a covenant with God that includes those who are still unjust. Until Jesus, a new covenant was needed after every sin, after every breach of the covenant with God. Jesus made a covenant once and forever.

00.55 Break [END FIRST & START SECOND SESSION (SEE GS2)]

01.00 Dialogue: The importance of the Bible
• Watch the video of #TwGOD Question 1.10 together: "Why is the Bible so important?"
• Discuss what you just heard. Ask the participants whether they see a connection between the covenant of God with Noah and Abraham in the Old Testament, and the covenant of Jesus for all humanity

in the New Testament? We will come back to this theme later (SEE MEETING 8).

01.10 Round Table 3: Moses and the Exodus
- Follow the indications of Worksheet 3.3.

01.35 Today's hero: Saint Augustine
- The Bible may seem very far away from daily life. Saint Augustine had a similar experience, but then found how the Bible could help him to be more himself!
- Watch the video of Saint Augustine via *Online with Saints*.
- Ask the participants whether they would like to be helped in their lives by the Bible, like Saint Augustine? What can we learn from his example?

Pray & Act

01.40 Synthesis & actualization
- Say in conclusion that the story of 40 years in the wilderness is the history of the love and faithfulness of God, who continues to feed his people, whatever he does. What does this mean for us here and now? The key word is the covenant: the formalised relationship of God with his people. The covenant was renewed after every sin, with Noah, Abraham, Moses. ... We are all part of this people. With Jesus, God's covenant with us is complete once and for all!
- Conclude with the question: "How can what I have learned nourish my personal faith and relationship with Jesus? How can I put this into action?" Speak briefly about this.

01.45 Closing prayer
- Go (if possible) to the chapel or church. Light the candles and sing a song.
- One of the participants can read Genesis 12:1-4a. Invite the participants to think for a moment in

silence: "Am I ready to go wherever God asks me to go, like Abraham? How would I respond? What things can hold me back from saying 'yes' to God?"
- After a few minutes of silence, hand out small sheets and pens. Invite the participants to write a very short letter to Jesus, asking for the courage to be able to say "yes" to God's Will like Abraham. "Even though you may not yet know what God is asking of you, do you desire to say 'yes'?"
- Say: "In a later meeting we will speak about how you can find the Will of God (SEE MEETING 9). For now, keep this letter with you as a reminder of your desire to follow God."
- Finish by praying together an Our Father and a Hail Mary.

01.58 Conclusion in the meeting room
- Remind participants of the date for the next meeting and present the dual challenge:
  - Read these Questions in the *Tweeting with GOD* book: 1.21 & 1.23.
  - "Interview" someone who reads the Bible on occasions, and ask what is the most important story for them and why?

TO PREPARE
- Bibles
- Video equipment (internet)
- *Tweeting with GOD* book & app
- Strips of paper for Scripture Charades OT (DL)
- Images for Round Table 1 (DL)
- Paper & pens

Worksheet 3

3.1 Scripture charades OT

Prepare a series of little papers with titles of Bible stories (SEE BELOW). Consider whether your group will know most of these stories. If not, prepare a list with all these titles and hang it on the wall so the group can see them as a help in guessing. You may wish to explain that, in general, Scripture simply is another word for Bible.

Explain that this activity is called Scripture Charades: "One of you gets up front and receives a note with the title of a Bible story written on it. You get 60 seconds to act this out with the group guessing. After 60 seconds, read aloud the brief summary for each of the Bible stories that were guessed. Then someone else gets 60 seconds to act out as many Bible stories as possible. The one who gets the most correct guesses wins."

Titles of Bible stories
- *Creation of heaven and earth* (GEN 1:1-2:3). How God created heaven and earth for us to live in.
- *Creation of Adam and Eve* (GEN 2:5-24). How God created man and woman.
- *Adam and Eve Fall into sin* (GEN 3:1-24). How the first man and woman sinned against God.
- *Noah's ark* (GEN 6:9-17). How Noah filled the ark with animals and survived a destructive flood.
- *The tower of Babel* (GEN 11:1-9). How the people in their pride thought they could build a tower to heaven.
- *Birth of Moses* (EX 1:8-2:10). Moses is placed into a basket on the river and raised by Pharaoh's daughter.
- *Moses and the burning bush* (EX 3:1-15). How God spoke to Moses from a bush and gave him his mission.
- *The ten plagues* (EX 7:6-11:10). How God struck Egypt with plagues to force Pharaoh to let the people go.
- *The exodus* (EX 14:1-31). How Moses led the Israelites out of Egypt. Start of 40 years in the desert.
- *Moses parting the Red Sea* (EX 14:9-31). How God let his people walk dry over the bottom of the sea.
- *Manna and quails from heaven* (EX 16:13-21). How God fed his people every day with bread and quails.
- *The Ten Commandments* (DEUT 5:1-22). How God gave Moses the Ten Commandments.
- *David and Goliath* (1 SAM 17:1-58). How David struck the giant Goliath with his sling and a single stone.
- *Jonah and the fish* (JON 1:1-17.2:10). How Jonah tried to run from God, and was saved by a big fish.
- *Daniel in the fiery furnace* (DAN 3). How the bad king threw Daniel in a furnace, and God kept him alive.
- *Daniel in the lion's den* (DAN 6). How God saved Daniel when the king threw him in a pit with hungry lions.

3.2 Round Table 1: Noah and God's covenant

- Prepare five images in advance: a rainbow, the bird of peace, Noah's ark, some animals, and some water.
- If participants do not know the story of Noah's ark yet, first read some excerpts from the text together (E.G. GEN 6:1-9.17; 7:1-4.23; 8:6-14; 9:8-13). Place the five pictures on the table and ask the participants to list elements of the story as they remember it. Try to come up together with a list of the most important elements of the story of Noah. You can complete the elements that were not mentioned:
  - God sees that the people behave badly.
  - Only Noah was a good man: God wants to start humankind all over again with Noah and his family.

- Noah must build an ark and bring together representatives of all animals.
- The 40-day deluge begins: everyone and everything drowned, except those in the ark.
- Noah sent a dove to see if he can get out: it returns with an olive branch.
- God gives the rainbow as a symbol of his promise (covenant in biblical words) never to destroy humanity again.

- Then speak together about the importance of this covenant of God with his people, with us. Note that there are many ecological elements in the story of Noah and the flood. Also, water generally represents chaos in the Bible. In this story, when the chaos (water) flows away, we are left with the beauty of creation, the animals, the twigs …

3.3 Round Table 3: Moses and the Exodus

1. Explain that participants will get to know the experience of the Exodus and the 40 years in the wilderness through some essential statements about the history of Israel.
2. Draw an (imaginary) line in the meeting room. All participants stand on the line to begin with. Indicate clearly which side of the line is "true" and which is "false."
3. Explain the rules: "I will read out statements, to which you will respond. You can express yourself by moving around in the room, in silence, so without speaking:
   - 1 big step right means you agree, 2 steps right means you totally agree;
   - 1 big step left means you disagree, 2 steps left means you very much disagree;
   - no steps means you remain neutral or do not know the answer."
4. To practice, you can read a statement like this: "I like Apple more than Android," "I like caramel chocolate ice cream with little pieces of real chocolate," "I have traveled to a country that speaks a language other than English," "I have dark eyes," etc.
5. Now move to the statements indicated below. Depending on the time available, you can use more or fewer statements. Once the participants have responded by moving around, you can ask them to share briefly about their response and about the deeper meaning of the statement.

Statements

- *Statement:* "The people of Israel built the pyramids of the pharaohs in Egypt." True or false?
  Reply: False! The people were in Egypt and worked for the Pharaoh, but it was not at the time of the pyramids (Ex 1:8-11). They came to Egypt many years before because of hunger in their country, at the invitation of the Israelite Joseph who was a high official of the Pharaoh (Ex 1:1-6). But now the people were oppressed by the Pharaoh because he was afraid of the great group of Israelites (Ex 1:12-14).
  Application: "God is with us even when we are in distress, when things do not work out, when we are exhausted, and he does not forget us."

- *Statement:* "Moses did not hold an election campaign and was not elected by the people of Israel." True or false?
  Reply: True! Moses was chosen by God to lead his people and help them to leave Egypt and slavery (Ex 3:9-10).

God spoke to Moses from the burning bush (Ex 3:1-6). At first, he did not want to respond to God's call, and God had to insist a lot before Moses accepted (Ex 3:11-14; 4:1-5.13-17).
Application: "Today too, God calls men and women to guide the Christian people. Are you ready to accept the call of God in your life?" (SEE MEETING 9).

- *Statement:* "Moses was a saint in everything." True or false?
Reply: False! For starters, he had killed someone (Ex 2:11-12). Furthermore, he obeyed only after God's insistence (Ex 3:11-14; 4:1-5.13-17). Also later, on the way through the desert, he did not always do what God asked him (Num 20:12).
Application: "God calls without distinction. He knows that we are all sinners: the Pope, the religious, the carpenter, the nurse. ... It is not sin that shows us the way, but the unconditional response to God's Will. Along the way we gradually advance in holiness" (SEE MEETING 16).

- *Statement:* "The Pharaoh let the people of Israel depart freely, without revolution or civil war." True or false?
Reply: True! But not before Moses insisted so much on behalf of the people and God sent ten plagues (Ex 5:1-2; 7:13-12:42). Although eventually Pharaoh let the people go free, he soon changed his mind and sent his army to bring them back (Ex 13:17-18; 14:9-31).
Application: "Sometimes you have to work hard and have a lot of patience to receive the gift of God – in this case freedom. But God is with us every moment" (SEE MEETING 6).

- *Statement:* "Moses was a magician who used magic to pass through the Red Sea." True or false?
Reply: False! The Bible says that the waters of the Red Sea separated not by magic, but by the miracle God performed. The people could pass across the seabed, while their pursuers drowned when the waters returned to their normal state (Ex 13:17-18; 14:9-31).
Application: "God helps his people also today. He often uses means or persons to send us a message that we had not thought of. Sometimes he even performs great miracles, but usually he helps us through daily experiences in which we can either recognize the hand of God or call them coincidence."

- *Statement:* "In the desert, God gave the people food to eat every day." True or false?
Reply: True! Every day there was a kind of heavenly bread, manna, fallen down from heaven, ready to be picked up (Ex 16:2-8). But the people were not satisfied with the manna: they wanted more, and other things (Num 11:4-15). They had great difficulty trusting God.
Application: "God wants to feed us, especially spiritually. He knows our needs, and we ask him daily to give us our daily bread in the Our Father. But do we trust in him? Are we happy with what he gives? Or do we always want more, always something else?" (SEE MEETING 13C).

- *Statement:* "The people were faithful to God like he was always faithful to them." True or false?
Reply: False! Every time, the people thought of themselves first, not of God's love and what he wanted for them (Ex 17:1-7). Every time they sinned again, and every time once more God forgave them (Ex 24:1-8).
Application: "God is always true to his word and to each of us. But often we are not faithful. We are selfish,

think first of ourselves or our family or circle of friends. We all need to ask for forgiveness from time to time" (SEE MEETING 13F).

- *Statement:* "A 'golden calf' is an award of God for very special people." True or false?
  Reply: False! The people wanted a more immediate contact with their God and did not want to wait until Moses came back with the answer to their request (Ex 32:1-35). They built a golden calf and worshipped it: they could make the calf say whatever they wanted. This may seem like an interesting approach, but in fact, they did not find true joy because they lacked the relationship with the living God.
  Application: "We constantly build dreams that are not based on the reality of God's love, but on the love of self. We build idols, false gods, and give these more attention than God and our neighbors. Examples of idols: fashion, money, power, my appearance, sex, material possessions, make-up, my projects. Deep within you, you know these do not bring any real joy."

- *Statement:* "The people wrote and voted on the Ten Commandments after their experience in the desert." True or false?
  Reply: False! The Ten Commandments come directly from God: these are the rules of life, written on two "tablets" of stone that Moses received on the mountain (while the people were building a golden calf) (Ex 31:18; 34:1-29).
  Application: "One can find traces of the content of the Ten Commandments in various civilizations in the world, also non-Christian. For example, the Universal Declaration of Human Rights of the United Nations shows their importance. Not only because some of its writers were Christians, but especially because the Commandments express a lifestyle that deeply corresponds with what and who we are as people. The Ten Commandments come from God, who knows us better than anyone, because he created us! The Commandments are the way by which we can find true happiness here and now" (SEE MEETING 17).

- *Statement:* "After 40 years in the wilderness, the people arrived in the land promised by God." True or false?
  Reply: "True! Moses saw the promised land but did not enter (NUM 20:1-12). It was the homeland of the Israelites for many generations until they were expelled from their land by enemies. You can read in the Bible how the story continues."
  Application: "God wants to bring us all to the promised land. Like the people in the desert, God is with us, but not everything is perfect yet. We suffer, we are sad, and we experience how hard it is not to sin. Our 'promised land' is heaven, where life will finally be perfect because we will continually be in the presence of our loving God, together with many other people" (SEE MEETING 8).

- Conclude by saying that today, too, there are people in exodus; they, too, are in search of the promised land. Do you know any contemporary examples? Responses may include: economic migrants, war refugees, victims of violence and discrimination, homeless people.
- Then ask in what sense we can say that each of us, alone and together, is also in exile, underway in the desert? Among the answers: We are all on the way to heaven, but have not yet arrived; we seek happiness here on earth, but it is never perfect; we too make big mistakes on the road, like the people in the desert.

Meeting 4: Prayer – Why should I pray and how can I do it?

This meeting aims to help participants discover how God is very close to them, and that they can reach out to him in prayer at every moment. Our focus will be on both personal prayer and community prayer. At the end of the meeting, participants will have learned about different ways to pray.

The meeting

One of the most common reactions when talking about prayer is: "I pray, but God does not listen to me." The proposed exercise will help participants perceive that when we experience silence in prayer it does not mean God is not listening. On the contrary! Even if no one else is listening to us, God always hears us. But prayer is not just a way to make our wishes come true: God desires to enter into a relationship with us. To help us express this relationship, we pray. In this course we aim at helping the participants to experience different forms of prayer themselves.

The bottom line is that we can pray in many ways: any way is fine, as long as we truly try to open ourselves to God, and are not just concerned with what we want. For that reason we look at the various categories of prayer, which show that prayer goes beyond just sending our shopping list to God: praise, supplication, asking for forgiveness, and thanksgiving.

Today's hero is Saint Monica. She totally focused on her prayer, because she knew she could do nothing without God's grace. She kept imploring his help and grace, also when it took very long before she received what she prayed for so ardently.

Prayer

When we speak of prayer, it is especially important to also put it into practice. In the first Round Table, the participants are invited to look back over the past week. The prayer time will be based on this review. You can invite the participants to address to God their worship, intercession, thanks, and requests for forgiveness. Leave everyone completely free to speak out loud or not. No one is forced to open their soul to the group if they do not want to. You could start with a time of worship of God in himself and continue with intercessory prayer for those in the community who need your prayers. Remember to

The Christian view of prayer

Objective of this meeting:
Discover how prayer can bring you closer to God; that various forms and categories of prayer can help you in your life.

Related Questions:
3.1, 3.2, 3.3, 3.5, 3.6, 3.7, 3.12, 3.14, 3.22

Dual challenge:
- Read these Questions in the *Tweeting with GOD* book: 3.1 & 3.3.
- At least once, make time for 3 minutes of prayer in silence.

add a prayer intention for the personal growth in faith of the participants.

Additional suggestions

- This can be a good moment to speak with your group for a few minutes about what you want to do during meeting 7: ACT – How can I help my neighbor? You can discuss what the best option is for your group, and what will need to be done in the coming time to prepare this charitable action.
- The *Tweeting with GOD* app contains a lot of prayers. Encourage the participants to explore these, both for their personal prayer and as a help to participate in Mass in many languages.
- For the first Round Table you could make scarves for blindfolding. This can help the participants to keep their eyes closed.
- During the prayer time you could pray the Chaplet of Divine Mercy (SEE #TwGOD APP > ⚜ > 🏛 > ⊕).
- One or two people can be invited to prepare a short presentation of the theme based on the Questions from the *Tweeting with GOD* book for the next meeting.

The gist of it

- Pray, relate, recap
- Round Table 1: Does God listen?
  - Activity: Review of your week
  - Does God listen even when you don't notice anything?
- Today's hero: Saint Monica

....

- Round Table 2: Forms of prayer
  - Video: Why should I pray, and how do I do it? (#TwGOD 3.1)
  - Do you pray? What forms of prayer do you know?
  - Mt 6:5-13. How can you pray, alone or together?
- Round Table 3: Categories of prayer
  - Activity: Pray with the review of your week
  - Should you only ask, or also praise, thank, and ask forgiveness?
- Closing prayer
  - Bring the prayers of the group to the altar
  - Thank, ask forgiveness, petition, and praise God
- Dual challenge
  - Read the #TwGOD Questions
  - Pray for 3 minutes in silence

Procedure for Meeting 4

Relate

00.00 Opening prayer
- Take a longer time for prayer than usual to start this session, following the indications for praying together (SEE WORKSHEET 4.1).
- Ask God's help to better understand in this meeting what it means to pray and why it is important for everyone.

00.10 Welcome: Find your prayer
- Follow the indications on Worksheet 4.2.

00.20 The previous meeting
- Engage in a simple and quick recap. What touched the participants most in the previous meeting? Are there new questions or ideas? How did they fare with the dual challenge?
  - Are there doubts about the Questions in the book *Tweeting with GOD*?
  - What was the most important Bible story for the interviewee?
- (The participants who prepared today's Questions can briefly present the theme).

Think

00.25 Round Table 1: Does God listen?
- Follow the indications on Worksheet 4.3.

00.45 Today's hero: Saint Monica
- Watch the video of Saint Monica via *Online with Saints*.
- Monica prayed for many years before she finally received what she begged of God. Ask: "Could you have such faith? How can her testimony help you in your life?"

00.55 Break [*END FIRST & START SECOND SESSION (SEE GS2)*]

01.00 Round Table 2: Forms of prayer
- Watch the video of #TwGOD Question 3.1 together: "Why should I pray, and how do I do it?"
- Ask: "Do you pray sometimes? How and when? What forms of prayer do you know?" Among the answers there will probably be the Our Father, the Rosary, Holy Mass, praying with the Bible. ... Write them down on a large sheet of paper.
- Explain that we can pray alone or together in community. Ask: "Can you give examples of some forms of community prayer? Circle these with a red marker. What are examples of prayer forms you can pray alone? Circle these with a green marker." Some terms will receive both a green and red circle.
- Continue: "So there are many ways to pray, both alone and together. In fact, prayer is not so much about how you do it, or what you say. It is mainly an expression of you reaching out to God. He wants to enter into a relationship with you. Does knowing this change the way you pray?"
- Read Matthew 6:5-6. Speak about this text and the reactions of the participants. You may wish to underline that we can pray anywhere, not only in church. For private prayer we just need some quietness like when we are alone in our room. Otherwise there are too many distractions!
- Now read Matthew 6:7-13. Speak together about difficult words and the thoughts of the participants.
- Conclude by saying that Jesus tells us himself that we do not need to use difficult words or complicated phrases to pray. Better not! Just speak from the bottom of our heart. And when we do not know how to pray, we can still pray the Our Father or another prayer from the *Tweeting with GOD* app.

01.20 Round Table 3: Categories of prayer
- Follow the indications on Worksheet 4.4.

01.40 Act
- In conclusion say that God is always here: "He sees you and listens to you, but often we do not realize his presence. You can pray alone or with others. The way you pray is not so important: above all it is important to *spend time* with God. You can start your day greeting God, ask his help during the day, and thank him before you go to sleep, asking forgiveness for what was wrong. To get started, you could resolve to make at least the sign of the cross whenever you wake up or go to sleep. Any form of prayer is fine, but remember that maintaining a relationship needs more than you sending up your shopping list!"
- Conclude with the question: "How can what I have learned nourish my personal faith and relationship with Jesus? How can I put this into action?" Speak briefly about this.

Pray

01.45 Closing prayer
- Go (if possible) to the chapel or church. Light the candles and sing a song.
- Ask two participants to bring the large sheet with the prayers before the altar or in front of an icon or a cross.
- Invite participants to stay a moment in silence to offer these intentions to God in prayer.
  - Then give some time to thank God, each in his or her heart or out loud.
  - Then invite them to ask the Lord for forgiveness, in silence or aloud.
  - Invite them to ask the Lord what they want, for others or for themselves, in silence or aloud.
  - Finally, praise God, worship him, simply recognize his greatness and his love, in silence or aloud.

- Conclude with an Our Father and a Hail Mary.

01.58 Conclusion in the meeting room
- Remind participants of the date for the next meeting and present the dual challenge:
  - Read these Questions in the *Tweeting with GOD* book: 3.1 & 3.3.
  - At least once, make time for 3 minutes of prayer in silence. You can choose a prayer from the *Tweeting with GOD* app or use another form of prayer. The important thing is to do nothing else for 3 minutes; this prayer time is your small offering to God.

TO PREPARE
- Bibles
- Video equipment (internet)
- *Tweeting with GOD* book & app
- *Online with Saints* app
- Sheet for review of the week (DL)
- Large sheets & markers
- Paper & pens
- Box or basket
- (Speaker to play music)

Worksheet 4

4.1 Opening prayer

1. If possible, go to a church or chapel. Perhaps participants can spend some time in front of the Blessed Sacrament in the tabernacle. Otherwise you can place chairs near an icon. Give participants a few minutes in silence to recollect themselves.
2. Give everyone a piece of paper and a pen. Ask them to write down an intention, something they would like to tell or ask God. For example, they may want to pray for someone who is ill, for work, for an exam to go well, for refugees. Tell them that these intentions will not be read by anyone.
3. Collect the papers in a box or basket.
4. Put the box or basket in front of the altar, the Blessed Sacrament, or the icon.
5. Make the sign of the cross. Introduce the prayer. You can start, for example: "Thank you, Lord, for bringing us together tonight. In this box are our prayers. Please hear them." Now tell the participants that they are free to pray aloud the intentions they had written down – if they feel like doing so.
6. When it has been silent for a few minutes after the last intention has been spoken aloud, conclude the prayer, saying, for example: "Please hear these prayers of ours, Lord. Help us tonight to be respectful and attentive to each other. Help us learn and grow. Our Father …" Make the sign of the cross.

4.2 Welcome: Find your prayer

- As a warm up, divide the group into two teams. Each team has at least one phone with the *Tweeting with GOD* app. Let them open the ⛪ "Pray" section, and then 🛐 "Catholic Prayers."
- Say: "As you can see, the 'Catholic Prayers' section of the app consists of 7 parts. I will mention the name of a prayer in the app, which you have to find as soon as possible in one of the 7 sections. The team that finds the prayer first gets 1 point."
- Get ready to keep score, and give the title of one prayer at the time:

– Glory Be to the Father	– Angel of God
– Benedictus	– Memorare
– Angelus	– Anima Christi
– Prayer to Saint Michael	– Act of Contrition
– The Rosary	– Te Deum
– Divine praises	– Stations of the Cross
– Hail Mary	– Sub tuum praesiduum
– Act of Hope	– Act of Love
– Regina Coeli	– Chaplet of Divine Mercy
– Our Father	– Prayer for the Pope
– Salve Regina	– Act of Faith
– Veni Creator	– Magnificat

4.3 Review of my week

- Say that the Bible tells us that God always listens to our prayers. Read the Bible verse 1 John 5:14. Do not discuss it now.
- Give each participant a copy of the table for reviewing their week:

Contentment	Annoyance
– I am thankful for …	– What unnerved me …
– I am satisfied, because …	– This bothered me …
– I am a bit proud because …	– I was angry because …
Joy	*Hope*
– It gave me joy that …	– I want to continue with …
– I was happy, because …	– I wish ever more …
– I was pleasantly surprised that …	– I need more courage to …

- Invite: "Take 5 minutes to look back over your week with the aid of this table, looking at what satisfied or upset you, what gave you joy or hope. You can divide the circle into four different-sized parts and write a few key words for each group."
- Then ask to form groups of two: "One of you closes their eyes and tells of the events of the week. Keep your eyes closed. The other listens for five minutes without saying anything, and without touching or reacting. At a signal, you switch roles. Use all the time available: speak for 5 minutes or remain silent." Optionally, you can play quiet music in the background so that the groups do not disturb each other too much.
- Then come all together and ask the participants to tell what was the easiest: talking or listening? "How was it to speak without receiving a reaction? Did you believe the other was listening all the time?"
- Then ask whether they can see a connection between what we just did and the way in which God hears our prayers? "Does it help you to have faith in God who listens to your prayers even when you do not experience any reaction? Unlike your friends, God is always listening! And he invites you to listen too: praying is not only speaking, it is also and especially listening to God." Speak together about this.
- To conclude, you can read the Bible verse 1 John 5:14 once more, and ask if everyone agrees with Saint John. Why or why not?

4.4 Categories of prayer

Write these four circles representing four categories of prayer on a screen or flip over:

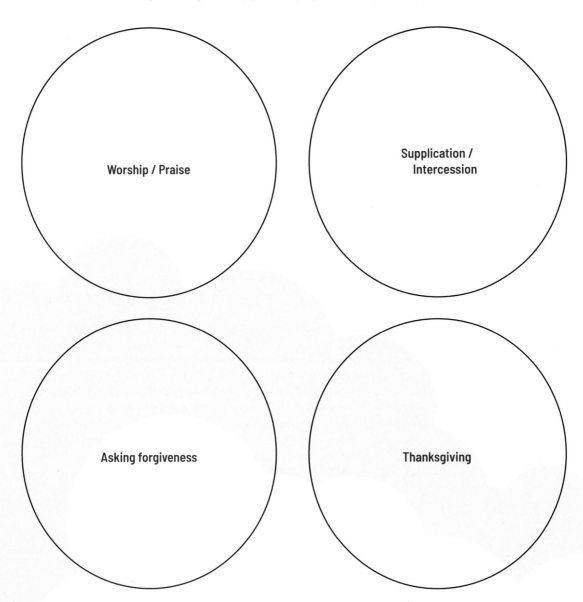

Worship / Praise

Supplication / Intercession

Asking forgiveness

Thanksgiving

- Explain that we can distinguish different kinds of prayer: worship (praise), asking (petitioning), thanking (thanksgiving), asking forgiveness (confession). Search together for examples of each prayer attitude.
- Explain: "Now take your sheets with the review of the week. You will receive some sticky notes. Write a few brief prayers or whatever you want to share with God, at least one for each of the four categories. Stick the notes on a large sheet, organized by prayer attitude (without reading them aloud). There will probably be especially intercessions for specific intentions."
- Conclude saying that each of the four categories of prayer is important. "You do not only ask your friends for help, you also thank them, you say sorry, and sometimes maybe congratulate (praise) them for who they are or what they do. It is the same with God! If you not only look for him when you need help but also just to spend time with him, you will gradually deepen your relationship with God! Just give it a try. During your day, make it a habit to simply say: 'Thank you, Father, 'Please, help me Lord, 'Praise to you, God!', or 'Sorry, Jesus!'"

Meeting 5: Your group's questions 1

This meeting about your group's questions forms an integral part of the course schedule. We have explained earlier how to approach this meeting (SEE GS8). If you need help to encourage the participants to ask questions, you can look back to the introductory pages (SEE GS9).

Sample procedure for Meeting 5

Relate

00.00 Opening prayer
- Choose a prayer from Appendix 5 or use the *Tweeting with GOD* app.

00.02 Welcome
- Decide on a warm-up activity (SEE APPENDIX 3.7).

00.15 The previous meeting
- Engage in a simple and quick recap. What touched the participants most in the previous meeting? Are there new questions or ideas? How did they fare with the dual challenge?
  - Are there doubts about the Questions in the *Tweeting with GOD* book?
  - What form of prayer did the participants choose for their 3 minutes of prayer?
- (The participants who prepared today's Questions can briefly present the theme).

Think

00.20 Round Table 1: First question
- Watch that all participants who wish to have the possibility of asking questions and presenting their view on the matter.

00.45 Today's hero: Choose from the app
- Choose the video of a saint that may help with the dialogue on today's theme.

00.55 Break [END FIRST & START SECOND SESSION (SEE GS2)]

01.00 Round Table 2: Second question / a new angle on the first question
- Make sure that the questions are discussed in depth. This might be a good moment for dialogue in small groups.

01.25 Round Table 3: Deepening the theme
- You can check among the questions on the website tweetingwithgod.com whether a video is available about today's theme.

Pray & Act

01.40 Synthesis & actualization
- Check whether there are any remaining questions, which you can briefly address at this point, or defer to another meeting.
- Conclude with the question: "How can what I have learned nourish my personal faith and relationship with Jesus? How can I put this into action?" Speak briefly about this.

01.45 Closing prayer
- Go (if possible) to the chapel or church. Light the candles and sing a song.

- Open the prayer, for example: "Lord Jesus, thank you for today's dialogue. We have been able to grow in our understanding of the theme, and we hope that this will bring us closer to you. Help us recognize your presence in our lives, and inspire us with your Holy Spirit to keep searching for the truth."
- You can repeat a prayer method from one of the previous meetings, or add a time of intercession with the group, for example.
- Conclude with an Our Father and a Hail Mary.

01.58 Conclusion in the meeting room
- Remind participants of the date for the next meeting and present the dual challenge:
  - Read the related Questions in the *Tweeting with GOD* book.
  - Define together what you will do for the second challenge.

- Bibles
- Video equipment (internet)
- *Tweeting with GOD* book & app
- *Online with Saints* app

The gist of it

- **Pray, relate, recap**
- **Round Table 1: First question**
  - Paying attention that all who wish can contribute
- **Today's hero: Choose from the app**

....

- **Round Table 2: Second question / a new angle on the first question**
  - Maybe work with small groups.
  - Make sure that the questions are discussed in depth
- **Round Table 3: Deepening the theme**
  - Check whether a video about the theme is available
  - Attention that everyone gets to say what they want to
- **Synthesis & actualization**
- **Closing prayer**
  - Ask the help of the Holy Spirit to find answers
- **Dual challenge**
  - Read the #TwGOD Questions related to the theme(s) covered
  - Define the second challenge together

Meeting 6: Good & Evil – Why is there evil if God created everything so good? What is grace?

The purpose of this meeting is to learn about God's grace. We will first see how all have the experience of evil and of personal sin. To break away from the influence of evil we have to prepare ourselves and open our hearts to receive the grace of God. The related #TwGOD Questions (SEE BOX) provide a set of arguments on the subject.

The theme of grace is essential, so we invite you to give it sufficient time and attention. Feel free to spread the content over multiple sessions. It is a theme around which our personal relationship with God evolves. God's grace is part of the foundation of all our faith and Christian life.

The meeting
It is perhaps not the first theme that we think of every day. Therefore, it may be useful to prepare the group with an activity (SEE APPENDIX 3.7). Once the participants mentally enter into this theme, there will certainly be much to discuss.

Questions may arise about miracles, magic, or exorcism. If you were to address these questions now – important as they are – you would risk losing the thread of this meeting. When there is a lot of interest in these issues you could address these in one of the meetings on your group's questions (SEE #TwGOD 3.18 & 4.18).

Note that this is not about the personal sin of the participants: during a later meeting, we will look at the importance of recognizing our personal sins and of asking forgiveness of the Lord (SEE MEETING 14). The important thing at this point is to recognize how we are all subject to evil as well as to the consequences of sin, and that we all need God's grace.

Prayer
Prayer is always important, and maybe even more so in this meeting. The question of evil and grace can only be understood when we grow in relationship with the God who is love. Only this love can overcome evil. Even if there will not always be definitive answers, the key is that the Lord is always near to help us with his grace.

> ## Evil, sin, and grace
>
> *Objective of this meeting:*
> Understand that the existence of evil is not according to the plan of God, who created us with a free will and supports us with his grace.
>
> *Related Questions:*
> 1.4, 1.34, 1.35, 1.36, 1.42, 4.12
>
> *Dual challenge:*
> - Read these Questions in the *Tweeting with GOD* book: 1.35 & 4.12.
> - Do something good for someone without others noticing.

That is why at the heart of the prayer of this meeting we ask for special graces for each participant. These can help and support them in their personal faith and their relationship with the Lord.

Additional suggestions

- To encourage mutual listening, you can suggest that each participant listens really well when others speak (SEE APPENDIX 3.5).
- An alternative for "Today's hero" could, for example, be Saints Olga and Vladimir. These people lived a life of sin and spiritual struggle, but in the end they found inner peace in their relationship with the Lord. This is the basis of every journey of faith, and therefore also of that of the participants.
- You could conclude – before the prayer – with a few questions that help participants to reflect on what they received during this meeting (SEE APPENDIX 3.6).
- One or two people can be invited to prepare a short presentation of the theme based on the #TwGOD Questions for the next meeting.

The gist of it

- **Pray, relate, recap**
- **Round Table 1: The experience of evil**
  - Activity: What are examples of evil today?
  - Why do humans do these things?
  - What about evil not caused by humans?
- **Round Table 2: The impotence of God**
  - Video: Why is there evil? (#TwGOD 1.35)
  - Why did God create us with a free will? Who is Satan?

....

- **Round Table 3: Grace**
  - What is grace in a Christian sense? (#TwGOD APP > QUESTION 4.12)
  - How to respond to God's grace?
- **Today's hero: Saint Lidwina of Schiedam**
- **Synthesis & actualization**
- **Closing prayer**
  - Write down special graces for your life with God
- **Dual challenge**
  - Read the #TwGOD Questions
  - Do something good without others noticing

Procedure for Meeting 6

Relate

00.00 Opening prayer
- Choose a prayer from Appendix 5 or use the *Tweeting with GOD* app.

00.02 Welcome: Quick thinking
- Follow the indications on Worksheet 6.1.

00.15 The previous meeting
- Engage in a simple and quick recap. What touched the participants most in the previous meeting? Are there new questions or ideas? How did they fare with the dual challenge?
  - Are there doubts about the Questions in the *Tweeting with GOD* book?
  - How did it go with the challenge of the last meeting?
- (The participants who prepared today's Questions can briefly present the theme).

Think

00.20 Round Table 1: The experience of evil
- Follow the indications on Worksheet 6.2.

00.40 Round Table 2: The impotence of God?
- Watch the video of #TwGOD Question 1.35 together: "Why is there evil?" Talk about what you have heard and seen.
- Ask: "If God is omnipotent, can he create a stone so heavy that he cannot lift it?" Talk about this for a moment.
- Explain that this question is often used to show that God is limited – which is contrary to our faith. But God cannot be captured by our human comparisons. If God limits himself (when he is born as a man), it is by his own

Will, out of love for us (SEE MEETING 8). Speak about this.
- Say that in his great love, God created us with free will. He hopes we will love him back. Nobody can be forced to love. Only when we are free can we freely choose to love God in response to his love for us. This means we also have the freedom not to choose for God. What can be the link between this freedom and the experience of evil? Does this help explain evil?
- The basic idea is that by giving us the opportunity to choose for him in freedom, God also gave us the possibility of another choice: to reject him and to reject his love. The latter is the origin of evil.
- Say in conclusion that in the Bible, evil is personified in the person of the devil, Satan. He is a creature of God who abused his freedom by choosing against God and his love. He is the enemy of God who seeks to tempt us to choose against love, against the light of God, to enter into darkness and misfortune – far away from God and the happiness he wants for each of us. Be cautious, but do not be afraid: the devil is only a creature and cannot hurt those who remain close to Jesus.

00.55 Break [END FIRST & START SECOND SESSION (SEE GS2)]

01.00 Today's hero: Saint Lidwina of Schiedam
- Read Colossians 1:24. How can Saint Paul rejoice in his suffering? Can you see any sense in what he says?
- Watch the video of Saint Lidwina of Schiedam via *Online with Saints*.
- Ask the participants whether they think suffering can be meaningful?
- Saint Lidwina suffered greatly in her life. She found certain sense in her pain because it brought her closer to God (SEE #TwGOD 1.37). This clearly does not

mean that we need to look for suffering. There is already far too much pain in the world, which is why Saint Paul claimed that Jesus' suffering is not complete. But if we are suffering, we can offer our pain to God. This is why Saint Paul could even rejoice in his suffering. What do the participants think about this concept?

01.15 Round Table 3: Grace
• Follow the indications on Worksheet 6.3.

Pray & Act

01.35 Synthesis & actualization
• Ask: "What do you remember most about this session?" and speak about it. The central message is that despite the experience of evil, we can be at peace because God is with us every moment and wants to help us with his grace.
• Conclude with the question: "How can what I have learned nourish my personal faith and relationship with Jesus? How can I put this into action?" Speak briefly about this.

01.40 Closing Prayer
• Go (if possible) to the chapel or church. Light the candles and sing a song.
• Distribute small papers and pens and place a basket before the altar.
• Say: "You can ask God for special graces for your life. This is not about a new bicycle, but something that can help you become closer to God. For example, to learn how to love, to pray, to read the Bible. ... Everyone can write down one or more graces they want to ask from God. Then fold the paper and take it to the basket before the altar."
• During the silence you can play contemplative music.
• End the prayer with an Our Father.

• The papers may be offered to God together with the gifts of bread and wine at the next Eucharist or destroyed by the moderator. Nobody should read them: These are prayers to God alone.

01.58 Conclusion in the meeting room
• Remind participants of the date for the next meeting and present the dual challenge for Meeting 7:
  – Read these Questions in the *Tweeting with GOD* book: 1.35 & 4.12.
  – Do something good for someone without others noticing.

TO PREPARE
– Bibles
– Video equipment (internet)
– *Tweeting with GOD* book & app
– *Online with Saints* app
– Box of matches & ashtray
– Sticky notes, papers & pens
– Large sheet & markers
– Small papers, pens & basket
– (Speaker for playing music)

Worksheet 6

6.1 Welcome: Quick thinking

1. Tell participants that this activity is about getting them thinking and sharing about good and evil.
2. Explain the rules: "I am going to pass around a matchbox. You will each light a match in turns. As long as the match is burning you can spout whatever comes to your mind about the topic. Anything goes: opinions, questions, ideas, memories, and so on. When you need to extinguish the match (before burning your fingers, please!), you must stop talking and pass the matchbox to the next person."
3. Before you start the activity, give the participants a minute to reflect on the topic. This is to prevent people from only repeating what others say.
4. Select the first person to light a match, give them the matchbox, and tell them to start.

6.2 Round Table 1: The experience of evil

Dialogue 1
- Distribute sticky notes and pencils.
- Start by saying that the experience of evil can be different for everyone, but we all experience evil in our lives.
- Ask the participants to write on each note an example of the experiences of evil in our world. The responses will include pain, death, disease, disasters, wars ...
- Let the participants stick their notes on a wall or another visible place.
- Say: "When you see all this, it is clear that the world is not perfect. Where do you think all this evil comes from?"
- Through the responses you will hopefully discover that there are two major groups of evil: one where humans are the author, and one where humans are not directly involved.
- Divide a large sheet in two and ask participants to sort the notes according to the origin of evil "man" or "nature." Participants might use the words "chance" or "fate" or "destiny," but these words do not express the ongoing relationship of God with creation.

Dialogue 2
- Talk first about evil caused by humans (theft, murder, wars ...).
- Ask: "Why do humans do these things?" And then: "Do you, too, contribute to the evil in the world by your sins?"
- The intention here is not so much to speak about the particular sins of the participants, but to stay on a more general level: We are all sinners.
- Ask: "What can we do to reduce the harm caused by humans?" Speak about it in the group.

Dialogue 3

- Then talk about the evil that is not caused by humans (disease, natural death, disasters ...). This second category of evil is not related to personal sin: for example, typically, disease is not caused by the sin of the sick!
- Ask: "Where does all this trouble come from? If God is so great, why does he allow it?" (Do realize that we cannot answer this question completely here on earth, but elements of an answer can be found).

6.3 Round Table 3: Grace

- Divide the group into small groups (SEE APPENDIX 3.1 & 3.2). Ask them to think for a moment: What makes me live (apart from material things)? Responses may include the love of a parent, friendships, being esteemed by others ...
- Then ask: "Which of these responses are linked to God? What have you done to deserve this?" Finally ask: "When we speak of 'grace,' what do you think it is?" Speak about it.
- In the *Tweeting with GOD* app, read the answer to Question 4.12. Ask what is the relationship between what you have just read and what we just said. And then what is grace in the Christian sense?
- Come back together in the group, and write the answers found on a large sheet. The answers include: a gift, God is near, he is here to help me ...
- Say that this is not automatic; we must accept the gift and collaborate with God's grace. Ultimately, grace is the help of God, freely given to grow in relationship with him in daily life.
- Ask: "How can we respond to the grace that God gives us?" To help the group, you can add: "I do not deserve the friendship of my friends, but I can show my gratitude: this will change me, lead me to act on behalf of others. Can it be the same in your relationship with God?"

Meeting 7: ACT – How can I help my neighbor?

The dual purpose of this meeting is to act charitably and to help others as a group, while participants discover the importance of volunteering, sharing, and attention to the other in order to practice their faith. The message of Jesus, the Gospel, is not only intended to be read and questioned intellectually: it is meant to be lived together with others!

There is a direct connection between knowing God and serving him in our daily lives. Think back to the five keys to *How to grow in faith* (SEE GS1): in addition to relating and thinking about the faith, groups using *Tweeting with GOD* live the other three components: they pray, celebrate, and act charitably.

Pray

Prayer is essential if we want to grow in the true knowledge of God and advance in a personal relationship with the Lord. Hence the importance of starting and ending each meeting with prayer (SEE #TwGOD 3.1). We propose to insert a full evening of prayer in the course (SEE MEETING 14), and to make time for a day of retreat (SEE MEETING 11). We have already spoken about personal and community prayer. Every prayer is both personal and collective, because we are never alone when we pray (SEE MEETING 4).

Celebrate

It is not Catholic to display serious faces all the time. God wants to communicate his joy to us (JN 15:11). If we believe that he loves us and saves us, then we can also be lighthearted. Humor can help a lot to make a deep and serious discussion more effective and to overcome hesitations or opposing views in dialogue. Not because faith is ridiculous, but just to see things in a proper perspective, so we can see what is really important: the unconditional love of God for all people. This love carries a promise of hope in itself. That is good news to celebrate together! (SEE MEETING 18)

Act

We would have lost the purpose of this course if it were only to look at intellectual knowledge. We hope that the experience of the participants in the meetings will lead them to grow in their personal relationship with Jesus. This friendship with God will in turn stimulate their true relationship with others and their desire to act charitably toward those in need.

> ## ACT - Help someone else
>
> *Objective of this meeting:*
> Volunteering in a nursing home, in the community, or with a charitable organization, with the purpose of putting what has been learned so far into practice.
>
> *Questions from Tweeting with GOD:*
> 1.35, 3.1, 3.50, 4.1, 4.7, 4.8, 4.9, 4.10, 4.45

Faith in Jesus is neither a mental nor a solitary exercise. One cannot be a Christian alone. God loves all people, especially those who face hardships. Jesus made himself very small to live among us. If we seek him in faith, we can also recognize his presence among people less well off than ourselves. Apart from prayer, we can help these people in many ways. At any rate we can help them recognize the love of Jesus which gives color and hope to all of life.

You might ask yourself what difference you can make, as you can never assist all those who need help in the world. Saint Mother Teresa said: "We can do no great things – only small things with great love." We can at least try to help those we meet. If all people did the same, the world would be very different! The following pages provide some ideas for charitable action. Ideally, this action should be considered a choice on the part of the group rather than a mandatory activity. Together, you can probably find many other ways to help others!

The gist of it

- Decide beforehand what you are going to do
- Prepare what you will need
- Pray, divide tasks, get started
- Be focused on the people you want to help
- Evaluate together

....

- Suggested activities
    - Entertaining in a nursing home
    - Helping the food bank
    - Meeting homeless people
    - Assisting the needy in the community
    - Holding a Church auction for charity
    - "Week of Mercy" in your community

Procedure for Meeting 7

Program

Preparation beforehand

- Decide (at an earlier meeting) with the group what you would like to do to help others (see the suggestions below). The best is to collectively agree on your project.
- You could invite a representative of a charity organization to one of your meetings. Ask this person about their work and how the group can help.
- See to the practical aspects: transportation, permits, clothing, safety, risk assessment, parental/guardian permission, resources, budget ...

Getting started

- Before beginning the charitable outreach, gather all participants together. Engage in a quick dialogue: this is not the moment for a long debate.
- Start with a short prayer to make it clear that you are doing this as an act of faith and love for the Lord and his people. If possible, have one of the participants say this prayer. You can ask for strength and divine inspiration for the group, and an open heart towards the people you will be meeting.
- Divide the tasks (together with a member of the charity organization) and get started.
- Always stay focused on the people you want to help: it revolves around them! Jesus loves each of them as he loves you too.
- If you want, you can hold breaks, with several or all group members discussing how things are going, whether they need help or whether they have any questions.

Conclusion

- Take time to talk about your experience after the event. Ask: "What do you think of this experience?

What have you learned? Are there things that surprised you? Do you think it was useful? Would you be willing to repeat this experience? Does it help you move forward in your personal faith?"
- End with a short prayer.
- You can also have a meal together to conclude the outreach, continuing to dialogue about the highlights and challenges of the experience.
- Remind participants of the date for the next meeting and the dual challenge of last time.

Suggestions

Nursing home

- You could go to a nursing home and organize games for residents.
- Take a bunch of old board games with you that residents are likely to enjoy.
- Prepare tasty snacks and drinks. Make the residents feel they are important and valuable to you!
- If there are musicians or singers in the group, they can play a few songs. You can also prepare a playlist with classics from the old days.
- Conversations will probably emerge between participants and residents. Take the time to truly listen to the people. You will notice that you do not always need to reply. Often they just want to share their story. The most important thing is that you are there for them in friendship and faith according to their needs.
- (If the experience is good, participants could individually decide to "adopt" a resident whom they will visit regularly thereafter – no longer under the responsibility of the moderator, but directly with the staff of the nursing home).

Food bank

- Come up with a way to help the local food bank to find means or help with distribution.
- For example, make a shopping list of products that the food bank could use (together with a representative of the food bank).
- Stand at the entrance of one or more supermarkets (first ask permission of the store manager).
- Distribute pieces of paper with one item printed on it to people who walk into the store and ask if they would like to buy this product for the food bank.
- Collect the products that people hand to you in boxes. Sort the products by kind; this saves the food bank work.
- You could hold a similar action at your school or in the parish at the end of Sunday Mass.

Homeless people

- You may also go out and meet homeless people.
- Most cities have organizations that work with homeless people. These organizations usually have daily or weekly activities that volunteers can help out at, such as serving breakfast or dinner.
- The key is not what you do, but how you do it. Do not be afraid to talk to the people you meet, and to listen to their story.

In the community

- You will also find people in need in your own community. You could talk to the priest or the charity committee and make a list of people who are in need for whatever reason.
- They may need help with all sorts of things:
  - tidying the garden
  - repairing a doorbell
  - painting a garden shed
  - purchasing heavy groceries
  - drinking tea with a lonely person
- Divide the tasks among yourselves and get started.

- For some (e.g. technical) tasks, you may want to ask other community members for help. If they want to assist you, great! After all, the goal is to help these people!
- You can also apply this to the church or school itself. Think cleaning and tidying the church/school building and its surroundings.

Church auction

- To raise money for charity you could organize a church auction, for example after Sunday Mass or an evening. This does require some preparation.
- Ask people to donate items which you will then sell at the auction. You will be surprised at how much people will give!
- Ask a capable person to function as auctioneer, if needed ask someone from outside of the group. The better the auctioneer, the more money you will raise!
- Divide the other tasks: have people show items, wrap items, and collect and count the money.

Week of Mercy

- If you want to go big, participate with your group in the organization of a "Week of Mercy" in the community or parish. Charitable activities will be held throughout the week. On Sunday, everyone and everything is brought to God in prayer. Both volunteer community members and people in need will be happy with such an initiative.

TO PREPARE
- A common idea
- Resources needed to execute it

Meeting 8: Christmas & Easter – Why is Jesus our "Savior"? From what do I need to be saved?

The purpose of this meeting is to recognize how everything that has been said so far leads to the mystery of the birth, death and resurrection of Jesus, celebrated at Christmas and Easter. In more traditional language, we will speak about God's great "plan of salvation." Only when we contemplate human existence and our personal life in the context of God's plan can we begin to see sense in the painful events surrounding the death on the cross and resurrection of Jesus.

You will often have to refer to the content of this meeting (AND #TwGOD 1.26-1.28). The theme of the death and resurrection of Jesus is truly the center of our faith. On the cross, all God's love and his desire for us to be with him converge and are realized. This is how our Savior saves us from having to be far away from God because of our sins.

The meeting

From the beginning, many had difficulty accepting the core of Jesus' message. This remains true today, too. When you speak about this issue in the group, the discussion can bring up questions like: "What do I need to be saved from? How could the death of one person change the fate of all? Is it not just past history?" That is great, for it shows the involvement of the participants.

We will begin the dialogue in this meeting by reflecting on joy, in connection to the question: "What brings me true and lasting joy?" From there we will move to the joy of Christmas, when God comes to live with us. Subsequently we contemplate the cross of Jesus: his suffering, his death and his resurrection became for us the door to the true joy of eternal life. We will briefly see how the dramatic events that precede Easter are celebrated in Holy Week. The activity of Jesus & Me helps the participants to see where they stand vis-a-vis Jesus.

Prayer

For the prayer, we propose to go see Jesus who is really present with his Eucharistic body in the tabernacle in the chapel or church (SEE MEETING 13C). If possible, organize Eucharistic adoration. If the participants do not know

Jesus and God's plan of salvation

Objective of this meeting:
Learn about the core of our faith and what God saves us from through the birth, suffering, death, and resurrection of Jesus.

Related Questions:
1.26, 1.27, 1.28, 1.29

Dual challenge:
- Read these Questions in the *Tweeting with GOD* book: 1.26 & 1.27.
- Make, find, or buy a cross and put it in your room. Talk with Jesus on the cross from time to time.

this form of prayer, it is important to introduce it briefly (SEE #TwGOD 3.14). You could, for example, start by reading the text of Question 3.14 together in the *Tweeting with GOD* app. Optionally, you could invite a participant or moderator to give a testimony of their personal experience with Eucharistic adoration (SEE APPENDIX 2).

Additional suggestions

- If the conversation risks faltering, it may be useful to invite the participants to talk in small groups for a moment. There are several proposals for this (SEE APPENDIX 3.1 & 3.2).
- You may wish to conclude the meeting – before the prayer – with a few questions that help to reflect on what is important for the participants at this moment (SEE APPENDIX 3.6).
- Your priest, deacon, or another pastoral worker may be invited to attend this session to talk about the core of our faith.
- One or two people can be invited to prepare a short presentation of the theme based on the #TwGOD Questions for the next meeting.

The gist of it

- Pray, relate, recap
- **Round Table 1: The true joy of living**
  - Find together examples of what brings happiness
- **Dialogue: Perfect happiness and the Incarnation**
  - Video: "Will there be steak and cake in heaven?" (#TwGOD 1.45)
  - How is Jesus' birth related to our perfect happiness?
- **Round Table 2: The cross and my salvation**
  - Dialogue around the cross: What does Jesus save me from?

....

- **Activity Jesus & me**
- **Today's hero: Saint Nicholas Owen**
- **Round Table 3: Jesus' resurrection at Easter**
  - What is the importance of the resurrection?
  - What happens during the Easter Triduum?
- **Synthesis & actualization**
- **Closing prayer**
  - Exposition of the Blessed Sacrament
  - Praise God for his love, sacrifice, and promise of life
- **Dual challenge**
  - Read the #TwGOD Questions
  - Make, find, or buy a cross and put it in your room. Talk with Jesus on the cross from time to time.

Procedure for Meeting 8

Relate

00.00 Opening prayer
- Choose a prayer from Appendix 5 or use the *Tweeting with GOD* app.

00.02 Welcome: Human knot
- Follow the indications on Worksheet 8.1.

00.10 The previous meeting
- Engage in a simple and quick recap. What touched the participants most in the previous meeting? Are there new questions or ideas? How did they fare with the dual challenge?
    - Are there doubts about the Questions in the *Tweeting with GOD* book?
    - Have they been able to do something for another without it being noticed?
- (The participants who prepared today's Questions can briefly present the theme).

Think

00.15 Round Table 1: The true joy of living
- Follow the indications of Worksheet 8.2.

00.25 Dialogue: Perfect happiness and the Incarnation
- Watch the video of #TwGOD Question 1.45 together: "Will there be steak and cake in heaven?" Speak with the group about difficult points, and search together for the central message.
- Explain that God wants true happiness for us, a joy that lasts forever. Here on earth we can know happiness, but there is always suffering and mourning too. The world is not perfect and we are limited. Yet God wants more for us. He wants us to live forever in his presence in true and perfect happiness: This is the best definition of heaven! Why do you think we say this? Speak about this.
- Then say that Jesus came to show how God wants to bring about this perfect happiness. It is only because of Jesus that we have access to God. God wanted to come very close to us. He was happy to give up the perfect happiness of heaven in order to be born as a man on earth, limiting himself in many ways. He became flesh, the Bible says, which is why we speak of the Incarnation (JN 1:14).
- We celebrate Jesus' birth as man at Christmas. God was never this close to us. Jesus told us everything we needed to know about the love of God for every human being. Why do you think Christmas is such an important feast? What exactly do we celebrate at Christmas?
- The Bible tells us: "This is the Will of God, your sanctification" (1 THESS 4:3). By trying to live with God in holiness or sanctity, we can come closer to him (SEE MEETING 16). It is only through Jesus that we can reach a level of sanctification that will bring us to God and the perfect happiness he wants for us. Without him, we cannot do this.

00.35 Round Table 2: The cross and my salvation
- Follow the indications of Worksheet 8.3.

00.55 Break *[END FIRST & START SECOND SESSION (SEE GS2)]*

01.00 Jesus & me
- Follow the indications of Worksheet 8.4.

01.20 Today's hero: Saint Nicholas Owen
- Watch the video of Saint Nicholas Owen via *Online with Saints*.
- Ask: "What connection do you see between our theme and the life of Saint Nicholas Owen?" And:

"Would you be willing to give your life for your friends like he did?"

01.25 Round Table 3: Jesus' resurrection at Easter
- Follow the indications of Worksheet 8.5.

01.35 Jesus & me revisited
- Follow the indications of Worksheet 8.6.

Pray & Act

01.40 Synthesis & actualization
- Come together and ask: "So, what is God's grand plan for us?" Jesus wants us to find true joy, to be happy and full of hope in this moment, and later forever with him in heaven, for which we are all predestined. God brings this about through Jesus. At Christmas we celebrate the fact that God himself came to live among us: he was never so close! At Easter we celebrate the fact that Jesus died for our sins, to make it possible for us to be reconciled with God. This is when he "saved" us from the devastating effect of our sins: therefore we call him our Savior. Thanks to him, we have a great future where before there was none! When he became alive again, he promised that we too could choose to live forever with God in perfect happiness.
- Conclude with the question: "How can what I have learned nourish my personal faith and relationship with Jesus? How can I put this into action?" Speak briefly about this.

01.45 Closing prayer
- Go (if possible) to the chapel or church. Light the candles and sing a chant.
- Give a short introduction on the exposition of the Blessed Sacrament and take time for Eucharistic adoration (SEE #TwGOD 3.14). If it is not possible to expose the Blessed Sacrament, remain in all simplicity before the closed tabernacle or before a crucifix or an icon.
- Take time to praise the Lord for his love, his sacrifice, his death, and the great hope of eternal life in him that he has obtained for us on the cross, and for the joy that he wants to give us already now!
- Invite the participants to spend a moment of silence with him, and to realize that they too are destined for this joy he wants to give.
- Conclude with an Our Father and a Hail Mary.

01.58 Conclusion in the meeting room
- Remind participants of the date for the next meeting and present the dual challenge:
  - Read these Questions in the *Tweeting with GOD* book: 1.26 & 1.27.
  - Make, find, or buy a cross and put it in your room. Talk with Jesus on the cross from time to time.

TO PREPARE
- Bibles
- Video equipment (internet)
- *Tweeting with GOD* book & app
- *Online with Saints* app
- Sticky notes & pens
- (Auction hammer & coins)
- Crucifix
- Eucharistic adoration

Worksheet 8

8.1 Welcome: Human knot

1. Decide if and how to split the group into smaller groups.
2. Explain the rules: "In a moment, you will be asked to get into a small group and kneel down in a tight circle. When I give the sign, everyone closes their eyes, and reaches out in the middle of the circle with both hands. Grab someone's hand with each of your hands." Explain: "I am going to pass around a matchbox. You will each light a match in turns. As long as the match is burning you can spout whatever comes to your mind about the topic. Anything goes: opinions, questions, ideas, memories, and so on. When you need to extinguish the match (before burning your fingers, please!), you must stop talking and pass the matchbox to the next person."
3. Continue: "When I invite you to open your eyes, you make sure that everyone is holding the hands of two different people. On my sign, carefully stand up, and untangle yourselves without letting go of anyone's hand. The group that untangles themselves fastest is the winner."
4. Explain at the end that untangling the knot is a little like being saved: "At the beginning it all seems one big mess, and only subsequently you start to see more clearly that there is a way out, where before there seemed none"

8.2 Round Table 1: The true joy of living

- Distribute sticky notes and pens. Say that the great plan of God for each of us is that we live in happiness! "Can you give examples of what brings happiness to people? Write these down, one on each sticky note." Among the points mentioned there will probably be: sweets, friendship, love, music, relationships, sex, family.
- Ask whether there are limits to happiness? Which? Speak about this. You will find that some joys are temporary (eating, pleasure, possessions, selfish desires), while other joys are permanent (friendship, love, joys that are not selfish).
- Subsequently, expose the sticky notes on the wall. Ask participants to think for a moment: "What example of happiness is most important for you?" Suggest choosing one sticky note per person. Then you can talk a moment about why these notes were chosen.

Auction of joy
- Optionally, you can hold an auction with the cards:
  - Apart from the sticky notes with examples of joy, you will need an auction hammer and coins.
  - Each participant receives 10 coins to bid on the joys. The idea is to bid only on the joys that are most important to you. The lowest bid is 1 coin, the highest is 4 coins: who offers 4 coins directly receives the sticky note with the joy.
  - During the auction, people receive directly what was purchased. They try to finish all their money.
  - Then ask participants to choose one sticky note they bought, choosing what is the greatest joy for them. You can take a moment to talk about the motivation for their choice.

8.3 Round Table 2: The cross and my salvation

- Place a large crucifix in the middle of the group.
- Read a brief biblical text in which Jesus announces his passion (Mk 8:31-33; 9:30-32; 10:32-34).
- Say: "God seeks a relationship with each of us. If I want to maintain a friendship with you, I have to invest my-self: we spend time together, I am open to your needs, I help you when it is needed, I am ready to sometimes sacrifice my own will for your good, or make other sacrifices. When I truly love you, I do not really care what happens to me as long as you are well and happy. Ultimately, I am even ready to bear a punishment in your place. Can you understand this? Do you think you can do something similar for someone you truly love?"
- Explain that God gives us more than anyone else: "He does this because he loves you deeply. He wants you to find true happiness in your life. God is infinitely good and the absolute opposite of every sin and all evil. He loves us greatly, but we cannot come in his presence as long as there are traces of sin in us. God and sin are like the two poles of a magnet: they simply cannot come together. Thus our sins are a barrier that prevents us to reach God. Before the death and resurrection of Jesus, the only destiny of the sinner was to be far from God forever (in fact, this is the definition of hell: never to be able to approach God who is love). Can you imag-ine a life far away from God? Would there be happiness?"
- Explain that Jesus wanted to change this barrier between us and God, and make our relationship with God possible. "When Jesus died on the cross which lies here in our midst, he obtained forgiveness for the sins of all people of all ages, making it possible for us to approach God! We said before that when you truly love someone, you might even be ready to undergo punishment for them. Jesus suffered on the cross out of love of you! So that you do not need to suffer all that! He did this to make it possible for you to approach God and be happy forever with him in heaven. Have you ever thought about the death of Jesus on the cross in this way? What does this mean to you? If you look at Jesus on the cross laying here in our midst, what do you think?"
- Conclude by saying that through his sacrifice out of love for us, Jesus sets us free, or "saves" us, of the effect of our sin, which would keep us far from God forever. "Thanks to Jesus, now you can be forgiven your sins (in the Sacrament of Reconciliation) and remain in a true relationship with God (see Meeting 13F & 14). So how do you say in your own words why Jesus is our 'Savior'?"

In this activity you will reflect together on where participants stand in relation to Jesus:

1. Decide if and how you want to split the group into small groups.
2. Explain the rules: "In a moment I will ask you to speak in small groups regarding the question: 'Where would I stand in relation to Jesus if he stood before me today?' Would you stand far away or close by? Would you be standing still? Would you be walking towards him or away?"
3. "Would you be standing or kneeling? With your back turned or facing him? Would you be looking up to his face? Would you be going to give him a hug?"
4. After the dialogue in the small groups, come back together. Explain: "I place a cross here in front representing Jesus. Then people from each small group in turn can take the place and position that reflects where they feel they are with Jesus at this moment."
5. Ask everyone to stay quiet and not to comment on the position people take. You may wish to play some quiet music as each group or person comes forward.

8.5 Round Table 3: Jesus' resurrection at Easter

- Sit around the crucifix once more. Explain that through his suffering and death, Jesus obtained forgiveness for our sins. Thus he made it possible for us to come close to God, who is the complete opposite of sin. The best news is that he did not remain dead: he rose from the dead. Just as Jesus was dead and became alive again to continue to live forever in perfect happiness with God, that now is also our future. The perfect happiness we spoke about before will be ours when we arrive in heaven. This is the ultimate expression of God's love for us. Why do we say this?

- Continue saying that we celebrate this greatest message of all at Easter. This is where Jesus' birth on earth, which we celebrate at Christmas, takes its deepest meaning. During Holy Week, the days before Easter, we want to live with Jesus through his suffering and death towards his resurrection: "Do you know what liturgical celebrations precede Easter on Thursday and Friday?"

- You can take some time to speak about what we celebrate during these three holy days, which we call the Easter Triduum. On Maundy Thursday we commemorate the Last Supper, where Jesus instituted the Eucharist and priesthood (SEE #TWGOD 3.30). On Good Friday we pray with Jesus as he dies for us on the cross (SEE #TWGOD 3.31). On Holy Saturday evening we go to Church to celebrate the resurrection of Jesus that took place during the night (SEE #TWGOD 3.32). And on Easter Sunday we continue to celebrate the resurrection (SEE #TWGOD 3.33).

- In conclusion you can say: "Do not worry if you cannot understand everything we said today. Even the Apostles had difficulty in understanding when Jesus said that he had to suffer, die, and become alive again. The most important message is that Jesus' suffering and death on the cross are very important to us, precisely because he did not stay dead: this is the great truth of the resurrection! Jesus lives at this moment and wants to be part of your life and help you carry your cross, so that one day your happiness will be perfect!"

- Briefly repeat the second part of the Jesus & Me activity, this time all together. The moderator stands in front, and everyone takes a place and position that reflects where they feel they are with Jesus at this moment.
- While they stay in their position, help the group to think about the following questions: "Did you take a different position than before? If so, are you closer or further away from Jesus? Did your position or attitude change? What does this mean for your personal faith and relationship with Jesus?"
- Just keep some silence between the questions. There is no need to talk about the answers with the group: this is about everyone's personal relationship with God.

Meeting 9: Pentecost – Do I have a vocation and what is the role of the Church?

The purpose of this meeting is to help participants discover that each of them is called by God. A vocation is not an obligation imposed by God. Rather, it helps to get rid of all the expectations of our surroundings and simply focus on being ourselves in the eyes of God, our Creator. Jesus has given us the Church to help us search for our vocation, especially through spiritual accompaniment.

The meeting
The meeting begins by looking at the lives of the participants so far. What happened? Where was God? A drawing helps to get clarity in this regard. Next is the question of how their live will continue: What role do they wish to give to God? What does this mean for their vocation? And then the important question: How can one know the Will of God? The meeting intends to raise awareness that everyone is called, and that discernment is needed to find one's personal vocation.

There are basic life decisions to make before making other choices. First, it is important to realize that both marriage and ordination/consecration are true vocations, and of equal value. If our vocation is marriage, we ask ourselves the question whom to marry. If our vocation is ordination/consecration, we can choose to live as a consecrated virgin, a religious sister or brother, a priest. When the participants arrive at the stage in their life when they must discern their vocation, it is better not to seek it just by themselves, but to find a spiritual director who can help to recognize God's calling. A debate among the participants follows.

Prayer
For the prayer we take a time of intercession for all vocations and professions that participants know, and also pray for those who bear responsibility in the Church.

This is not the time to speak concretely of the personal vocation of each individual, for it is better to discuss that privately with a spiritual director. Yet this time of intercession may help participants who wish to take the search for their own vocation seriously.

Your vocation and the Church

Objective of this meeting:
Everyone has a vocation; learn how to discover your personal calling in relation to the Church community.

Related Questions:
3.50, 4.2, 4.3, 4.4, 4.5, 4.50

Dual challenge:
- Read these Questions in the *Tweeting with GOD* book: 4.3 & 4.4.
- Think about what vocations could be possible for you. Ask the Lord to help discern what you should do with your life.

It could be useful to prepare the names of some possible spiritual directors, in case a participant asks how to find one. This can be a lay person, a sister, or a priest in your community, but also someone who lives further away. If necessary, spiritual guidance can also be offered via videocall.

Additional suggestions

- Alternatives for Today's hero could be Saint Francis de Sales and Saint Jane de Chantal, masters of spiritual accompaniment.
- One or two people can be invited to prepare a short presentation on the theme based on the Questions from the *Tweeting with GOD* book for the next meeting.

The gist of it

- Pray, relate, recap
- Intro: The path of life
    - Draw: What does your life's journey look like?
    - God in my past; God in my future
- Round Table 1: Finding God's Will
    - Video: 5 steps to get to know God's Will (#TwGOD 4.6)
    - How do you make choices? How can I do God's Will?
- Round Table 2: Pentecost and the Church
    - Acts 2:1-6: What happened at Pentecost?
    - How does your vocation serve all the Church?
....
- Round Table 3: Call to sanctity
    - Why is our first calling to become holy?
    - What fundamental vocations are there in the Church?
- Today's hero: Saint John Paul II
- Debate: Vocations
    - Is ordination/consecration more difficult than marriage?
- Synthesis & actualization
- Closing prayer
    - Pray with 1 John 4:1-3
    - Intercessory prayer for vocations and tasks
- Dual challenge
    - Read the #TwGOD Questions
    - Think of possible vocations

Procedure for Meeting 9

Relate

00.00 Opening prayer
- Choose a prayer from Appendix 5 or use the *Tweeting with GOD* app.

00.02 Welcome: Throwing balls
- Follow the indications on Worksheet 9.1.

00.10 The previous meeting
- Engage in a simple and quick recap. What touched the participants most in the previous meeting? Are there new questions or ideas? How did they fare with the dual challenge?
  - Are there doubts about the Questions in the *Tweeting with GOD* book?
  - Did they find a crucifix and speak from time to time with Jesus on the cross?
- (The participants who prepared today's Questions can briefly present the theme).

Think

00.15 Introduction: The path of life
- Follow the indications on Worksheet 9.2.

00.35 Round Table 1: Finding God's Will
- Follow the indications on Worksheet 9.3.

00.50 Round Table 2: Pentecost and the Church
- Follow the indications on Worksheet 9.4.

00.55 Break *[END FIRST & START SECOND SESSION (SEE GS2)]*

01.00 Round Table 3: Call to sanctity
- Explain that we can distinguish different levels of calling. Our first calling that we all share is to holiness or sanctity! Saint Paul wrote that it is God's Will for all of us to become holy (1 THESS 4:3). In the words of Jesus: "Be perfect as also your heavenly Father is perfect" (MT 5:48). What he means is that God wants us to become ever more perfect in love. That is what it takes to become a saint (SEE MEETING 16). An important help towards holiness is the Sacrament of Baptism (SEE MEETING 13A). As Saint Paul says: "You were washed, you were sanctified, you were justified in the name of the Lord Jesus Christ and in the Spirit of our God" (1 COR 6:11). What does this mean for you? How can you become more perfect?
- Secondly, within this first calling to holiness, we are all called to one of the following fundamental vocations at the service of the Church community: marriage (or single life), celibacy in priesthood, or the consecrated life. Each of these are in principle choices for all your life, and thus only one of these options is God's Will for you. Can you see yourself in one of these callings? You do not need to say which, but it is good to think about what God might be asking of you. Speak about this.
- Thirdly, within your life's vocation, you are be called to specific tasks at the service of the Church. These can be very different, and can change with time. We need to break through some presuppositions here: not all married women are called to become mothers, not all priests will have a parish, not all religious live in a Benedictine monastery, and not all single lay people are sad spinsters, just to name a few. There are endless possibilities here. But before you take a decision about what you will do on a daily basis, you need to go back to the second point and find out your life's vocation.

01.10 Today's hero: Saint John Paul II
- Watch the video of Saint John Paul II via *Online with Saints*.

- Ask: "How can his testimony help us in our lives?" And: "Can you believe that he became what he was by doing the Will of God?"

01.15 Vocations debate
- Follow the indications on Worksheet 9.5.

Pray & Act

01.40 Synthesis & actualization
- Say in conclusion that vocation is a calling from God: "He does not want to limit or condition your life - you are always free to accept or refuse your calling. But God who knows you inside out promises that if you accept your vocation, you will be able to be profoundly yourself and find true happiness. There will still be trouble and suffering, but these cannot get to your inner joy, as this comes from God and from knowing that you do what you have to do. We are all called to become holy. Just as the Apostles started their mission at Pentecost, the beginning point of the Church, every vocation is at the service of the Church community. The most important options for your personal vocation are marriage or celibacy in priesthood and the religious life. Each of them can be deeply fulfilling, but only one is for you. The basic message of this meeting is: find out God's Will for you, and you will find real and lasting joy!"
- Conclude with the question: "How can what I have learned nourish my personal faith and relationship with Jesus? How can I put this into action?" Speak briefly about this.

01.45 Closing prayer
- Go (if possible) to the chapel or church. Light the candles and sing a song.
- Pray, for example, "Lord, here I am. I still have a lot of questions and do not understand everything.

But I want to do your Will in my life because I know this will bring me true joy. Help me to seek and find the vocation that you propose to me."
- Read the Bible text 1 John 4:1-3. Invite the participants to pray for a moment in silence, asking God that they will be able to recognize the inspiration of the Holy Spirit for themselves. That they may stay close to Jesus and with him search for their personal vocation.
- Conclude together with a series of intercessions: each participant can mention any vocation or task in life, and all respond, "Lord, hear our prayer." Do not forget to pray for those who bear responsibility in the Church.
- Conclude with an Our Father and a Hail Mary.

01.58 Conclusion in the meeting room
- Remind participants of the date for the next meeting and present the dual challenge:
  - Read these Questions in the *Tweeting with GOD* book: 4.3 & 4.4.
  - Think about what vocations could be possible for you. Ask the Lord to help discern what you should do with your life.

TO PREPARE
- Bibles
- Video equipment (internet)
- *Tweeting with GOD* book & app
- *Online with Saints* app
- Paper & color pencils & pens
- Sheet with arguments for the debate (DL)
- (Speaker for playing music)

Worksheet 9

9.1 Welcome: Throwing balls

1. Make sure every participant has a sheet of paper and a pen. Ask them to write four facts about themselves, like their favorite food, sport, color, and language. Have them scrunch the paper into a ball.
2. Explain the rules: "When the music starts, you can throw your ball around the room. Pick up the ball that lands nearest you, and throw it to the other side of the room. When the music stops, pick up the ball nearest to you. Now unfurl the paper, and find the one who wrote these four facts."

9.2 Introduction: The path of life

- Make sure everyone has a sheet of paper and pencils at their disposal.
- Explain: "We are going to make a drawing of your life's journey so far. It does not necessarily need to be an artistic rendering. You can write or draw as you wish. We will look at the most important moments in your life up to this moment, and then also look forward. Find a quiet place somewhere in the room, making sure you can hear my voice clearly."
- "For starters, draw a horizontal line in the middle of your sheet. This line represents today. Now draw the road of your life, starting with the road of your past life, continuing beyond the horizontal line towards the future. What does the journey of your life look like? Is it a bumpy road or quite straightforward? Are there roadblocks, or are you moving forward rather smoothly?"
- "Now write or draw some significant moments in your life so far on the left side of the road. Think of things like family, friends, school/work, sports, music, faith ..."
- "Continue on the left side, writing or drawing the desires or hopes that you have for the future. Think of family, study, professionally, financially, faith ..."
- "We now move to the righthand side of the road. Think of the moments that God was present in a special way in your life. Use another color, indicating these moments in writing or by drawing."
- "Let's move on towards the future: Where do you feel God is calling you to next?"
- Obviously this can be a very private exercise. There is no need to share the drawings with the other participants. This is about everyone's personal life's journey with God.

9.3 Round Table 1: Finding God's Will

- Explain that on the path of our life, we constantly have to make choices: "We all know from experience that making a choice is not easy and it is even more difficult if the choice is final. When we choose one option, others vanish, they are no longer possible for us! Yet choosing can also be liberating. Maybe you have had the experience of feeling relieved when you finally made your decision. We build up ourselves and our lives through the choices we make. How do you see this?"
- Then say: "Your vocation is God's calling, addressed to you personally – your place in life so to say. The Will of God does not come from outside you, but from deep in yourself. God created you, he loves you, and knows what will make you truly happy in your life. Indeed, your vocation is to be deeply yourself. God's Will for you is just that. But how can you be yourself in the depths of your heart? How could you discover the Will of God?"
- Watch the video of #TwGOD Question 4.6 together: "5 steps to get to know God's Will." Speak about it.
- Ask to recap the 5 steps that were proposed in the video, and speak about how these can help the participants in their life.
- In our course so far, we have already spoken about the fact that God loves each of us, that we can meet him in prayer, and that it is good to always seek to learn more about faith and God. The video spoke about the importance of "discernment." What is that?
- Then explain that it is the task of each of us to discern what is good for us, what God wants for us. But it is easy to make a mistake and make a wrong choice that we will regret later. "If you want to make a fundamental choice in your life, speak about it with a spiritual director. This may be a religious sister, a priest, or someone who prays and loves God. They will help you in the name of the whole community of the Church. It is not prudent to make difficult choices all by yourself, as we easily deceive ourselves. Does anyone have experience with spiritual accompaniment? Maybe the moderator?"

9.4 Round Table 2: Pentecost and the Church

- Explain that Jesus himself called the Apostles for their mission (MT 10:1-4). He taught them for three years, and promised them a helper who would assist them to speak about God with love and authority (JN 14:16-17). This helper is the Holy Spirit (SEE MEETING 13B). "The Holy Spirit will help you too to live your vocation, first of all to become holy (1 PET 1:2), but also to speak about the faith to others (ACTS 1:8)."
- Read Acts 2:1-6. The Apostles, who fled into a closed room in Jerusalem after the death of Jesus and were very afraid, are now speaking with such inspiration that they manage to reach out with the message of Jesus to people from all the world! Their vocation is no longer just for themselves, but for the good of the entire Church and all humanity. "What does that mean for your own vocation?"
- "Your children may bring you joy. However, you raise them not just for fun, but so they can become good members of the community. As a priest you may immensely enjoy preaching, but you preach in the first place to help the faithful. Thus, your vocation is never just for yourself, but always at the service of the entire Church."

9.5 Vocations debate

Introduction

- Explain that even before finding a nice girl or a handsome boy to marry, we will have to discern whether it is our vocation to marry or not: "Maybe God is calling you to make a vow to celibacy in priestly or consecrated life. You can promise fidelity to someone in marriage, just as you can also pledge fidelity to God in ordination or consecration. In the latter case, you choose freely not to get married and not have sex, for love of God. Can you imagine that?"
- "If you find it is your vocation to get married, you are faced with the choice of your partner, and later maybe with questions like how many children you can responsibly raise. After choosing celibacy, you will face the choice of, for example, becoming a priest, religious, or consecrated lay person. So, let's see in a little more detail the differences between ordination/consecration and married life."

Indications for the debate

- The purpose of this exercise is to demonstrate that both marriage and ordination/consecration have difficult and joyful aspects. With God everything is possible! So, rather than looking at the practical side, it is better for us to search deeply within ourselves for God's Will for us.
- The idea is to hold a debate. The roles are played by participants: two participants imagine they are consecrated or a priest, and two others imagine being married (not necessarily to each other!). Another participant is the moderator who leads the discussion. To keep the debate lively, distribute the arguments only to the debaters from each side, so that they do not know the arguments of the other side. The moderator of the session has both arguments. The other participants can help when one side has no arguments left.
- It is not necessary to be too serious: humor can help a lot.
- The moderator introduces the debate and asks the question: "Which of you has the hardest vocation?"
- After a possibly hesitant beginning, the debaters are likely to launch fully into the debate without the help of the moderator.
- Below, we give some arguments that can help the debaters.

The difficulties of Ordination/consecration

- My tasks in the community or the responsibility for the souls of others can be very heavy.
- Everyone looks to me all the time; I do not have much time for myself.
- God is perfect in everything and I have to try to reflect this in my lifestyle.
- Sometimes I feel lonely. On the other hand, the community's attention can be overwhelming.
- I am woken up at night to assist a dying person as a sister in the hospital or as a priest.

The difficulties of Marriage

- The responsibility for my family can be very difficult.
- My children correct me all the time and they think I'm not fashionable.
- I change babies' diapers all the time, also at night, clean up after sick kids …
- I never have a quiet moment: even in the bathroom the children know where to find me.
- I have to get up during the night to pick up my older kids from the nightclub (and teach them to drink reasonably).

- I have to find new ways to speak about Jesus in a world that seems to be quite far from him.
- I work day and night for minimum wages.
- I do not have a sexual relationship, and have to keep a proper physical distance from others.
- I promised to be obedient to my boss, the bishop / superior and have to do what they say.
- ...

- I have to be very creative to make everyone in the family happy.
- Children are expensive.
- My partner does not always want to have sex when I want, and then I have to wait. Still I remain faithful and keep a proper physical distance from others.
- I cannot always do what I want: there is also the will of my spouse and our children.
- ...

The joys of Ordination/consecration
- I can take a quiet moment of prayer every day, and this is "work."
- As I have my habit or clerical dress, I never need to think about what I will wear.
- I have the joy of sharing the lives of people who come to the convent or parish, at moments of great joy and great sorrow.
- It is a great joy to help people find their way (back) to God through conversation and prayer.
- I find joy in my fidelity to God, also in the way I live my sexuality.
- I know I live my vocation; this gives me great inner joy and energy to dedicate myself to it.
- When I go back to my room after a long day, I can be alone in tranquillity.
- I'll never know unemployment.
- I'm glad to be part of the Church, in the first place in my community or my parish.
- ...

The joys of Marriage
- It is a joy to spend time together and to share our love with our children, for example, at the dinner table.
- I can always ask my family for advice on how to dress today – but opinions differ!
- I cannot describe my joy when I see my children running towards me after a brief absence.
- It is a joy to pray as a family and to pass on our faith to our children.
- We are loyal to each other and express our love also in our sexual relationship.
- I know I live my vocation; this gives me great inner joy and energy to dedicate myself to it.
- When the children finally fall asleep, I enjoy a special moment with my spouse.
- In a family there is always something to do.
- I'm glad to be part of the Church, first of all in our family, the domestic church.
- ...

Meeting 10: Your group's questions 2

This meeting about your group's questions forms an integral part of the course schedule. We have explained earlier how to approach this meeting (SEE GS8). If you need help to encourage the participants to ask questions, you can look back to the introductory pages (SEE GS9).

Sample procedure for Meeting 10

Relate

00.00 Opening prayer
- Choose a prayer from Appendix 5 or use the *Tweeting with GOD* app.

00.02 Welcome
- Decide on a warm up activity (SEE APPENDIX 3.7).

00.15 The previous meeting
- Engage in a simple and quick recap. What touched the participants most in the previous meeting? Are there new questions or ideas? How did they fare with the dual challenge?
  - Are there doubts about the Questions in the *Tweeting with GOD* book?
  - Have participants been able to think about vocations possible for them (without necessarily mentioning which)?
- (The participants who prepared today's Questions can briefly present the theme).

Think

00.20 Round Table 1: First question
- Watch that all participants who wish to have the possibility of asking questions and presenting their view on the matter.

00.45 Today's hero: Choose from the app

- Choose the video of a saint that may help with the dialogue on today's theme.

00.55 Break [END FIRST & START SECOND SESSION (SEE GS2)]

01.00 Round Table 2: Second question / a new angle on the first question
- Make sure that the questions are discussed in depth. This might be a good moment for dialogue in small groups.

01.25 Round Table 3: Deepening the theme
- You can check among the questions on the website tweetingwithgod.com whether a video is available about today's theme.

Pray & Act

01.40 Synthesis & actualization
- Check whether there are any remaining questions, which you can briefly address at this point, or defer to another meeting.
- Conclude with the question: "How can what I have learned nourish my personal faith and relationship with Jesus? How can I put this into action?" Speak briefly about this.

01.45 Closing prayer
- Go (if possible) to the chapel or church. Light the candles and sing a song.

- Open the prayer, for example: "Lord Jesus, thank you for today's dialogue. We have been able to grow in our understanding of the theme, and we hope that this will bring us closer to you. Help us recognize your presence in our lives, and inspire us with your Holy Spirit to keep searching for the truth."
- You can repeat a prayer method from one of the previous meetings, or add a time of intercession with the group.
- Conclude with an Our Father and a Hail Mary.

01.58 Conclusion in the meeting room

- Remind participants of the date for the next meeting and present the dual challenge:
  - Read the related Questions in the *Tweeting with GOD* book.
  - Define together what you will do for the second challenge.

> **TO PREPARE**
> - Bibles
> - Video equipment (internet)
> - *Tweeting with GOD* book & app
> - *Online with Saints* app

The gist of it

- Pray, relate, recap
- Round Table 1: First question
  - Paying attention that all who wish can contribute
- Today's hero: Choose from the app

....

- Round Table 2: Second question / a new angle on the first question
  - Maybe work with small groups.
  - Make sure that the questions are discussed in depth
- Round Table 3: Deepening the theme
  - Check whether a video about the theme is available
  - Attention that everyone gets to say what they want to
- Synthesis & actualization
- Closing prayer
  - Ask the help of the Holy Spirit to find answers
- Dual challenge
  - Read the #TwGOD Questions related to the theme(s) covered
  - Define the second challenge together

Meeting 11: RETREAT – How do I give myself completely to God in prayer?

A retreat is a time when we temporarily leave everyday life behind to give ourselves completely to God in prayer (SEE #TWGOD 3.17). It is recommended to follow a retreat with all the participants to help them grow in faith (and if applicable prepare to receive the Sacraments). Here we propose a schedule for a one-day retreat, which could also be extended over several days.

Silence

This is a serious retreat with a lot of silence and time for personal prayer. Do not immediately conclude that it would be too difficult for your group. If they have never experienced a retreat, it is a unique opportunity to do so in a safe environment. Many groups are positively surprised by the experience and the benefits of silence. That said, you are obviously free to adapt the program if necessary.

We propose texts to introduce the times of prayer. The purpose is mainly to advance in the personal relationship with God and to listen to him.

Preparation

Discuss together how you will organize your retreat:

- Choose where you would like to go. This can be a monastery or a place of pilgrimage where they receive groups. If you stay in the parish, be sure to be disturbed as little as possible.
- Possibly invite someone to guide the day: a sister, a priest, or another close friend of God. If you cannot find anyone, you can direct the retreat yourself.
- It is advisable not to talk for most of the day and to seek God in the silence of prayer. To help keep silent during breaks, you can play quiet music in the background.
- Read the retreat program carefully and discuss where you can best hold the various parts of the program. The subject is "silence": leave all stress behind to find the silence that will help people listen to God.
- Ensure that all participants have a copy of the schedule or display it in a central location. Use a bell to draw attention to the next part of the program, so that no one needs to check their phone to see the time.

Retreat

Objective of this meeting:
Start listening to God in silence and temporary solitude.

Related Questions:
3.1, 3.2, 3.3, 3.4, 3.5, 3.6, 3.7, 3.8, 3.9, 3.10, 3.11, 3.12, 3.13, 3.14, 3.17

Suggestions

- Prepare as much as possible in advance to avoid disturbance and wasting time during the retreat.
- Ask external volunteers to help with practical things like making coffee, tea, and lunch. This way, participants can focus completely on the retreat.
- During this retreat, there is no place for mobile and other communications. To be "online" with God, it is best to disconnect yourself temporarily from social media and other distractions.
- If participants are very active, it may be good to add some exercise in the program. For example, you can offer to go for a stroll in the afternoon. You could possibly suggest maintaining the silence for at least part of the way.

The gist of it

- Welcome
- Morning prayer in the church
- Today's hero: Saint Teresa of Avila
- First thematic introduction
- Introduction to personal prayer
- Personal prayer
- Midday prayer in church
- Lunch
- Silence
- Second thematic introduction
- Personal prayer
- Coffee or tea in silence
- Introduction to a closing reflection
- Silent prayer in church
- Collective closing prayer
- Looking back
- Closing

Procedure for Meeting 11

Introduction

10.00 Opening
- Switch off mobile devices.
- Follow the indications on Worksheet 11.1.

10.15 Morning prayer in the church
- You can compose a morning prayer with biblical texts and songs. Depending on the group, you could also pray the morning prayer of the breviary.
- The most important thing is to ask God to help you to leave daily life behind in order to meet him in silence and peace.

The meeting

10.35 Today's hero: Saint Teresa of Avila
- Explain that it may seem so far away from daily life to make time for prayer. You are not alone. Also the saints had difficulty in discovering the beauty of silence and prayer.
- Watch the video of Teresa of Avila via *Online with Saints*.
- Keep a few minutes of silence to let people con- template what they have just seen and heard.

10.45 First introduction in the meeting room
- Follow the indications on Worksheet 11.2.

11.00 Introduction to personal prayer
- Explain that you will now spend time in personal prayer, in silence, in a place of your choice. You can go to the chapel or church with a lighted candle, sit before the tabernacle or statue of Mary, walk in the garden or in the park, stay in a corner of the hall, or just here in the meeting room. Choose a place and body position that will help you seek God in silence.

- Here are a few suggestions:
  - "Do not fear the silence: it is only by remaining silent that you can learn to listen to God. Do not speak among yourselves; leave others free to pray. Do not worry when things become boring: sometimes patience is needed while you are crossing an arid spiritual desert before finding water. Do not give up too quickly, take the time to pray: that is the reason you are here today! Try to make the most of this opportunity to spend some quality time with God.
  - Make good use of the time: we reserved a full hour for prayer. You are of course not obliged to pray during all that time, but do respect the silence and give the opportunity to others to pray.
  - Start your prayer by reading the Bible passage again slowly and choose two or three points you want to meditate on together with God. Begin your prayer with the sign of the cross and conclude with a formal prayer such as the Hail Mary or Our Father. Finish with the sign of the cross. Thus you mark the time that you devote completely to God."
  - As a guide, you can use the text "Praying with a passage of the Bible" in the *Tweeting with GOD* book (SEE APPENDIX 4).

11.15 Personal prayer
- Everyone finds a place where they feel good praying in silence, using the text 1 Kings 19:11-14.

12.15 Midday prayer in church
- Gather for a brief time of worship with beautiful songs of praise. Depending on your group, you can also pray Midday prayer from the breviary.

12.45 Lunch
- If you think this is feasible, invite the participants

to eat in silence. After a prayer, play gentle music. Make a real effort not to speak, leaving everyone to the thoughts that come to them. Make sure that food is distributed evenly on the tables, so that participants do not need to get up or ask others to be served. Take your time to eat: try tasting and chewing the food more carefully than usual.

13.45 Silence
- Participants can choose their own way to pass the time: taking a walk, sitting in church, reading ... but without speaking!
- If the surroundings and weather permit, they can go for a walk in a garden or park. Invite them to think about the nature around them: this can be a nice starting point to talk with God about creation! They can also, for example, pray while walking.

14.30 Second introduction in the meeting room
- Follow the indications on Worksheet 11.3.

15.00 Personal prayer
- Everyone prays alone in silence, there where they feel comfortable, using the text Luke 10:38-42.

16.00 Coffee or tea in silence

16.30 Introduction to a closing reflection
- Follow the indications on Worksheet 11.4.

16.45 Silent prayer in church
- Personal prayer following the indications given. Provide paper and pens if necessary.

Conclusion

17.15 Collective closing prayer
- Take a moment together to thank God for this day. Sing praise and thanksgiving songs, share your prayer intentions and ask God's blessing.

- Everyone can offer a prayer intention and light a candle on the altar.
- You can also use Appendix 5 of the book *Tweeting with GOD* to reflect on this day in silence.
- Finish with an Our Father and a Hail Mary: "Ask Mary to help you find moments of silence to really listen to God, also in daily life."

17.45 Coffee, tea, and cookies in the room
- Look back over the day together: "What did you like? What did you find difficult? Have you experienced God's presence today? Would you like to repeat such a day? Why or why not? No one is obliged to share their personal experiences. What happens between you and God cannot be for everyone."

18.30 Closing
- Remind participants of the date of the forthcoming meeting and the dual challenge of last time.

TO PREPARE
- Bibles
- *Tweeting with GOD* book
- Paper and pens
- Program
- A vase with water and sand at the bottom
- (Speaker for playing music)

Worksheet 11

#11.1 Opening

- Let us start with an image: take a vase filled with water, with sand or mud at the bottom. Look, the water is beautiful and clear. But if I stir it, it turns brown and cloudy and cannot see through it anymore. If I let this mixture sit still for an hour, then all the sand will sink to the bottom and I will once again be able to see through the water.
- It is the same with our mind and our spirit. When I am constantly moving, literally or figuratively, because of constant stimulation, then my mind is like the vase with muddy water. It is a cloudy mass, and I cannot see through it. I cannot distinguish things well. But when I relax, then my ideas settle. I can once again think clearly and see things that I had not noticed before. Today we want to give your life's "vase" time to rest so that the cloudiness can settle, allowing you to see God and yourself better.
- Perhaps you have experienced that sometimes there is a lot of noise in the world. So much, in fact, that we must shout to make ourselves heard. In such a situation, it is not easy to hear how God speaks, especially as his voice can often be heard only in silence. That is why we want to spend this day in silence, for a change. We have already spoken a lot with each other at our meetings. Now we will be silent together in order to be able to listen to God.
- Some people very consciously choose to spend some moments in silence from time to time. They disconnect from Instagram and Facebook, check their WhatsApp and email less frequently and sometimes even turn off their phone! And these people are often far from religious. So even beyond religious considerations, people need silence to keep functioning.
- Silence can be scary at first. Whenever there is a moment of silence in a conversation, we try to fill it with small talk. But silence can help our spirit in a powerful way. Today we will practice keeping silent and experience the power it gives us for our search of God.
- This requires everyone's cooperation. First – if you did not do so already – switch off your mobile devices completely. Make a real effort not to speak with each other today. It is really easy to go sit somewhere hidden and whisper, but then you miss the goal of this day. Allow yourself and others to experience the silence. Even if you have trouble believing in God, you are still able to remain silent. We should all keep silent from time to time: to listen to better ourselves, to find peace of mind, to make time and space to focus our attention on God.

#11.2 First introduction

- Look up 1 Kings 19:11-14 and ask someone to read it aloud.
  - Elijah was a prophet, someone who was chosen by God to speak on his behalf. But it became too much for this holy man and he had what would now be called a "burnout." Discouraged, he lies under a bush and falls asleep (1 KINGS 19:4-5). God gives him to eat and drink, but this is not enough to pull him out of his depression. When God asks him what he is doing, Elijah rants about everything that is going wrong.
  - So, God tells Elijah he has to come out, not to give up, but to get up and keep going. Elijah is instructed to wait for God. God is not in the thunderstorm. He is not in the rumble and tremor of an earthquake. He is also not in the roaring of the blazing fire. God is the whisper of a soft breeze. In the middle of the stormy noise of the day, of the earthquake of our activities, of the roaring fire of all our desires, it is difficult to recognize that soft breeze, and to listen to God's wise whispering voice. We all need silence.
  - Not being silent at times can be very dangerous. Just look at Elijah. In the chapter preceding the passage we just read, Elijah was very successful when he called on God to help him, to show that God can work miracles (1 KINGS 18:21-39). Responding to Elijah's prayer, God set a heap of wet wood ablaze (God is therefore also in fire, at the right moment). Thus, everyone could see that the Lord is the one true God, not the false idol god (Baal). But right after, Elijah collapses. He is obsessed with his own holy zeal and can no longer be silent to listen to what God said to him. He lets himself be radicalized and loses the connection with God. Blinded and dumbed by this spell of self-conceit, Elijah orders the killing of many prophets of the false god Baal. He then flees and suffers a "burnout." He must learn to listen to God again. And then he is told that his career as a prophet has come to an end: God consecrates Elisa as his successor!
  - Being silent on time is thus literally vital. Just as Elijah's gaze was clouded when he could no longer be silent, so is it vital for you to be silent every once in a while. Elijah shows the disastrous consequences that a clouded gaze can have! Only in silence can the sand in the vase settle, allowing you to see clearly. Then you can recognize, step by step, how God is present in your life: he made you, he loves you, he sent Jesus to bring you to him, he is always there for you. And he wants to relate to you and talk to you. Even now. God especially wants to speak to you in your prayer. You can really learn to listen to him and to devote time to him. Ask Jesus to pray for each of us, that we can be silent and see God's path with us more clearly.

- Look up Luke 10:38-42 and ask someone to read it aloud.
  - The two sisters, Martha and Mary, show two ways of being with Jesus, and each is good in its own way. They are good friends of Jesus, who regularly visits them and their brother Lazarus.
  - Martha is a strong woman. At that time, it was not customary that a woman be the head of a household, let alone that she personally invites a man to her home. Jesus may have been accompanied by an entire company of Apostles and disciples. There was so much to do to prepare meals and drinks for the guests, as prescribed by the rules of hospitality!
  - It is therefore understandable that Martha becomes annoyed with Mary for not helping her, and cuts in bitterly: "Lord, do you not care that my sister is leaving me to do the serving all by myself? Please tell her to help me!" It should have been normal to share the house duties. But here, something completely different is at stake.
  - It may be helpful to look at another Gospel passage for a moment. When Jesus raises Lazarus their brother from the dead, both sisters play an important role (Jn 11:17-32). Their opposing personalities are also evident. Both are disappointed and sad because Jesus did not come in time to heal their brother before he died. Martha comes running toward him, while Mary waits for Jesus at her home, and only when he calls her she throws herself at his feet, weeping.
  - Perhaps you recognize yourself in one of the sisters, or maybe you are a little like both. The passionate, active busybody personality of Martha, and the more cautious, searching, welcoming nature of Mary. We should be active Christians, attentive to those around us, especially to tell them about Jesus. We are often very busy and think we are doing useful work.
  - But sometimes it goes wrong … we get completely absorbed by our busy life, even finding pride in our busy agendas: "Look at everything I am doing!" We happen to be so busy that we do not find time for Jesus. And he so much would like to meet you regularly, not only for Mass on Sunday, but also for a moment of prayer during the week!
  - He says that Mary has chosen the better part. Our lives are not about what we do, but who we are in the presence of God. We are all children of God and therefore brothers and sisters in Jesus, so we must engage with others and help them where possible. But it starts with the fact that we are all children of God: he is the beginning and the future of our life. Our activity has little meaning if it does not come from our relationship with God.
  - This is why it is so important to regularly leave things aside, like Mary – even important things – and direct ourselves completely to the only thing of real importance. This is what we want to do during this retreat. Step back for a moment and look at what is really important in life and what is just superficial. On this basis, you could perhaps make some resolutions later in the day.
  - Currently, there is really only one thing that is important: you too can be seated at Jesus' feet. Silently. Then tell him everything that you have in your heart. Above all, listen to what he has to say! Find a place that suits you to pray, as you just did, and spend lots of time in the presence of Jesus.

#11.4 Introduction to a closing reflection

- If possible, go to the chapel or church and ask the participants to bring paper and pen.
- After a brief moment of silence, you can read Irma's email aloud. She is a young person who wrote a letter to Mary:
  - "Dear Mary, I often wonder: how much attention do I actually give to the people around me? Like this morning when I was at grandmother's. She told me about something she experienced, but although I think I nodded at the right moments, I was actually thinking of the fun evening I spent with my friends last night. And when my friend sent me a message today, I quickly responded with a smiley and I hurried back to see the film I was watching. Was that really enough?
  - I also wonder if I spend enough time with God. In fact, I currently do not know how I should do it. But I know that God made me and loves me. I would like to spend time with my Father in heaven every day! But so many things happen in a day. I do want to make time for him, but there are so many other things I want to do. Should I be clearer in my choices? Do I have to live more consciously? Maybe you could pray for me, Mary, that I may learn to prioritise and choose to live for the most important things in my life. Irma."

- Slowly pronounce the following sentences, observing a pause between sentences, to allow participants to reflect:
  - "This is a good time to reflect on your daily life. Do I spend enough time in silence? Do I give enough attention to the people around me? Do I regularly direct my attention to God and, if I do, does it 'work' or is it hard to become silent and quiet?"
  - "You may have experienced that 'just hearing God's voice quickly' does not work. You really have to take the time. That is why we will pray in silence now. Think of the questions that were just asked, and how you can find more silence in your life. Try to come up with some very concrete ideas and write down your resolutions. For example: not using your cell phone in your bedroom, one night a week without television and with a good book, making an annual retreat in a monastery. Like before, you can go to the church or another quiet place where you feel close to God."

Meeting 12: Sacraments & Liturgy –
What are sacraments? What is liturgy?

This meeting aims at helping participants discover the importance of the sacraments for their daily lives as aids to move forward on their path with God. They will get to know the seven sacraments, which are celebrated in the context of the liturgy.

As the introduction to the Rite of Christian Initiation of Adults states (NO. 7), the participants' questions are very important (SEE GS2). *How to grow in faith* can very well be used as a course in preparation for the sacraments. We do not receive the sacraments only for ourselves, but also for the good of the larger community of God: "Whatever gift of grace you received from God, place it at the disposal of others as good stewards of his manifold grace" (1 PET 4:10-11). For example, the gifts of the Holy Spirit (SEE MEETING 13B) accompany the call addressed to every Christian to live their relationship with the Lord with conviction, and thus to testify to their great love for God and neighbor.

The meeting

A main tool in this meeting is a memory card game on the sacraments. In a playful way, the participants get to know the seven sacraments, their main effect, and the principle liturgical action by the appointed minister. If they already know the sacraments and their main effect, this will serve as a reminder. Otherwise, the proposed exercise will give them an overview of the seven sacraments and their fruits. This will give them the basic understanding for the subsequent dialogue about the sacraments and the grace God confers on us through them.

A dialogue follows about the liturgical celebration that brings about the sacrament: the external forms (visible signs) of the liturgy signify and bring about the outpouring of God's grace (invisible reality). Hence the importance of the liturgy: without it we cannot receive the sacrament. In principle, liturgy is always celebrated with (representatives of) the community present. This is an action of prayer of all the community, and everyone is invited to join in with the prayer for the particular person or persons who receive a sacrament. The link between the sacraments and the church goes back to Jesus, who appointed the Apostles as leaders of the Church and instituted the sacraments.

Sacraments and liturgy

Objective of this meeting:
Perceive how the seven sacraments and the liturgy are essential in the everyday life of a Christian.

Related Questions:
3.25, 3.25, 3.26, 3.27, 3.35, 3.36, 3.37, 3.38, 3.40, 3.41, 3.42, 3.43

Dual challenge:
- Read these Questions in the *Tweeting with GOD* book: 3.24 & 3.35.
- Look around in a Catholic church near you and find items related to the sacraments, like the baptismal font, confessional, altar, tabernacle, holy oils.

For today's hero we suggest Don Bosco, who invited his young people always to confess their sins and receive Communion in order to grow on their path with God

Prayer
The prayer session foresees a time of intercessory prayer for people who are preparing to receive specific sacraments, anywhere in the world. Obviously, you can include those who have received these sacraments, and try to live with the grace received in the sacrament. It is also a good moment to thank the Lord for the sacraments that the participants have possibly already received in their lives or will receive in the near future.

Additional suggestions
- Once created, the Sacraments Memory game (SEE WORKSHEET 12.1) can be played at dead moments during later meetings.
- The dual challenge foresees a visit to the church. You could decide to visit the church together with the group, for example next Sunday.
- One or two people can be invited to prepare a short presentation of the theme based on the Questions from the *Tweeting with GOD* book for the next meeting.

The gist of it

- **Pray, relate, recap**
  – Which are the seven sacraments?
- **Round Table 1: God's presence in the sacraments**
  – Why did Jesus give us the 7 sacraments?
  – What is a sacrament? What is sacramental grace?
- **Today's hero: Saint John Bosco**

....

- **Round Table 2: The seven sacraments**
  – Small groups: What kinds of sacraments are there?
  – Plenary: What grace do the sacraments give?
- **Round Table 3: The liturgy**
  – What is the liturgy? What is the liturgical year?
  – Who administers the sacraments?
- **Synthesis & actualization**
- **Closing prayer**
  – Intercessory prayer for people who receive a sacrament
- **Dual challenge**
  – Read the #TwGOD Questions
  – Find items related to the sacraments in a Catholic church

Procedure for Meeting 12

Relate

00.00 Opening prayer
- Choose a prayer from Appendix 5 or use the *Tweeting with GOD* app.

00.02 Welcome: Sacraments Memory
- Print the cards for the Sacraments Memory game and cut them out (SEE WORKSHEET 12.1).
- Explain that you are going to play Sacraments Memory in pairs. Every pair receives a set of Memory cards, together with an answer key.
- Mix up the cards. Place them in neat rows with the text facing down.
- The first player turns over any two cards (all players try to remember the position). If the two cards match, keep them.
- Keep playing until the cards do not match. Turn the non-matching cards back over.
- It is now the turn of the other player.
- The game is over when all cards have been matched. The player with the most matches wins.
- After finishing the game, play the second round without the answer key.

00.25 The previous meeting
- Engage in a simple and quick recap. What touched the participants most in the previous meeting? Are there new questions or ideas? How did they fare with the dual challenge?
  - Are there doubts about the Questions in the *Tweeting with GOD* book?
  - How did it go with the challenge of the last meeting?
- (The participants who prepared today's Questions can briefly present the theme).

Think

00.30 Round Table 1: God's presence in the sacraments
- Follow the indications of Worksheet 12.2.

00.45 Today's hero: Saint John Bosco
- Watch the video of Saint John Bosco via *Online with Saints*.
- Say that Don Bosco told the young people he worked with over and over again to confess their sins in order to receive God's forgiveness, and go find him at Mass. To visit Jesus in the Blessed Sacrament kept in the church, where he is always waiting for us. Don Bosco wanted to show that God chose the sacraments as a means to be very close to us. What can we learn from him? Do you want to be as close to God as possible? How can you do this?

00.55 Break [END FIRST & START SECOND SESSION (SEE GS2)]

01.00 Round Table 2: The seven sacraments
- Follow the indications of Worksheet 12.3.

01.20 Round Table 3: The liturgy
- Explain that the sacraments are celebrated during the liturgy: this is a public prayer form which follows a set ritual. These set gestures and words show that it is not the celebrant but the grace of God that is central to the celebration. During the liturgy we are united with all other believers and even with the saints in heaven: all together we worship God! Ask participants to express in their own words what the liturgy is.
- Add that Jesus appointed the Apostles as leaders of the Church, and entrusted the celebration of the seven sacraments to them. Their successors, the bishops, are helped by the priests and deacons to celebrate the liturgy and the sacraments. The

sacraments are a gift of Jesus himself to the entire Church community. Therefore, in principle sacraments are celebrated during the liturgy in the presence of some members of the community. Speak about this together.

- State that the Church has its own schedule for the year, based on the liturgy. We call this the liturgical year, which starts with Advent, four weeks before Christmas. Speak together about the liturgical year. Some questions can be helpful: "When do we celebrate Christmas? What other great liturgical feasts do you know?"
- Have someone write all these feasts on sticky notes. When you have no more ideas, try to order all the liturgical celebrations chronologically throughout the year: Advent, Christmas, Lent, Easter, Pentecost, Ordinary time (SEE #TwGOD 3.26-3.27).
- Explain that the liturgy uses different colors to distinguish seasons and celebration (SEE #TwGOD 3.25). Maybe the participants have noticed some colors and their use. Speak about this. In the Latin Rite we use:
  – White (or silver, gold) for the joyful celebration of feasts;
  – Red for the Holy Spirit and sacrifice of life;
  – Purple for penance and mourning (funerals);
  – Green for ordinary time.
- Look up the scheme of the liturgical year in the *Tweeting with GOD* book (SEE #TwGOD 3.26). Now check which important liturgical celebrations you are missing among the sticky notes. Speak together about the seasons, the celebrations, and the colors used in liturgy.

Pray & Act

01.40 Synthesis & actualization
- Conclude that God knows that we need his help in order to approach him. He comes especially close to us in the seven sacraments; these are a very concrete way to receive a special grace from God. He wants to be part of your whole life, especially at the key moments when you receive the sacraments. We celebrate the sacraments together with the community in the liturgy.
- Check whether there are any remaining questions, which you can briefly address at this point or defer to another meeting.
- Conclude with the question: "How can what I have learned nourish my personal faith and relationship with Jesus? How can I put this into action?" Speak briefly about this.

01.45 Closing prayer
- Follow the indications of Worksheet 12.4.

01.58 Conclusion in the meeting room
- Remind participants of the date for the next meeting and present the dual challenge:
  – Read these Questions in the *Tweeting with GOD* book: 3.24 & 3.35.
  – Look around in a Catholic church near you, and find items related to the sacraments, like the baptismal font, confessional, altar, tabernacle, holy oils.

TO PREPARE
- Bibles
- Video equipment (internet)
- *Tweeting with GOD* book & app
- *Online with Saints* app
- Sacraments Memory (DL)
- Sticky notes & pens

Worksheet 12

12.1 Sacraments Memory

Key to the sacraments

	Key to the sacraments	Effect (SEE #TWGOD 3.35)	Action	
	7 SACRAMENTS	**We receive God's grace** through the working of the Holy Spirit and the ministry of the Church	*Visible sign of an invisible reality*	
For all Catholics	BAPTISM	**We are born again:** we start a new life with Jesus, freed from sin, and become members of the Church.	*Pouring water*	Initiation
For all Catholics	CONFIRMATION	**We grow in faith:** the Holy Spirit binds us to the Church in a special way and makes us adults Christian.	*Laying on of hands & anointing on forehead*	Initiation
For all Catholics	EUCHARIST	**We are fed:** Jesus offers his own life, body and blood, as food.	*Offering bread & wine*	Initiation
For all Catholics	RECONCILIATION	**We are forgiven:** God forgives our sins, for which we ask pardon in confession.	*Laying on of hands & absolution*	Healing
For all Catholics	ANOINTING OF THE SICK	**We are healed:** we are given strength, hope, and comfort from God when faced with disease or even death.	*Anointing on forehead and hands*	Healing
Particular vocations	MATRIMONY	**We form a family:** a man and a woman form an intimate union of love and life before God, and welcome children as gifts of God.	*Consent: promises of the spouses*	Service of communion
Particular vocations	HOLY ORDERS	**We are given deacons, priests, and bishops:** God gives us men whom he himself has called to administer the sacraments in his name.	*Laying on of hands & prayer*	Service of communion

Memory cards

Print these cards (on two colors of paper or with different backs):

7 SACRA-MENTS	We receive God's grace	7 SACRA-MENTS	*Visible sign of an invisible reality*
BAPTISM	We are born again	BAPTISM	*Pouring water*
CONFIRMA-TION	We grow in faith	CONFIRMA-TION	*Laying on of hands & anointing on forehead*
EUCHARIST	We are fed	EUCHARIST	*Offering bread & wine*
RECONCILIA-TION	We are forgiven	RECONCILIA-TION	*Laying on of hands & absolution*
ANOINTING OF THE SICK	We are healed	ANOINTING OF THE SICK	*Anointing on forehead and hands*
MATRIMONY	We form a family	MATRIMONY	*Consent: promises of the spouses*
HOLY ORDERS	We are given deacons, priests, and bishops	HOLY ORDERS	*Laying on of hands & prayer*

12.2 Round Table 1: God's presence in the sacraments

- Begin by asking: "At what point in your life have you ever felt the presence of God? At what moments or events in your life do you think we need God's presence and help most?"
- Explain that Jesus gave the Apostles seven sacraments. In this way, God wants to be very close through his gift of love. The sacraments are signs of God's presence at a particular moment in your life. Every sacrament is a kind of doorway to God. For a moment we are directly connected with him through the love and grace he wants to give us. The effect of this gift of grace is visible in many ways, for example, in the life of the saints. "With the help of God's grace received in the sacraments, you too can live as a saint!"
- Ask: "Have you already received one or more sacraments? Which?" And then: "How important are the sacraments for the life of the Church?"
- Say that the sacraments are defined as "visible signs of an invisible reality" (SEE #TwGOD 3.35). "How do you understand this phrase? What is the visible sign of the Sacrament of Baptism? (pouring water). And what is the invisible reality? (the grace that makes one a child of God)." Speak about this together.

12.3 Round Table 2: The seven sacraments

- Make small groups (SEE APPENDIX 3.1 & 3.2) and make sure each group has a set of Sacraments Memory cards. Explain:
- "First organize the sacraments into two groups, without looking at the key: 'for all Catholics' and 'for particular callings.' Then try to individualize the sacraments of initiation, healing, service of communion."
- "Subsequently try to link the descriptions of the effect of the sacraments to the corresponding sacrament. Likewise with the principle action that makes the sacrament happen."
- "When you are done, use the key to check whether the answers were correct."
- "Now take some time in your little group to speak about every sacrament. What does this sacrament do? When would you receive it? No worries when you do not find the answer: subsequently we'll talk about the sacraments together. Be sure to remember the questions you cannot answer in your small groups."

- Come back all together: "Now try to list each of the seven sacraments, when you receive it, and what grace it gives in particular – without checking the answer key:
  – Baptism (SEE MEETING 13A, #TwGOD 3.36),
  – Confirmation (SEE MEETING 13B, #TwGOD 3.37),
  – Eucharist (SEE MEETING 13C, #TwGOD 3.44-3.50),
  – Reconciliation (SEE MEETING 13F, #TwGOD 3.38-3.39),
  – Anointing of the Sick (SEE MEETING 13E, #TwGOD 3.40),
  – Matrimony (SEE MEETING 13D, #TwGOD 3.43),
  – Holy Orders (SEE MEETING 13E, #TwGOD 3.41-3.42)."
- Ask: "How many times can we receive the sacraments?" (Eucharist, Reconciliation and Anointing of the Sick several times, the other sacraments only once – Matrimony can be received again after the death of a spouse).

- Say in conclusion that as we said at the beginning, the sacraments are signs of the special presence of God at specific times in our life. "Would you like to receive one or more sacraments now that we have talked about them? Which in particular?"
- Note that the course schedule includes meetings about each of the sacraments (SEE MEETING 13), so you can defer the participants' specific questions until these meetings.

12.4 Closing prayer

- Go (if possible) to the chapel or church. Light the candles and sing a song.
- Open the prayer, for example: "Lord Jesus, thank you for giving us the sacraments and the liturgy. Help us recognize how close you are to us at every moment, and how we can receive your grace in a particular way in the sacraments. Help us realize the importance of the sacraments of initiation, healing, and service of communion for our daily lives. Be with us at this moment and help us to live not for ourselves, but for you and for other people."
- This is a good moment to pray together for the people who will receive or recently have received any of the sacraments. Invite the participants to mention names of people or groups, formulating their prayers aloud. Do not forget to also ask God's grace for the participants themselves:
  – For those who prepare to become part of the family of Jesus in Baptism ... For ourselves ...
  – For those who will receive the Sacrament of Confirmation ... For ourselves ...
  – For all the faithful who are participating in the celebration of the Eucharist ... For ourselves ...
  – For all who want to receive God's forgiveness for their sins in Reconciliation ... For ourselves ...
  – For all the sick who seek strength and healing in the Anointing of the Sick ... For ourselves ...
  – For the individuals seeking their calling, the couples preparing to get married, and for all married couples ... For ourselves ...
  – For those who seek their vocation, for our deacons, priests, and bishops ... For ourselves ...
- Pray, for example: "Dear God, we thank you for your presence in our lives and in the lives of people around the world. Thank you for the strength and support you want to give us through the sacraments, which express your desire to be with us at every moment of our lives. Help us to grow in our understanding of the value of the sacraments for our personal journey with you. Be with us at every moment!"
- Conclude with an Our Father and a Hail Mary.

Meeting 13: Sacramental grace – What happens in each of the Sacraments?

The following six meetings aim at giving an overview of the sacramental grace received in the Sacraments. Each of these meetings is intended to be part of the course program. In case the course is used to prepare for one or more sacraments, you can add additional meetings to the program, for example about the liturgy (the layout of which follows for each sacrament after the worksheet). You could add additional meetings as needed on the basis of the respective Questions in the book *Tweeting with GOD*.

The sacramental part is the same for all rites. The liturgical celebration covers the Latin Rite only. For an introduction to the Oriental rites you could look up Questions 3.51-3.55 in the *Tweeting with GOD* app.

The sacraments of initiation

Baptism, when received as an adult, is not the beginning of a faith journey. The journey has started long before, and the candidate gradually grows in faith. The various steps envisaged by the Rite of Christian Initiation of Adults accompany the candidate towards a new beginning with God in Baptism. After the essential moment of Baptism, various rites explain the centrality of this sacrament for every Christian (SEE THE LITURGY OF BAPTISM).

The same Spirit is present in all the sacraments, but at the time of Confirmation we are permanently marked by the Holy Spirit. This is the "confirmation" or strengthening of the grace of Baptism. It is good to reflect on the role of the sponsor (SEE WORKSHEET 13B.6). A Confirmation saint can accompany the Confirmation candidate throughout their Christian life (SEE WORKSHEET 13B.7; #TwGOD 4.16). The rite of Confirmation explains the essence of this sacrament (SEE THE LITURGY OF CONFIRMATION).

The Eucharist is the source and summit of Christian life, the bishops present at the Second Vatican Council declared (SEE #TwGOD 2.48). Receiving Communion for the first time is an

The gift of the sacraments

Objective of this meeting:
See how God's sacramental grace – received through the working of the Holy Spirit - confirms the link with Jesus and his Church, and helps us to live as convinced Christians.

13A Baptism related Questions:
1.4, 1.22, 1.26, 1.32, 1.34, 1.45, 2.30, 3.15, 3.22, 3.35, 3.36

13B Confirmation related Questions:
1.31, 1.32, 1.33, 2.30, 3.34, 3.36, 3.37

13C Eucharist related Questions:
2.30, 2.35, 3.14, 3.25, 3.44, 3.45, 3.46, 3.47, 3.48, 3.49, 3.50

13D Matrimony related Questions:
3.43, 4.19, 4.20, 4.21, 4.32

13E Holy Orders & Anointing of the Sick related Questions:
2.1, 3.40, 3.41, 3.42, 4.4

13F Reconciliation related Questions:
3.38, 3.39, 4.12, 4.13, 4.14

important moment. The explanation of the liturgy of the Eucharist covers the Latin rite (SEE THE LITURGY OF MASS). For the Byzantine rite of the Eucharist, see the *Tweeting with GOD* app (> ⚒ > ⛪).

The sacraments of service of communion
Preparation for marriage is often a (re)discovery of the faith for the spouses. In this sense it is proper not only to focus on the Sacrament of Matrimony and the immediate preparations of the couple, but to embed these sub-jects in a larger and broader understanding of the faith as a whole. The essence of marriage is well expressed in the central rites of the liturgy (SEE THE LITURGY OF MATRIMONY). The Sacrament of Holy Orders is conferred after the election by the Church in the liturgy of ordination (SEE THE LITURGY OF HOLY ORDERS).

The sacraments of healing
The theme of forgiveness is central to every rela-tionship and therefore also to the relationship with God. His forgiveness is related to our redemption by Jesus through his suffering, death, and resur-rection (SEE MEETING 8). Sin limits us in our freedom and we all need the liberating experience of God's forgiveness. The liturgy of the Anointing of the Sick forgives sins and implores God's strength for the sick (SEE THE LITURGY OF ANOINTING OF THE SICK). The liturgy of Reconciliation is simple, in order that everyone has access to this important sacrament of healing (SEE THE LITURGY OF RECONCILIATION).

....

Suggestions when preparing for sacraments

- Insert one or more special meetings about the sac-ramental liturgy, helped by the Worksheet about the "Essential Moment" of the celebration, and the double page about the liturgy of the sacrament.
- Prepare, together with participants, the prayer inten-tions for the liturgy. At least two elements deserve special attention: firstly, the life of faith of the candi-dates with the grace of the sacrament, and secondly, as a consequence also the needs of their neighbors (SEE #TWGOD 3.45). Before you start writing these inten-tions, ask the Holy Spirit to inspire you.
- Visit the church together with the candidates, and walk them through the liturgy. This will give rise to new questions, and possibly very interesting dialogue in another setting.

Procedure for Meeting 13A Baptism

Relate

00.00 Opening prayer
- Choose a prayer from Appendix 5 or use the *Tweeting with GOD* app.

00.02 Welcome: Jesus' story
- Follow the indications on Worksheet 13A.3.

00.15 The previous meeting
- Engage in a simple and quick recap. What touched the participants most in the previous meeting? Are there new questions or ideas? How did they fare with the dual CHALLENGE?
  - Are there doubts about the Questions in the *Tweeting with GOD* book?
  - What items related to the sacraments did you find in the church?
- (The participants who prepared today's Questions can briefly present the theme).

Think

00.20 Introductory dialogue
- Follow the indications on Worksheet 13A.4.

00.35 Round Table 1: He washed my sins away
- Follow the indications on Worksheet 13A.5.

00.55 Break [END FIRST & START SECOND SESSION (SEE GS2)]

01.00 Dialogue: The canyon of sin
- Follow the indications on Worksheet 13A.6.

01.10 The celebration of Baptism
- Explain that Baptism is essential, as it brings new life with God. For this reason, nothing more is needed than water and the words we just men-tioned. In case of need, anyone can baptize, as long as they intend to baptize as Jesus told us to do (SEE THE LITURGY OF BAPTISM). Why do you think Jesus chose to use water for administering this sacrament?
- Water is needed for life: without it nothing grows, nothing prospers, nothing lives. Without Baptism there is no life in God. But water can also be dangerous, it can even cause your death. Baptism is a serious matter, it is about life and death. In order to make space for God in ourselves, our old selfish self must die, so that we can be born again to a new life with God. He is love and relationship in himself (SEE MEETING 1). We are baptized in his name: Father, Son, and Holy Spirit (SEE WORKSHEET 13A.1). What does this mean for you?
- An infant can be baptized very early in life, and its parents will teach it about the faith. The early Christians developed a procedure of several phases for preparing adults to be baptized, which we still use. It helps to gradually grow in faith and understanding of God's love. We call this the *Rite of Christian Initiation of Adults*, abbreviated in English as RCIA (SEE WORKSHEET 13A.2). Why would there be such a long process in preparation for Baptism?

01.20 Today's hero: Saint Martin of Tours
- Watch the video of Saint Martin of Tours via *Online with Saints*.
- Martin drastically changed his lifestyle when he asked to be prepared for Baptism. He felt he had to give up his military career and made new choices. From that moment onwards he started living only for God. How can his example help you?

01.30 Round Table 3: The Holy Spirit in Baptism and Confirmation
- The Apostle Peter preached: "Repent, and be baptized every one of you in the name of Jesus Christ

so that your sins may be forgiven; and you will receive the gift of the Holy Spirit" (Acts 2:38).

- Ask the participants to take out the *Tweeting with GOD* app, and open it at Question 3.36. Read from the Wisdom of the Church: "What are the effects of Baptism?" Ask: "What does this list of effects of Baptism say about the Holy Spirit? What does this mean for us?"
- Then read in the same app at Question 3.37 from the Wisdom of the Church: "What happens in Confirmation?" Ask: "What does this text say about the role of the Holy Spirit in Confirmation? What does this mean for us?"
- "You are now discovering for yourself how the sacraments of Baptism and Confirmation are connected. A continuous working of the Holy Spirit in your life can be discerned. How does this influence you?" Talk about this, and then ask: "What does this continuity mean for your life as a Christian?"
- "In Baptism you receive the Holy Spirit, who wants to help you believe in the love of God the Father and the presence of Jesus in your life. In Confirmation, the help of the Holy Spirit is 'confirmed' in you (SEE MEETING 13B): you are called to share your faith with others – in the first place by living yourself as a good Christian and thus making a difference in the world. You do not only live for yourself, but especially for the love of God, brought to you by the Holy Spirit."

Pray & Act

01.45 Synthesis and actualization
- Ask the participants to enlist the main graces received in baptism (becoming a child of God, member of the Church, receiving the Holy Spirit, forgiveness of sins). It is a good custom to (privately) celebrate the date of your baptism as it marks the beginning of your new life in God.

- Conclude with the question: "How can what I have learned nourish my personal faith and relationship with Jesus? How can I put this into action?" Speak briefly about this.

01.50 Closing prayer
- Follow the indications on Worksheet 13A.7.

01.58 Conclusion in the meeting room
- Remind participants of the date for the next meeting and present the dual challenge:
  - Read these Questions in the *Tweeting with GOD* book: 1.4 & 3.36.
  - Find in the *Tweeting with GOD* app a prayer to the Holy Spirit, and pray this alone or with some others.

TO PREPARE
- Bibles
- Video equipment (internet)
- *Tweeting with GOD* book & app
- *Online with Saints* app

Worksheet 13A

13A.1 Essential moment of Baptism

The essential moment of baptism is when the celebrant pours water over the head of the candidate three times, saying: "(*name*), **I baptize you in the name of the Father, and of the Son, and of the Holy Spirit."**

Follow the "explanatory rites" which underline several key gifts the candidates receive in baptism:
- The anointing with holy oil (chrism) shows that through the Holy Spirit, they now share in his mission as a king who treats people justly, a prophet who speaks about God's love, and a priest who brings people to God.
- They are clothed with a white garment: a new life has started as a child of God, cleansed from all their sins.
- They receive a lighted candle, which shows that like Jesus they are to be a light to the world.
- With infants, the celebrant lightly touches their ears and mouth, praying that they may soon be able to listen to God's Word, and speak about it.

Normally, adults receiving baptism are confirmed directly after baptism and participate in the Eucharist for the first time.

13A.2 Rite of Christian Initiation of Adults

The *Rite of Christian Initiation of Adults* (RCIA) is a process that helps people to gradually discover the Catholic faith and their relationship with God. *How to grow in faith* can accompany candidates on this journey, notably because the ritual indicates the importance of giving generous space for the candidates' questions (SEE GS3). The procedure of the RCIA for becoming a Christian and receiving the sacraments is based on the customs of the early Church. Traditionally the candidates for baptism are called "catechumens," literally, "those being instructed" in the faith.

The phases of the RCIA procedure, including preparation, celebration, and follow-up of the sacraments of initiation are as follows:

1. **Precatechumenate:** evangelization and inquiry by the candidates. This phase concludes with the rite of acceptance as "catechumens," students of the faith.

2. **Catechumenate:** growth in faith, marked by several rites. This phase can take a longer time, and concludes with the rite of election or enrolment of names: the Church ratifies the catechumens' readiness to be further prepared. If possible, the election takes place on the First Sunday of Lent.

3. **Purification and enlightenment:** immediate preparation for receiving the sacraments. This phase ideally takes place during Lent, and concludes with the celebration of the sacraments of Christian initiation: Baptism, Confirmation and Eucharist. The ideal moment to receive these sacraments is at Easter, when we celebrate Jesus' resurrection.

4. **Post-baptismal catechesis ("mystagogy"):** the newly initiated Christian (sometimes called "neophyte") continues their journey of growing in faith. It is an intense phase of deepening the faith and living the experience of the sacraments, together with all the Christian community.

13A.3 Welcome: Jesus' story

1. Have the group sit in a circle. Pick the person who will start.
2. Slap in a slow rhythm, first twice on both legs, then clap your hands once, twice on both legs, clap hands ...
3. All join in the rhythm and the first person says: "Jesus says, Jesus says, Jesus says, Jesus says ..." At the dots, the player says the first two words of a sentence.
4. Then the person next to them does the same, repeating the first word and adding their own: one word for the legs, one for the hand clap. Thus slowly a sentence is formed. When someone says "full stop" the sentence is finished. A new one can be started, so that a story can be created.
5. If a player makes a mistake, they have to start the next round.

13A.4 Introductory dialogue

- Read Matthew 28:19-20. These are Jesus' words to the Apostles after his resurrection. It is just one of the many times that the Bible tells us how important Baptism is. Why would Baptism be so important? Have a first exchange about this question.
- Read Matthew 3:13-17. Jesus wanted to be like us in everything (except in sin). Thus he even asked to be baptized. At least two things are significant in this text. As soon as he was baptized, the heavens opened and the Holy Spirit came over Jesus. Knowing that he wanted to be like us in everything, why is this point so important for us?
- So a first gift of Baptism is that we receive the Holy Spirit, who wants to help us live our faith. Now, let's have a look at the second significant element in this Bible text. God said "This is my Son, the beloved, with whom I am well pleased" (MT 3:17). Why do you think this is so important?
- When anyone is baptized, God is saying silently: "This is my beloved child, with whom I am well pleased." By asking for baptism, we definitively accept God as our father, and he confirms that we are his child! So, in baptism, we become a child of God. Never will we be completely alone any more, for as we heard in the first Bible text, Jesus promises to be with us always. "What does this promise mean to you?"
- "There is another reason why we will never be alone: we share the same father with all Christians. So, from the moment of your baptism, you suddenly have many brothers and sisters around all the world! Baptism therefore also makes you a member of the Church. Have you ever thought about Baptism in this way?"
- In summary, through baptism, we become children of God, members of the Church, and receive the Holy Spirit. And then there is a very important fourth element of Baptism ...

- Explain the following situation: "Suppose I give you a ripe mango or a big fat burger to share right now, without giving you any tools or crockery. You just can't avoid getting your hands dirty … and when you're done and want to wash, I wryly inform you there is neither water nor tissues, and suggest that we continue our dialogue. Most of us will feel uncomfortable or even mentally blocked, and can only talk freely again after cleaning their dirty hands and mouth. Do you recognize this situation?
- Did you ever feel dirty because you did something wrong morally? When there was no dirt to be seen, and still you felt filthy and blocked?
- Sin is a reality we all experience. The Bible says that we are all dirty with sin (Is 64:6; 1 Jn 1:8-9). We always have the option to choose for the good, but so often let ourselves be seduced to choose what is bad. Sin has terrible consequences: it blocks you in your relationship with God until you are able to get washed. Therefore everyone is encouraged: "Get up, be baptized, and have your sins washed away" (Acts 22:16). For the sins you commit after baptism, there is another sacrament, that of Reconciliation (see Meeting 13F). Baptism is a decisive moment in your life, and the beginning of a life with God's grace. Speak together about what Baptism does.
- It is helpful to distinguish between two kinds of sin. We already spoke of our personal sins. There is another kind of sin. The first sin of mankind, the original sin, was committed by Adam. That first sin stained all the next generations, including us. We could say that this original sin is something like a virus that runs through our veins from conception, and which is genetically passed on to the next generation. We need an antidote to be healed from this virus. Jesus came to bring this antidote, and the remedy he gave is baptism. Baptism washes away both original sin and all our personal sins. Speak about the distinction between original sin and personal sin.
- How is it possible that simple water takes away sins, and brings us very close to God? This is all connected to the salvation that Jesus wants to bring us. Think back for a moment to our meeting about salvation (see Meeting 8). Jesus gave his life out of love for us, so we would be able to reach out to God and live forever. His death brought us life. After his death on the cross, Jesus' side was pierced by one of the soldiers. Water and blood flowed out of his side (Jn 19:34). This is often interpreted as a symbol for the life-giving sacraments. How are the sacraments linked to the salvation that Jesus wants for each of us?
- The first Christians were adults who asked to be baptized. Like all parents, Christians want to give their children everything that is good for them. If Baptism is so good, then we cannot keep this from our child until they come of age. We want them to live the grace of Baptism from childhood: to live as a child of God, with the help of the Holy Spirit, free from the burden of the sin of past generations. Therefore it became the custom to baptize children. The only difference with adult Baptism is that children have not yet committed personal sins. "Can you understand the desire of these parents? Would you baptize your children – if you had any?"
- "So, God gave the Sacrament of Baptism to wash away your personal sins, and also original sin. The water of baptism washes all the past sins away and unblocks you, so that you are open to receive God's grace."

13A.6 Dialogue: The canyon of sin

- Read Ezekiel 36:25-28. In Baptism we are as if reborn; we start life again with God at our side (JN 3:5). "How would you describe this new life that Baptism gives?"
- "The water of Baptism does not only wash your sins away, it also restores your communion with God. You could see the effect of your sins as a deep canyon. You stand on one side of the canyon, and God is at the other side, with no way for you to get over the canyon. God wants to change that situation. He opens a water lock, and the canyon fills with water. Now you only have to swim to get to him. Or he even gives you a rowing boat. But you yourself have to decide to swim or get into the boat and start rowing towards God. How do you see this situation? Do you want to get across the canyon?"
- "Do you have the experience of being on a bus with other people for a long ride, with everyone sitting in their own corner without talking to each other? Individualism at its worst. But then something unexpected happens: the bus has to stop and can no longer continue its journey, for example, because the bus breaks down (or because there is this wide canyon). Suddenly all passengers start to talk to each other and relate. That is what God wants for us, to create community among ourselves. Swimming or rowing across the canyon by yourself can be dangerous. But when you are with others, you can help each other to get over the canyon of sin, and reach out to God through the means (the water in the canyon) he has given us. Does this image help you understand better what Baptism is about? How?"

13A.7 Closing prayer

- Go (if possible) to the chapel or church. If possible go to the baptismal font, and pray around the font. Light some candles and sing a song to the Holy Spirit. Between [brackets] are some indications in case this is used as a baptismal course.
- Pray, for example: "Dear Lord, thank you for helping us understand the fundamental importance of the Sacrament of Baptism (received in this baptismal font). [Help us to prepare ourselves to receive this sacrament with an open spirit]. Help us to live the grace of our Baptism every day. You come very close to us when we are baptized, and promise to never let us go. Give me the grace to never let you go too."
- Spend a few minutes in silence. If the participants are already baptized, let them give thanks for their Baptism, and ask God's help to realize the importance of that sacrament for their daily lives. [If they are preparing to receive Baptism, they can ask God in their hearts to help them live towards that great day].
- Then pray: "Come, Holy Spirit, fill the hearts of your faithful and kindle in them the fire of your love. Send forth your Spirit and they shall be created. And you shall renew the face of the earth" (SEE #TWGOD 3.9).
- After a few more minutes of silence, conclude with an Our Father and a Hail Mary.

Liturgy 13A: The liturgy of Baptism

It is possible to be baptized as a child at the request of the parents, or as an adult at one's own request. Baptism is the beginning of life in Christ. It is a grave and life-changing moment for the candidate. Therefore, the liturgy foresees a long path of preparation for adults asking to become Christian. Children who receive the sacrament will be educated in the faith by their parents.

The celebration

An adult usually follows the RCIA (SEE WORKSHEET 13A.2). The rite of Baptism itself is mostly the same for both infants and adults. The sacrament can be administered during Mass (ideally during the Easter Vigil) or outside Mass. In the latter case, the procedure is followed as presented, omitting the "Liturgy of the Eucharist" (SEE BOX).

Church architecture expresses the importance of baptism with a baptismal font (SEE #TwGOD 3.22), traditionally at the cold dark north side: Baptism brings us from darkness to the light.

The liturgy

- The actual liturgy of Baptism starts after the readings and the homily with prayer and the litany of saints: all saints are asked to pray for the person who is going to start their journey with Jesus to become one of the saints themselves! A prayer follows to keep all evil and harm far from them (prayer of exorcism). If applicable, the candidate is anointed with the oil of the catechumens.
- Then the water is blessed – or if it is already blessed, the celebrant thanks God for the blessed water that generates life. This is not only intended in an ecological way: the water of Baptism gives life in a spiritual way, in the sense that in Baptism one is born again in the Spirit (JN 3:3-6), and as a child of

God. Just as Jesus died and became alive again, baptism symbolizes the death and resurrection with Christ, who rose on the third day.

- The candidate renounces sin and professes their faith in God. As Baptism washes away all preceding sins, this is a very serious moment. For future sins, the baptized will need the Sacrament of Reconciliation (SEE MEETING 13F).
- Now we come to the constitutive moment when the person is baptized in the name of the Father, Son, and Holy Spirit. Three times water is poured over the head of the candidate. It is like at Jesus' baptism (by triple full immersion in the river Jordan), when the Father exclaimed: "this is my beloved child."
- The explanatory rites follow after Baptism (SEE WORKSHEET 13A.1).

The celebrant

The sacraments of initiation are in principle administered all together in the same celebration, as to express the unity between these three. However, the bishop can ask to withhold the Sacrament of Confirmation, for example, so the newly baptized can be properly confirmed by the bishop himself. The right to receive the Sacrament of Baptism is deemed so important that – lacking an ordained minister – anyone can baptize in an emergency, because Jesus himself linked this sacrament to the salvation he preached (MK 16:16, SEE MEETING 8). Even a non-Christian can do so, as long as they intend to baptize the person into the faith as professed by the Catholic Church, and with the words mentioned above.

Liturgy of Baptism

Opening
- Welcome & penitential preparation
- Opening prayer

Liturgy of the Word
- Reading(s)
- Psalm
- Gospel
- Homily

Celebration of Baptism
- Interrogation
- General intercessions
- Litany of Saints
- Prayer of exorcism
- (Anointing with the oil of the catechumens)
- Blessing of the water
- Renunciation of sin and profession of faith
- Baptism
- Explanatory rites

Liturgy of the Eucharist
- Prayer over the gifts
- Preface & Eucharistic prayer
- Rite of Communion
- Prayer after Communion

Conclusion
- Blessing & dismissal

TO PREPARE
- RCIA procedure / meeting the parents
- Repeating the responses with the candidates
- Rite of Baptism
- Choice of readings
- Intentions for the general intercessions

Procedure for Meeting 13B Confirmation

Relate

00.00 Opening prayer (SEE APPENDIX 5)

00.02 Welcome: Sanitary Bible sharing
- Follow the indications on Worksheet 13B.2.

00.10 The previous meeting
- Engage in a simple and quick recap. What touched the participants most in the previous meeting? Are there new questions or ideas? How did they fare with the dual challenge?
  - Are there doubts about the Questions in the *Tweeting with GOD* book?
  - What prayer to the Holy Spirit did you pray?
- (The participants who prepared today's Questions can briefly present the theme).

Think

00.15 Introductory dialogue: Everyone their task
- Follow the indications on Worksheet 13B.3.

00.35 Round Table 1: Confirmation and the Holy Spirit
- Follow the indications on Worksheet 13B.4.

00.55 Break [END FIRST & START SECOND SESSION (SEE GS2)]

01.00 Round Table 2: The gifts of the Holy Spirit
- Follow the indications on Worksheet 13B.5.

01.15 Today's hero: Saint Dominic Savio
- Watch the video of Saint Dominic Savio via *Online with Saints*.
- Ask: "How can the Sacrament of Confirmation help you to start living like this saint?"

01.25 Round Table 3: The celebration of Confirmation
- Read Acts 8:14-17. Ask: "What is being said in this passage?"
- Explain: "The Apostles prayed for baptized Christians by laying on hands. This is how they received the Holy Spirit. We are reading an account about the ceremony of Confirmation! Later, the Apostles passed their ministry on to the bishops, who are their successors today (SEE MEETING 2 & 12B). This is why it is normally the bishop who celebrates the Sacrament of Confirmation. If necessary, he may delegate a priest. Speaking of which, do you know who our bishop is?"
- "There are two central elements in the Confirmation liturgy. At some point, the bishop (or his delegate) extends his arms and hands over you all and prays an ancient prayer." Distribute a paper with the prayer of the bishop (SEE WORKSHEET 13B.1) and say: "Read these words carefully: what do you notice in particular?" We hope that the participants recognise the 7 gifts of the Holy Spirit. Furthermore they may can see that this sacrament is the "confirmation of Baptism": there is a continuity.
- "The second essential element of the sacrament is when you come to the bishop (or his delegate), with your sponsor (godmother or godfather). The bishop marks your forehead with sacred oil (chrism), saying: 'Be sealed with the gift of the Holy Spirit.'"
- Ask: "How would say in your own words what the gift of the Holy Spirit brings you in the Sacrament of Confirmation?"

Pray & Act

01.40 Synthesis and actualization
- Conclude by reminding that each of us is a child of God and he loves us infinitely. "Therefore, he wants to mark you with his sign, the invisible and per-

manent mark of the Holy Spirit. His love is with you always. The bishop confirms this through his prayer and the anointing with sacred oil. When you have received all three sacraments of initiation, this marks the beginning of your life as a mature Christian in the Church."
- Conclude with the question: "How can what I have learned nourish my personal faith and relationship with Jesus? How can I put this into action?" Speak briefly about this.

Conclusion

01.45 Closing prayer
- Go (if possible) to the chapel or church. Light the candles and sing a song. Between [brackets] are some suggestions in case this is used as a Confirmation course.
- Pray, for example: "Holy Spirit, we come here in prayer to thank you for the Sacrament of Confirmation. Help us accept in faith what we do not yet understand intellectually. Help us to welcome you as the one who wants to be with us always."
- Each participant receives paper and pen. Explain: "We will spend a moment in silence, during which you can thank God for all that you are and all you have received. Then think of a special grace you want to ask for your Christian life [on the occasion of your Confirmation]. Something that will help you on your path with God, like a stronger faith, a better understanding of God's love, a greater capacity to speak about him. Write down the grace you are asking and pray the Lord to grant you this gift."
- [After some moments of silence, invite participants to bring a copy of this sheet to their sponsor who accompanies them to Confirmation. Ask them to pray for you to receive that grace.]
- Conclude with an Our Father and a Hail Mary.

- [At the end of the meeting, give everyone a sheet that explains how to choose a saint for Confirmation (SEE WORKSHEET 13B.7), a companion for the road. When participants have chosen a Confirmation saint, they can ask him or her to pray for the grace they desire].

01.58 Conclusion in the meeting room
- Remind participants of the date for the next meeting and present the dual challenge:
  - Read these Questions in the *Tweeting with GOD* book: 1.32 & 3.37.
  - Take up the sheet with the grace you want to ask from God, and pray that God will grant you what is good for you.

TO PREPARE
- Bibles
- Video equipment (internet)
- *Tweeting with GOD* book & app
- *Online with Saints* app
- Several toilet rolls
- Bicycle & sticky notes
- Paper & pens
- Sheet with the words of the bishop (DL)

Worksheet 13B

13B.1 Essential moment of Confirmation

The essential moment of Confirmation is twofold:

1. The bishop (or his delegate) and the priests present extend their hands over all the Confirmation candidates, while the bishop alone says:

    "All-powerful God, Father of our Lord Jesus Christ, by water and the Holy Spirit you freed your sons and daughters from sin and gave them new life.

    Send your Holy Spirit upon them to be their Helper and Guide. Give them
    — the spirit of wisdom
    — and understanding,
    — the spirit of right judgment
    — and courage,
    — the spirit of knowledge
    — and reverence.
    — Fill them with the spirit of wonder and awe in your presence.

    We ask this through Christ our Lord. Amen."

2. Each Confirmation candidate approaches the bishop (or his delegate). With his thumb impregnated with holy oil (chrism), he marks the forehead of the candidate with the sign of the cross, saying:

    "Be sealed with the gift of the Holy Spirit."

13B.2 Welcome: Sanitary Bible sharing

1. Pass around a toilet roll and ask everyone to rip off how much they would usually use.
2. When everyone has their supply of toilet paper, have them count their squares.
3. Inform the group that the number of squares dictates the number of truths they have to share about the Jesus and/or Bible. No repetition allowed.

- Read Ephesians 4:4-7 ,11-13 and speak about the text. Saint Paul sees the Church community as the body of Jesus: each Christian is like another part of his body. In all our variety as people, we are united in Jesus. There is one Holy Spirit, and one Baptism that precedes the Sacrament of Confirmation (SEE MEETING 13A & 13B). We all receive God's grace in a different way, and we all have a different task to fulfill – inspired and guided by the same Holy Spirit.
- Place a bicycle in the middle of the group and distribute sticky notes with pens. If you do not have a bicycle, draw one schematically on a large sheet of paper. Explain that the group is like this bicycle. Ask the participants to indicate which part of the bicycle corresponds to themselves: "If you good at giving strength, mark the pedals with a sticky note with your name; if you good at leading, put your name on the handlebars; if you can carry, stick your note on the rack; if you are great at braking in time, put your name on the brakes. You might also be good at transmitting, generating energy, giving light …"
- The sticky notes will probably be stuck all over the bicycle. This is in line with the Scripture text we just read: everyone has their own gifts and task to fulfil.
- Next hand out red sticky notes and ask: "What is the role of the Holy Spirit in our group?" Ask the participants to stick their note at the spot on the bicycle where, in their opinion, he is present. If necessary, you can explain that the Holy Spirit gives strength (pedals), support (rack), direction (handlebars), gives light (lamp), accelerates (transmission), generates (dynamo), calms down (brakes) … The idea is to perceive how each member of the group is important in a different way, and that the Holy Spirit is everywhere to inspire, give strength …
- "There we are: the Holy Spirit is wherever we are! He helps us in our personal task and vocation (SEE MEETING 9). Any vocation is not just for yourself, but for good of the entire Church. Therefore, we can compare this bike to the Church community. Why do you think we say this?"
- "In the Church, all are called to contribute, each according to their ability, and not to live only for themselves. Instead, we are called to add something to the whole. After all, the Church is a community of brothers and sisters in Jesus: we are family!"

- If we want to be truly of service to the Church community, we will need to be connected to Jesus. The Holy Spirit wants to help us do so. In the Sacrament of Confirmation we receive the Holy Spirit in a special way.
- Read Ephesians 4:14-15 and speak about it. This is a very rich text, which continues what we discussed just above.
- First of all, Saint Paul tells us that when we receive the Holy Spirit, we must no longer be like children who are easily distracted from the path they are following. Rather, he tells us to grow up in Jesus. The Sacrament of Confirmation wants to help us to live as grown-up Christians who try to follow Jesus day by day in their lives. In what way does the Holy Spirit act?
- The help of the Holy Spirit does not arrive by magic: from our end we will need to do what we can to be faithful and grow in faith, hope, and love. We will make mistakes; we will need forgiveness (SEE MEETING 13F): it takes time and investment to become holy (SEE MEETING 16). "How do you think the Holy Spirit wants to help you?"
- Saint Paul reminds us to "speak the truth in love" (EPH 4:15). He refers to the task of every Christian to tell others about the liberating message of Jesus. And to do so with the love that Jesus has for us. If in the Sacrament of Confirmation we are more closely united to Jesus, then we will have to try to live more closely in his love too. What does this mean?
- Finally, Saint Paul tells us that we are at the service of the entire body of Jesus (EPH. 4:16). What does he mean by this?
- Conclude that thus we have discovered several essential elements of the Sacrament of Confirmation: it helps us
  1. to be more connected to Jesus,
  2. to become grown-up Christians who take their responsibility seriously,
  3. to speak about his message wherever we go, and
  4. to be of service to the entire Church community.
  "How can you recognize the help of the Holy Spirit in your daily lives?"
- This question is also answered by Saint Paul, when in another letter he summed up the 12 fruits of the Holy Spirit (GAL 5:22-23). These are essentially signs that we are progressing on the path to God. Look up the 12 fruits in the *Tweeting with GOD* app or book (SEE #TwGOD 1.32; #TwGOD APP > 🕮 > ♟ > ◉). Talk about these briefly without searching to be exhaustive at this point.

13B.5 The 7 gifts of the Holy Spirit

- Hand out paper and pens. Invite the participants to take a few minutes to make a short list of the gifts they want to ask from God for their Confirmation. We will come back to these in a few minutes.
- Then explain that traditionally we distinguish the 7 gifts of the Holy Spirit. Read Isaiah 11:2-3 and try to list the 7 gifts with the help of the *Tweeting with GOD* app (SEE #TwGOD APP > 🕮 > ♟ > ◉). Note that sometimes the Bible translation expresses the last two gifts as one: "piety" and "fear of the Lord."
- "Now compare the list of gifts you wanted to ask from God with the 7 gifts of the Holy Spirit. What do you notice?" Speak about this together.

- "By his gifts, the Holy Spirit wants to help you to move forward on your path with God." Briefly discuss each gift of the Holy Spirit, starting with those which the participants think they most need (SEE #TwGOD 1.32).

13B.6 The role of the sponsor

"Candidates for Confirmation, as for Baptism, fittingly seek the spiritual help of a sponsor. To emphasise the unity of the two sacraments, it is appropriate that this be one of the baptismal godparents" (CCC 1311).

The role of your sponsor (godmother or godfather) is essentially twofold:
- To give an example of Christian life and help you prepare for the sacrament, as well as help you find answers to your questions.
- To pray for you, asking God's grace for your Confirmation, and to continue to accompany you in prayer after Confirmation. This is why participants ask their sponsor to pray for the special grace they want to ask from God at their Confirmation.

The sponsor is not committed only to you but also to God. Therefore, there are some criteria to be a sponsor:
- they have received the three sacraments of initiation: Baptism, Confirmation and Eucharist
- they are at least 16 years old
- they are not the father or mother of the Confirmation candidate
- they live an active Christian life and participate regularly in the life of the Church.

13B.7 Choosing your Confirmation saint

Your parents gave you your name at your birth. Your name gives you an identity, and others address you by that name. At your Baptism, you are baptized by your baptismal name(s). God knows you by name!

Now that you are preparing for your Confirmation, you can choose a name for yourself. The bishop can confirm you with that name. This is always the name of a saint, which may be added after your baptismal name. Your Confirmation name is mostly known to God and the Church. It is a sign of your new life with God that begins with your Confirmation.

This name binds you in a particular way to a saint: you can let yourself be inspired by their example and their gift to God. You can ask your Confirmation saint to pray for you. You have a special friend in heaven who can be a hero in the faith for you, and also a friend in your daily life.

To choose a saint, you can find inspiration in the *Online with Saints* app or elsewhere. You can choose a saint because you see parallels between their life and yours, or choose the name of a (grand)parent or another person you admire. Or you can simply re-elect the saint of your baptismal name. Do not forget to ask them regularly to pray for you!

Liturgy 13B: The liturgy of Confirmation

The Confirmation liturgy follows a defined sequence. This is not a simple public act or a rite of passage: during the Liturgy of Confirmation, God acts in a very concrete and definitive manner in the life of the person who is confirmed. The liturgy is not ours: it is given to us by the Tradition of the Church. Therefore, it is important to follow the order and official texts of the ritual. This is an act of faith: by following the ritual we express that what happens in the liturgy is beyond us. In this way, we let God act without the risk of placing our own ideas and proposals before his. Each Bishops' Conference has approved the liturgical texts for the administration of the Sacrament of Confirmation. In general, the liturgy always follows the same layout.

The celebration

Usually the Sacrament of Confirmation is received during a Mass. Simply said, it is a "normal" Mass, in which the ritual of Confirmation is inserted just after the homily. One can choose to use the readings of the Mass of the day or those suggested in the ritual for the Sacrament of Confirmation. If Confirmation is administered outside of Mass, the procedure below is still followed, omitting the "Liturgy of the Eucharist" (SEE BOX).

It may be useful to organize a visit to the church beforehand and practice together so that all know what will happen during the Confirmation liturgy. The goal is to help the participants become comfortable with how the liturgy proceeds and learn the answers to give.

No other specific place in the church is dedicated to this sacrament. It is very closely linked to baptism (and thus to the baptismal font). There may also be a specially designed place in the church where the three holy oils are preserved.

The liturgy

- The actual liturgy of the Sacrament of Confirmation begins with the calling by name of the Confirmation candidates. Sometimes they are asked to come before the bishop (or his delegate), who then delivers a brief homily.
- Then the bishop addresses the Confirmation candidates, asking them to renounce evil and profess their faith. It is useful for the candidates to review the answers in advance (during their visit to the church).
- The bishop calls on those present to pray. After a pause, he extends his arms, together with the priests present, to lay hands on all the Confirmation candidates together. Only the bishop pronounces the words of the prayer, asking God for the gifts of the Holy Spirit (SEE WORKSHEET 13B.1).
- Then the candidates come one by one before the bishop (or the delegated priest). They are accompanied by their sponsor, who lays a hand on their shoulder. The bishop marks the forehead of the candidate with the sign of the cross with holy oil (chrism), pronouncing the words of Confirmation (SEE WORKSHEET 13B.1). Then he exchanges a sign of peace with the newly confirmed.
- Mass continues as usual. Often, the Confirmation candidates prepare the general intercessions and read the intentions.

The celebrant

The Sacrament of Confirmation is celebrated by the bishop or a priest delegated specifically for that task. Although this is not always possible, ideally the Confirmation candidates briefly meet the bishop before the celebration for a convivial moment of exchange and to receive a word of encouragement. The bishop is not only the local leader of the Church, but also a successor of the Apostles, which brings us closer to Jesus.

Confirmation liturgy

Opening
- Welcome & penitential preparation
- Opening prayer

Liturgy of the Word
- Reading(s)
- Psalm
- Gospel

Liturgy of Confirmation
- Calling of the Confirmation candidate(s)
- Homily
- Renewal of the baptismal promises
- Laying on of hands & prayer
- Anointing with holy oil (chrism)
- General intercessions

Liturgy of the Eucharist
- Prayer over the gifts
- Preface & Eucharistic prayer
- Rite of Communion
- Prayer after Communion

Conclusion
- Blessing & dismissal

TO PREPARE
- Meeting of the candidates with the bishop
- Repeating the responses with the candidates
- Rite of Confirmation
- Choice of readings
- Intentions for the general intercessions

Procedure for Meeting 13C Eucharist

Relate

00.00 Opening prayer
- Choose a prayer from Appendix 5 or use the *Tweeting with GOD* app.

00.02 Welcome: Rolling balls
- Follow the indications on Worksheet 13C.2.

00.10 The previous meeting
- Engage in a simple and quick recap. What touched the participants most in the previous meeting? Are there new questions or ideas? How did they fare with the dual challenge?
  - Are there doubts about the Questions in the *Tweeting with GOD* book?
  - How was it to pray for the specific grace you want to ask from God?
- (The participants who prepared today's Questions can briefly present the theme).

Think

00.15 Introductory dialogue: Do this in memory of me
- Follow the indication of Worksheet 13C.3.

00.30 Round Table 1: Community
- Around the year 155, Saint Justin Martyr wrote a testimony of how Mass was celebrated at his time. Distribute this description of the Eucharistic celebration, and ask participants to read it (SEE WORKSHEET 13C.4).
- Explain: "As you can see, it is the same as what we do today (SEE LITURGY OF THE EUCHARIST). You will probably notice that the celebration of the liturgy is still the same in essence. You will also notice that the celebration starts with the community, which has a central place in the Eucharistic celebration."

- "We have seen before that the New Testament sees all the faithful together, the Church, as the Body of Jesus (1 COR 12:12-31). Each of us has another role to play (SEE MEETING 9). We are all united in Jesus. This becomes very concrete in the Eucharist: we all receive the same Body of Jesus. Do you think that also brings us very close to each other?"
- "During Mass, which we always celebrate with others, this is expressed for example in the sign of peace that we share (with a handshake, an embrace, a kiss ...). Justin called this 'the kiss.'"It is not intended as an awkward moment where we have to get out of our individualistic bubble to quickly shake hands with a half smile before re-entering our bubble. It is a moment where we share and even celebrate that together we are the body of Jesus. He is present in our community. Does this help you see why the Church is so important?"
- The community paid together for the bread and wine, with the money from the collection. Every gift is a little sacrifice. Together with our good works, intentions, and prayers, they are our small offering to God. Members of the community like the Mass servers bring the gifts to the altar in the name of all of us. The priest offers them to God, and asks us to join him in prayer: "Pray ... that my sacrifice (offering) and yours may be acceptable to God." Then something very special happens: our humble gifts of bread and wine are changed by God into Jesus' Body and Blood. God not only accepts our gift, but makes it better than anything we can imagine. What kind of offering can you bring to the altar during the Eucharist?
- We sometimes speak of the "sacrifice of Mass." That is because at Mass we are united with

Jesus' one sacrifice of his life on the cross (SEE MEETING 8). Jesus changes our small sacrifice into the sacrifice of his Body and Blood, offered once and for all on the cross for our benefit. He wants to give you everything he has, he even offers you his life, so you can find life with God! Can you imagine a greater gift? Should Mass bring you closer to people who suffer?

- At the end of Mass, we are sent forth: "Go in peace." This is not just a kind wish from the part of the deacon or priest, but it is a mission. If we really have received Jesus' own body at Mass, he is really with us also when we leave the church. Strengthened by his physical presence in us, we now are being sent out to live as good Christians, not just for ourselves, but open to others who need help. Do you think you are able to do this?

00.55 Break [*END FIRST & START SECOND SESSION (SEE GS2)*]

01.00 Today's hero: Blessed Carlo Acutis
- Watch the video of Blessed Carlo Acutis via *Online with Saints*.
- Ask: "What does Carlo's love for the Eucharist tell you?" And: "Does he inspire you to do something similar?"

01.10 Round Table 2: Jesus' presence
- Follow the indication of Worksheet 13C.5.

01.25 Round Table 3: John 6
- Follow the indication of Worksheet 13C.6.

 # Pray & Act

01.40 Synthesis and actualization
- In the Eucharist we meet Jesus himself, who sacrificed his life for us.
- Conclude with the question: "How can what I have learned nourish my personal faith and relationship with Jesus? How can I put this into action?" Speak briefly about this.

01.45 Closing prayer
- Follow the indication of Worksheet 13C.7.

01.58 Conclusion in the meeting room
- Remind participants of the date for the next meeting and present the dual challenge:
  - Read these Questions in the *Tweeting with GOD* book: 3.25 & 3.28.
  - Participate in the Eucharist in your local church on a weekday (obviously without skipping the Sunday Mass). What differences do you note with the Sunday?

TO PREPARE
- Bibles
- Video equipment (internet)
- *Tweeting with GOD* book & app
- *Online with Saints* app
- Sheets of (news)paper
- Sticky notes & pens
- Sheets for Round Table 1 (DL)
- Image for Round Table 3 (DL)

Worksheet 13C

13C.1 Essential moment of the Eucharist

The celebration of the Eucharist consists of two essential parts.
- The first is the coming together, listening to Word of God with readings, homily, and prayers. The essential words come from the Bible, the Word of God.
- The second is the offering of bread and wine, the consecration in thanksgiving, and communion. The essential words come from Jesus at the Last Supper.

There are various Eucharistic prayers. Have you ever noticed how there are several elements that come back, although the text is different. Here we look at the text of Eucharistic Prayer II:

Epiclesis, in which we ask the Father to send the Holy Spirit: "Make holy, therefore, these gifts, we pray, by sending down your Spirit upon them like the dewfall, so that they may become for us the body and blood of our Lord Jesus Christ."

Institution narrative, or "words of institution," doing what Jesus told us to do at the Last Supper: "At the time he was betrayed and entered willingly into his Passion, he took bread and, giving thanks, broke it, and gave it to his disciples, saying:

Take this, all of you, and eat of it, for this is my body, which will be given up for you *[=consecration of the bread]*.

In a similar way, when supper was ended, he took the chalice and, once more giving thanks, he gave it to his disciples, saying:

Take this, all of you, and drink from it, for this is the chalice of my blood, the blood of the new and eternal covenant, which will be poured out for you and for many for the forgiveness of sins. Do this in memory of me *[=consecration of the wine]*."

Anamnesis, in which we remember the passion, resurrection, and glorious return of Jesus: "We proclaim your death, O Lord, and profess your resurrection until you come again."

Intercessions, in which we pray for the pope, the bishops, and all the Church, the living and the dead: "Remember, Lord, your Church ... together with *(name)* our pope and *(name)* our bishop and all the clergy. Remember also ... all who have died in your mercy. ... Have mercy on us all, we pray, that with ... all the saints who have pleased you throughout the ages, we may merit to be coheirs to eternal life, and may praise and glorify you through your son, Jesus Christ."

13C.2 Welcome: Rolling balls

1. Give everyone a sheet of (news)paper, and tell them to roll it into a tight ball.
2. Ask the participants to stand at one end of the room, and place a target at the other side (for example, a waste paper basket).
3. Everyone can throw their ball one by one. The person who gets their ball closest to the target wins.

13C.3 Introductory dialogue: Do this in memory of me

- Distribute sticky notes and pens. Ask the participants to write down ways in which people remember someone who is no longer with them, one on each sticky note. They will probably refer to objects like photos, jewellery or other things used by the person. Or maybe letters or postcards they once wrote. Parents may conserve the first locks of hair of their child, or their first tooth. People who lost a loved one sometimes carry a lock of hair or a photograph in a locket.
- Place all the sticky notes on the wall. Explain that these things help us to remember, to feel close to these people. But it does not bring them back: it is only a memory. What really unites us is the love we once shared, a love that continues to live in our heart. That love is real and present, and deep in ourselves we know that this love cannot die (SEE #TwGOD 1.43). "Do you recognize this?"
- Jesus is present in a similar way in our lives. This presence becomes even much more concrete in Mass, which we also call the Eucharist. When he was together with his friends one last time on the evening before he would suffer and die on the cross, Jesus took bread and said: "This is my body, which is given for you. Do this in memory of me" (LK. 22:19). He then did the same with wine, saying, "This is my blood." Jesus wanted to be remembered, so that he would stay united with us in love. And it worked: Today we still remember what Jesus did, and we still do so by taking bread and wine like he told us to do. What is the difference between all these memories on the wall, and the way Jesus is present in the Eucharist?
- For starters, Jesus said it himself: "This *is* my body," "This *is* my blood." He did not say, "this is like my body" or something similar. And then there is the community of the Apostles: they kept repeating what Jesus did with bread and wine. Had he not told them, "Do this in memory of me" (LK 22:19)? The Apostles knew that they had to take Jesus' words literally. Do you see why?
- Saint Paul wrote: "All who eat and drink without discerning the body, eat and drink judgment against themselves" (1 COR 11:29). He thus called upon his readers to discern that Jesus is really present with his body and blood in bread and wine. If they did not see this, they had better not receive Communion, he said. How does this confirm our understanding that the Eucharist is truly Jesus' body and blood?

13C.4 Round Table 1: Community

- "On the day we call the day of the sun, all who dwell in the city or country gather in the same place.
- The memoirs of the Apostles and the writings of the prophets are read, as much as time permits. When the reader has finished, he who presides over those gathered admonishes and challenges them to imitate these beautiful things.
- Then we all rise together and offer prayers for ourselves … and for all others, wherever they may be, so that we may be found righteous by our life and actions, and faithful to the commandments, so as to obtain eternal salvation.
- When the prayers are concluded we exchange the kiss [of peace].
- Then someone brings bread and a cup of water and wine mixed together to him who presides over the brethren. He takes them and offers praise and glory to the Father of the universe, through the name of the Son and of the Holy Spirit, and for a considerable time he gives thanks (in Greek: *eucharistian*) that we have been judged worthy of these gifts. When he has concluded the prayers and thanksgivings, all present give voice to an acclamation by saying: "Amen."
- When he who presides has given thanks and the people have responded, those whom we call deacons give to those present the "eucharisted bread, wine and water and take them to those who are absent."

[ST. JUSTIN, APOLOGETICS 1, 65-67: CCC 1345]

13C.5 Round Table 2: Jesus' Presence

- Open your Bibles and read the very last phrase of the Gospel of Saint Matthew (MT 28:20). Jesus promised to be present in our lives, and does so in a very concrete way during the Eucharist. Speak about this.
- During Mass, Jesus is present in various ways. As soon as you come into the church, you can be sure that he is present in the tabernacle in front of the church or sacrament chapel. There we conserve the bread that was changed into Jesus' body during a previous Mass. His living presence in the church building is indicated by the light that burns continuously. Therefore it is a good custom to genuflect or bow as a greeting to Jesus before you sit in your place. What is a tabernacle? (SEE #TwGOD 3.14, 3.21). Does that continuously burning light comfort you as a sign of Jesus' presence?
- Jesus is also present in the community. As we have just been reminded, together we form the body of Jesus. And the community is larger than you can see. For starters, also the sick and those unable to come are included. Furthermore, we are united with all the Christians around the world. And thinking even larger, we are also united with the saints in heaven (and pray for the people in purgatory). All together we form the Church, the body of Jesus (SEE MEETING 13B). How does it help you to realize that you are not alone at Mass?
- You may have noticed that after every reading we hear: "The Word of the Lord," or "The Gospel of the Lord," and we respond with a word of thanks. That is because Jesus is also present in the readings: he is the Word of God, as we saw much earlier (SEE MEETING 2). Saint John called Jesus the Word, who was God, and came to us in order to bring us to God. He spoke of Christmas using these deep words: "The Word became flesh and lived among us" (JN 1:14). What does this mean to you?

- For God, his word equals his action: whatever God says, happens. Look at the creation: "And God said, 'Let there be light'; and there was light" (GEN 1:3)! When we listen to the Word of God in the readings, we are invited to discover the deepest message that he wants to give us today. And that message is always the person of Jesus, the Word of God. Have you ever thought about the readings at Mass in this way?
- The lectern from which we read from the Bible is sometimes called the table of the Word (SEE #TwGOD 3.21). Then the altar is the table of the Eucharist. On both tables, Jesus is present and offers himself to us. So, during the Eucharist, Jesus is present in many ways, but in a special way in his living Word, and concretely in his body and his blood that he offers to us in Communion.

13C.6 Round Table 3: John 6

- Show the group an image of a caterpillar, a cocoon, and a butterfly. Ask the participants to explain how exactly the caterpillar changes into a butterfly.
- Explain: "We are not able to really explain what happens in that cocoon, how the transformation takes place. But we still believe in both caterpillars and butterflies. We know that a true change, a metamorphosis, takes place, although we do not know how."
- "Maybe this example helps us to think about what happens at Mass, when bread and wine change into the body and blood of Jesus. We cannot explain how it happens, but we know that in the Eucharist Jesus is not only present in memory, but he is really there! You see bread, but in reality it is Jesus. You see wine, but it is Jesus. Do you see the analogy with the butterfly?"
- "The difference is of course, that in the case of the butterfly you can see with your own eyes that it has changed, whereas the body of Jesus looks like just bread. You need to look with the eyes of the faith in order to recognize that this is truly the body of Jesus. Do you want to have such faith?"
- "If you have difficulty in understanding this, you are not alone. Take out your Bibles and read John 6:51-58." Speak together about this text.
- "Also the people who heard Jesus say that he wanted to give his flesh as bread to eat debated what he meant. Jesus told them to take his words literally: unless you eat my flesh and drink my blood, you have no life in you. Jesus is very clear here! When the people protest that he cannot really mean that he offers his flesh and his blood to them, Jesus confirms once more that he intends exactly that! So Jesus himself confirms that he is concretely present in the Eucharist, which he instituted at the Last Supper, saying 'Take this, all of you ... do this in memory of me'!"

13C.7 Closing prayer

- Go (if possible) to the chapel or church. Find a place near the tabernacle. Light the candles and sing a song to the Holy Spirit.
- Pray: "Lord Jesus, you are present (here) in the tabernacle, which I can find in every Catholic church. Help me to learn to recognize your presence in the Sacrament of the Eucharist. You know how difficult it is to see your presence in what looks like bread and wine. But you also know my desire to get to know you better. Be present here, as we thank you for your life and your presence in our lives."
- Find a time during which you can praise Jesus for who he is and what he gives. Everyone can contribute. This is not the moment to ask, but rather to spend time with Jesus in praise and thanksgiving.
- [Pray especially for those preparing to receive their First Holy Communion].
- After a few minutes of silence, you can pray: "Lord Jesus, you are the Word of God. Help me to understand how you speak to me. You offered your life for me. Help me to recognize your offer in the Eucharist. In turn, I want to offer you my life. Give me strength to do so, and to live not only for myself, but especially for you and for other people. Through Christ our Lord. Amen."
- Conclude with an Our Father and a Hail Mary.

Liturgy 13C: The liturgy of the Eucharist

In the liturgy, God is central, not man. Therefore, we follow the texts of the given liturgy as faithfully as possible. The Mass book (Missal) and book of readings (Lectionary, Gospel book), have been beautifully designed to show our respect to God.

Because God is central, traditionally Church architecture tries to orient the apse of a church towards the East. This is not always possible, but a laudable endeavor as it is said that Jesus will return from the East at the end of times (CF. E.G. MT 24:27; ZECH. 14:4). We celebrate the greatest gift of God to us – Jesus' presence in the Eucharist – facing east as an assembly waiting for Jesus (the celebrant usually faces the faithful and leads the congregation in prayer).

The celebration

The liturgy of the Eucharist is a joint celebration of the whole congregation. Everyone joins in and has a role. Do not think that sitting in the pews means that you have no role: everyone present is called to play an active part in the joint liturgical prayer of the entire community. The Eucharist is defined by the Second Vatican Council as the "source and summit" of Christian life. Of all the seven sacraments, the Eucharist is the direct encounter with Jesus himself.

The liturgy

- The Liturgy of the Eucharist consists essentially of four parts. The first part contains the opening with a procession and the sign of the cross. The penitential rite in which we ask God forgiveness, remits any venial sin for which we are truly sorry (SEE MEETING 13F). On Sundays and feasts we chant the Gloria to praise God in himself. Then the celebrant prays the opening prayer.

- The readings follow, which together with the homily and the intercessions form the "table of the Word" on which Jesus offers himself as an example and inspiration. The Creed is prayed on Sundays and solemnities.
- Next is the offertory of bread and wine which will be used during the liturgy of this Eucharist. The gifts of bread and wine are brought to the altar and offered to God. The celebrant prays the preface and the Eucharistic prayer in the name of all present. At the moment that the priest prays the words of Jesus at the Last Supper (SEE WORKSHEET 13C.1), all kneel in awe for the great mystery that has been revealed to us.
- Mass concludes with a prayer, a word of thanks (community announcements) and the blessing by the priest, after which we are sent out into the world to do good, and to proclaim the Gospel of Jesus.
- In the above, we have not mentioned the way of celebrating Mass (e.g. the Divine Liturgy) according to one of the Eastern rites, which would be different. See the app for an introduction to the Eastern rites (SEE #TwGOD 3.51-3.55).

The celebrant

The celebrant of the Eucharist is the priest (or bishop) only. Without them, there is no Eucharist. The deacon assists them. He helps to distribute Communion once Mass has been celebrated. There are many more roles to play, however: faithful are needed to read the readings, the prayers, to bring the gifts to the altar, to serve Mass, to sing in the choir, to distribute communion, to prepare the sacristy …

Liturgy of the Eucharist

Opening
- Entrance procession
- Welcome & penitential preparation
- (Gloria)
- Opening prayer

Liturgy of the Word
- Reading
- Psalm
- (Second reading)
- Gospel
- Homily
- (Creed)
- General intercessions

Liturgy of the Eucharist
- Prayer over the gifts
- Preface & Eucharistic prayer
- Rite of Communion
- Prayer after Communion

Conclusion
- Blessing & dismissal

TO PREPARE
- A pure heart
- Rite of the Eucharist
- Intentions for the general intercessions

Procedure for Meeting 13D Matrimony

Relate

00.00 Opening prayer
- Choose a prayer from Appendix 5 or use the *Tweeting with GOD* app.

00.02 Welcome: Two truths and a lie
- Follow the indications on Worksheet 13D.2.

00.10 The previous meeting
- Engage in a simple and quick recap. What touched the participants most in the previous meeting? Are there new questions or ideas? How did they fare with the dual challenge?
  - Are there doubts about the Questions in the *Tweeting with GOD* book?
  - How was it to participate in weekday Mass? What differences did you note with Sunday Mass?
- (The participants who prepared today's Questions can briefly present the theme).

Think

00.15 Introductory dialogue: The wedding at Cana
- Read John 2:1-11. Focus on the first two verses and ask: "What strikes you in this passage?"
- "After years of growing up and learning privately, Jesus is about to start what we call his public life, the approximately three years during which he preached the Gospel. It is significant that he performs his first sign at a wedding (JN 2:11). Thus he shows how important marriage is for God and for humanity. Why would this be, do you think?"
- "Usually in texts about Jesus he is the main actor. Not so here: he is merely present as a guest, apparently accompanying his mother to the celebration. Yes, in a while he will perform a great miracle, but he is not involved with the marriage itself. He might at least have preached at the wedding ceremony. But the Bible text does not mention anything like that. Why not, do you think?"
- "We do not need God's intervention to get married. Marriage is already part of how he created man and woman. God said at their creation: 'It is not good that the man should be alone' (GEN 2:18) and 'Therefore a man leaves his father and his mother and clings to his wife, and they become one flesh' (GEN 2:24). These are fundamental texts for understanding marriage. Can you see this?"
- "Marriage is so much part of what God intended for humankind, that in the Catholic liturgy husband and wife themselves administer the sacrament to each other. The representative of the Church is merely present as a witness of the Church, to register the new marriage bond, and to implore God's blessing over the couple (SEE WORKSHEET 13D.1). So, Jesus does not need to celebrate the marriage, as the couple marry themselves. But he is present to bless them abundantly, which is symbolically expressed by the abundance of the very good wine he gives them to celebrate (SEE MEETING 18)." Speak about this together.

00.30 Round Table 1: Canon law
- Begin by reading the three rules for a successful marriage by Pope Francis (SEE WORKSHEET 13D.3).
- Explain that the Church has its own set of laws, which we call canon law, after the Greek canon which means "rule" (SEE #TwGOD 4.11). These laws are based on God's revelation in the Bible and through the Tradition of the Church (SEE MEETING 2). Their ultimate aim is to help us reach the salvation intended by Jesus (SEE MEETING 8): the very last article says that "the salvation of souls must always be the supreme law in the Church" (CANON 1752). The canons on matrimony give a quick insight into the essential elements of this sacrament.

- Form small groups (SEE APPENDIX 3.1 & 3.2) [or work in couples]. Distribute sheets with canon 1055-1056 (SEE WORKSHEET 13D.4).
- Ask the groups to study the text together, and to make a list of the essential elements of Matrimony.
- After some 5 minutes come back together. On a large sheet write down the essential elements found by the groups. Speak about each point briefly. Christian marriage is:
  - Between one man and one woman
  - A lifelong partnership: indissoluble – "what God has joined together, let no one separate" (MK 10:9)
  - Unity between the two – a faithful and exclusive relationship
  - For the good of the spouses – their well-being and happiness
  - Open to children – ready to share their love and collaborate with the Creator
  - A sacrament between two baptized – they share in the love of God himself

00.45 Today's hero:
Blessed Luigi and Maria Quattrocchi
- Watch the video of Blessed Luigi and Maria Quattrocchi via *Online with Saints*.
- These two people brought the Christian vision on marriage to life in their relationship. They called themselves an ordinary family. What made them so extraordinary?

00.55 Break [END FIRST & START SECOND SESSION (SEE GS2)]

01.00 Round Table 2: Love and dedication
- Follow the indication of Worksheet 13D.5.

01.20 Round Table 3: The celebration of marriage
- Follow the indication of Worksheet 13D.6.

Pray & Act

01.40 Synthesis and actualization
- Ask whether there are any burning questions remaining. To round off you can say that God intended marriage as the deepest expression of the love he laid in his creation. Marriage is not only for the good of the spouses, but also for the good of all the community. Selfless love may be rare nowadays, but it still is the foundation stone of a happy and stable marriage.
- Conclude with the question: "How can what I have learned nourish my personal faith and relationship with Jesus? How can I put this into action?" Speak briefly about this.

01.45 Closing prayer
- Follow the indication of Worksheet 13D.7.

01.58 Conclusion in the meeting room
- Remind participants of the date for the next meeting and present the dual challenge:
  - Read these Questions in the *Tweeting with GOD* book: 3.43 & 4.19.
  - Read the blessing of the spouses (SEE WORKSHEET 13D.1), searching for elements of what was said in this meeting.

TO PREPARE
- Bibles
- Video equipment (internet)
- *Tweeting with GOD* book & app
- *Online with Saints* app
- Box of matches & ashtray
- Sheets for Round Table 1 (DL)
- Large sheet and markers

Worksheet 13D

13D.1 Essential moment of Matrimony

The exact text is decided by the Bishops' Conference. Usually there are various options from which the spouses can choose. The essential moment is indicated in bold. The spouses stand in presence of the celebrant, join their right hands, and say, for example:

"I (Joseph), take you (Mary), to be my wedded wife to have and to hold from this day forward, for better, for worse, for richer, for poorer, in sickness and in health, to love and to cherish till death do us part.

I (Mary), take you (Joseph), to be my wedded husband to have and to hold from this day forward, for better, for worse, for richer, for poorer, in sickness and in health, to love and to cherish till death do us part."

The celebrant blesses the rings with a prayer (and holy water). Then the husband places the ring on his wife's ring finger, saying, for example, "receive this ring as a sign of my love and fidelity." The wife does the same to her husband.

After Communion, or after the general intercessions, the celebrant, with hands extended over bride and bride-groom, prays the nuptial blessing, for example: "Holy Father, maker of the whole world, who created man and woman in your own image and willed that their union be crowned with your blessing, we humbly beseech you for these your servants, who are joined today in the Sacrament of Matrimony. May your abundant blessing, Lord, come down upon this bride, Mary, and upon Joseph, her companion for life, and may the power of your Holy Spirit set their hearts aflame from on high, so that, living out together the gift of Matrimony, they may (adorn their family with children and) enrich the Church. In happiness may they praise you, O Lord, in sorrow may they seek you out; may they have the joy of your presence to assist them in their toil, and know that you are near to comfort them in their need; let them pray to you in the holy assembly and bear witness to you in the world, and after a happy old age, together with the circle of friends that surrounds them, may they come to the Kingdom of Heaven. Through Christ our Lord. Amen."

13D.2 Welcome: Two truths and a lie

1   Sit in a circle. One participant has to make three statements about anything they choose. Two are true, and one is a lie. Don't make the lie too obvious.
2.   Now the group tries to guess which statements is a lie.
3.   You can add some competition by keeping score of who guessed right, and who was able to trick the group.
4.   In conclusion you may have a brief dialogue about the observation that it is easy to lie, but is it good for a relationship?

13D.3 Three rules for a successful marriage

"Living together [in marriage] is an art, a patient, beautiful, fascinating journey. It does not end once you have won each other's love. Rather, it is precisely there where it begins! This journey of every day has a few rules that can be summed up in three ...

- 'Can I, may I?' This is the polite request to enter the life of another with respect and care. One should learn how to ask: may I do this? Would you like for us to do this? Should we take up this initiative, to educate our children in this way? ...
- 'Thank you.' It seems so easy to say these words, but we know that it is not. But it is important! We teach it to children, but then we ourselves forget it! It is important to keep alive the awareness that the other person is a gift from God — and for the gifts of God we say thank you!
- The third: 'I'm sorry.' In life we err frequently, we make many mistakes. We all do. In general each of us is ready to accuse the other and to justify ourselves. It is an instinct that stands at the origin of so many disasters. Let us learn to acknowledge our mistakes and to ask for forgiveness."

[POPE FRANCIS, *ADDRESS TO ENGAGED COUPLES PREPARING FOR MARRIAGE*, 14 FEBRUARY 2014]

13D.4 Round Table 1: Canon Law about the Sacrament of Matrimony

Canon 1055 §1. The matrimonial covenant, by which a **man and a woman** establish between themselves a **partnership of the whole of life** and which is ordered by its nature to the **good of the spouses** and the **procreation and education of offspring**, has been raised by Christ the Lord to the dignity of a **sacrament** between the baptised.

Canon 1056. The essential properties of marriage are **unity** and **indissolubility**, which in Christian marriage obtain a special firmness by reason of the sacrament.

13D.5 Round Table 2: Love and dedication

- Make small groups [or work in couples]. Ask them to read Saint Paul's letter to the Ephesians 5:21-33 together, and think about the following questions:
  – Why is this text not what it may look like at first sight, a suppression of women's rights?
  – What would the deeper meaning of this text be?
  – Does the text become more acceptable if we read "husbands" where it says "wives" and vice versa?
  – Why is it important for a successful marriage that the spouses be subject to one another?
- Come back together and speak about the text. As it may lead to strong reactions, especially from the women, let's make clear from the outset: for the Church, men and women have absolute equal value, and have the same basic rights (SEE #TWGOD 2.16). One is not lower or worth less than the other. At the same time, man and woman both have their own qualities, they are not the same. Thankfully, for their difference is the basic rea-

son for marriage in the first place. Briefly exchange opinions on this.

- The key to understanding this text is the first line: "be subject to *one another*" (Eph 5:21). Yes, wives are called to be subject to their husbands, but look at the men: they have to love their wives as Jesus Christ loved the Church. Jesus was God, but he subjected or humbled himself out of love for all of us by becoming man (see Meeting 8). That was not enough, he even further humbled himself by taking the form of a slave (Phil 2:7-8), and accepting death as a criminal on the cross. Why? Out of love! To make us holy and thus save us (see Meeting 8). Saint Paul tells men to do the same for their wives. Now who is getting the better part?
- Interchanging the words "husbands" and "wives" in the text can be helpful. It does not make them the same in everything, but it underlines their absolute equality in value. This helps to see the deeper meaning of this text with regard to their relationship within marriage. How do you see this?
- We could replace the words "subjecting yourself" with "leaving space for the other to flourish." Does this change your view of this text?
- The bottom line is that for married life to work, you will have to be ready to give up your own wishes, desires, and dreams for the sake of the other. What may seem easy when you have butterflies in your belly, can be much more difficult when you are settling in your married life. It sometimes demands real effort to leave each other not just enough space to breathe, but to flourish. In this sense, Saint Paul shows deep understanding of human nature. Can you see this?
- Married life is no longer about two individuals, but about a couple united for the whole of life who have become "one flesh" (Gen 2:24). As they will still be two minds, marriage is a lifelong exercise of giving oneself up for the sake of the other. If both have this attitude, marriage will work marvelously, principally because the reason for this self-denial is deeply shared love. A love which reflects the love of God, who gave up his life for us Precisely this is the reason why marriage is a sacrament, a doorway to God's love, so to speak (see Meeting 12). He is love himself, and is present in every loving relationship. Just as God shared his love with us, every married couple is invited to share their love with people around them, and in a special way with their children – if they receive this gift.

13D.6 Round Table 3: The celebration of marriage

- Marriage is a gift, not only to the spouses, but to the whole community. These two people will form a new and stable union: together they stand strong, united by their love, a love they can share with whoever needs it. Therefore, marriage is a public act, performed in the presence of a representation of the entire Church community. Before the essential moment of marriage, the representative of the Church asks the couple whether they have come out of their own free will and whether they are free to get married. Why is this important?
- If they are forced into marriage, or already married to someone else, for example, the marriage will be invalid. Only freely chosen and accepted love can last throughout the life of the spouses.
- We know that couples can encounter difficulties, and that sometimes they see no other way forward than by separation. They need to be accompanied with love and understanding by the Church community. If we admit that life on earth is not perfect just yet, we are all in great need of such love and understanding. Still, the

principle of marriage is that it is intended as a lifetime commitment by the spouses.

- Read Matthew 19:3-9 and speak about this. Jesus is very clear in his teaching. If at the creation God indeed planned that marriage would make man and woman into a new unity that would for the spouses' entire life, then who are we to separate them? During the wedding ceremony, the representative of the Church asks the two whether they intend a lifelong union in line with Jesus' words: "What God has joined together, let no one separate" (MT 19:6). Do you think such lifelong union is possible?
- The next question is whether they want their union to be open to children, and collaborate with God in sharing their love with their kids. At the creation, God told the first couple to "Be fruitful and multiply" (GEN 1:28). We are called to do the same. At the same time, God gave us responsibility as stewards all the creation (GEN 1:28; 1 COR 4:1-2). Also procreation should be done in a responsible way. Some couples cannot have children for medical or other reasons (SEE #TWGOD 4.32). But selfishly excluding children from the outset of marriage goes against the deepest intentions of our Creator and therefore against the very essence of Matrimony. Can you see this?
- The exact moment of marriage is when they exchange their vows, expressing their consent. The promise to be husband or wife, "to have and to hold from this day forward, for better, for worse, for richer, for poorer, in sickness and in health, to love and to cherish till death do us part" (SEE WORKSHEET 13D.1). Do these words have a deeper meaning in the light of what has been said so far?

13D.7 Closing prayer

- Go (if possible) to the chapel or church. Light the candles and sing a song to the Holy Spirit.
- Pray, for example: "Dear Lord, you started your public life at the wedding at Cana. Today we have thought about the true meaning of marriage. Help us to see how you are present everywhere love is shared. In a few moments of silence, we want to pray for all our intentions."
- Spend some time in intercessory prayer for the happiness of couples in marriage, for their family life, for those facing difficulties, for those who do not see how they can continue together …
- Conclude with an Our Father and a Hail Mary.

Liturgy 13D: The liturgy of Matrimony

The liturgy of Matrimony is a formal moment, with formal words. It is more than just a contract between two people: here a man and a woman are dedicating themselves for the remainder of their lives to each other in love. They do so in the presence of God and the Church, represented by the celebrant and the faithful present. The text for the liturgy is pre-established and approved by the Bishops' Conference.

The celebration

Marriage can be celebrated during Mass, or outside Mass, depending on various circumstances. If celebrated during Mass, the ritual for Matrimony is inserted just after the homily. After the Our Father comes the Nuptial Blessing. If Mass is not celebrated, the procedure below is still followed, omitting the "Liturgy of the Eucharist" (SEE BOX). The nuptial blessing follows directly after the general intercessions.

Often it can help a lot to calm the nerves of the spouses to literally walk through the liturgy of Matrimony in the church, showing where they will stand and when, and practicing their responses.

The liturgy

- The actual celebration of Matrimony starts with the questions of the celebrant to the spouses, asking whether they have come out of their own free will without constraint, and whether they are lawfully free to get married. They are also asked to confirm that they intend a lifelong union, and – if applicable – to accept children as a gift from God.

- The spouses join their right hand and declare their consent to each other, saying that they want to love and cherish each other until the death of one of them (SEE WORKSHEET 13D.1). The celebrant receives the consent in the name of

Liturgy of Matrimony

Opening
- Welcome at the door
- Entrance procession
- Opening prayer

Liturgy of the Word
- Reading(s)
- Psalm
- Gospel
- Homily

Liturgy of Matrimony
- Calling of the witnesses
- Questions before the consent
- Consent of the spouses
- Reception of the consent by the Church
- Blessing and giving of rings
- General intercessions

Liturgy of the Eucharist
- Prayer over the gifts
- Preface & Eucharistic prayer
- Our Father
- Nuptial blessing
- Sign of peace & Communion
- Prayer after Communion

Conclusion
- Blessing & dismissal
- (Dedication to our Mother Mary)
- Signing of the marriage record

the Church: from now on these two people are married.
- The rings are presented and blessed. Husband and wife place the ring on each other's ring finger, usually telling them to receive this ring as a sign of their love and fidelity (SEE WORKSHEET 13D.1).
- (If Mass is celebrated, it continues as usual with the general intercessions, and proceeds until after the Our Father.)
- The celebrant extends his hands over the husband and wife and prays the words of the nuptial blessing, asking God to bless this couple (SEE WORKSHEET 13D.1).

The celebrant
The ministers of the marriage consent are the spouses themselves. The celebrant merely assists as the spouses administer the sacrament, and accepts this in name of the Church. It is a natural right to get married, so that it would not be correct to impede people from marrying because of a scarcity of ordained ministers, for example. Therefore, a lay person can be delegated to accept the consent. In many cases the celebrant will be a deacon, priest, or bishop.

TO PREPARE
- Meeting of the spouses with the celebrant
- Repeating the responses with the spouses
- Rite of Matrimony
- Choice of readings
- Intentions for the general intercessions

Procedure for Meeting 13E Holy Orders & Anointing of the Sick

Relate

00.00 Opening prayer (SEE APPENDIX 5)

00.02 Welcome: Unfortunately ... fortunately
- Follow the indications on Worksheet 13E.3.

00.10 The previous meeting
- Engage in a simple and quick recap. What touched the participants most in the previous meeting? Are there new questions or ideas? How did they fare with the dual challenge?
  - Are there doubts about the Questions in the *Tweeting with GOD* book?
  - What did you find in the text for the blessing of the spouses?
- (The participants who prepared today's Questions can briefly present the theme).

Think

00.15 Introductory dialogue: Common priesthood and ordained ministers
- Follow the indications on Worksheet 13E.4.

00.30 Round Table 1: The celebration of ordination
- Explain that the Sacrament of Holy Orders is always administered by a bishop through the laying on of hands and the ordination prayer. Distribute the extract from the ordination prayer for a bishop (SEE WORKSHEET 13E.1). Ask the participants to read the text carefully in silence, searching for the main elements of the episcopate.
- Ask participants to speak with their neighbor about what they found. Then write all elements on a large sheet.
- Explain that the main tasks of deacons are to assist the bishop in his service to the poor, to administer the Sacraments of Baptism and Matrimony, and to assist bishops and priests during Mass. What elements from the sheet apply to the deacon? Mark these in yellow. Write down any other elements people come up with.
- Explain that priests are ordained to assist the bishop by celebrating the sacraments (except Holy Orders), teach and proclaim the faith, and help the bishop in the governance of the Church. What elements from the sheet apply to the priest? Underline these in green. Some tasks will apply to both deacons and priests.
- Explain that every priest serves for some time as a deacon before being ordained. And when a bishop is ordained, he usually has served as a priest for years. The bishop is a direct successor of the Apostles. At his ordination, he receives the fullness of the sacrament of Holy Orders in order to serve, govern, administer the sacraments, and teach the faith. Are there any tasks left on the sheet that are the sole responsibility of the bishop?
- Looking at the sheet, do you get a better idea of what the Sacrament of Holy Orders encompasses? Do you see the differences and parallels between the degrees of ordination? What else do you discover?

00.45 Today's hero: Saint Alphonsus Liguori
- Watch the video of Saint Alphonsus Liguori via *Online with Saints*.
- Alphonsus was a great lawyer, but he gave it all up. In what aspects of his life do you recognise the task of the deacon, in which tasks the priest, and where the bishop?
- His attention to the poor is a good example of the main task of the deacon: assisting the bishop in his care for the poor and sick. His love for preaching and inspiring people in their spiritual life are priest-

ly tasks. And his governance decisions regarding the training of priests is an episcopal task. So in his life, Alphonsus experienced all three degrees of ordination.

00.55 Break [END FIRST & START SECOND SESSION (SEE GS2)]

01.00 Round Table 2: Anointing of the Sick
- Follow the indications on Worksheet 13E.5.

01.15 Today's hero: Saint Teresa of Calcutta
- Watch the video of Saint Teresa of Calcutta via *Online with Saints*.
- Mother Teresa did whatever she could to help poor and sick people. Her sisters, assisted by medical staff, tried to help them get better and get up again. But more than through her own handiwork, Mother Teresa believed in the working of God's grace. That is why she always called a priest to administer the sacraments to the sick, including the Anointing of the Sick. Thus she cared for both the body and the soul of the sick. Speak about this together.

01.25 Round Table 3: The sacrament of death or life?
- Follow the indications on Worksheet 13E.6.

Pray & Act

01.40 Synthesis and actualization
- God gave us deacons, priests, and bishops to help us stay in touch with him, and be strengthened by the sacraments. One of the sacraments of healing is that of Anointing of the Sick, which gives first of all spiritual healing, and possibly also physical healing.
- Conclude with the question: "How can what I have learned nourish my personal faith and relationship with Jesus? How can I put this into action?" Speak briefly about this.

01.45 Closing prayer
- Go (if possible) to the chapel or church. Light the candles and sing a song.
- Distribute small sheets and pens, and ask people to write down the names of the sick and elderly people they want to pray for in particular. They can place these names in a basket in front of the altar.
- After some minutes of silent pray, say, for example: "Lord, we bring these people and their afflictions to you, and ask you to be with them, strengthen them, and help us care for them. Give them health in spirit and body. Not our will, but your Will be done."
- Now invite the participants to pray for your bishop(s), your priest(s), and/or your deacon(s). Everyone who wishes to can formulate a prayer intention, after which all reply, for example: "Lord, hear us."
- Conclude with an Our Father and a Hail Mary.

01.58 Conclusion in the meeting room
- Remind participants of the date for the next meeting and present the dual challenge:
- Conclude with the Our Father and the Hail Mary.
  - Read these Questions in the *Tweeting with GOD* book: 3.40 & 3.41.
  - Visit a sick person and/or send a card to someone in need to show that you are with them in thought and prayer.

TO PREPARE
- Bibles
- Video equipment (internet)
- *Tweeting with GOD* book & app
- *Online with Saints* app
- Large sheet & markers
- Essential words of Ordination (DL)
- Essential words of Anointing (DL)
- Basket, small sheets & pens

Worksheet 13E

13E.1 Essential moment of Holy Orders

There are two essential parts of ordination, indicated in bold:

1　First **the laying on of hands by the bishop** in silence.

2.　And then the **prayer of ordination by the bishop**, of which we give an abstract here:

– For the ordination of a deacon:
"Lord, look with favor on this servant of yours, whom we now dedicate to the office of deacon, to minister at your holy altar. Lord, send forth upon him the Holy Spirit, that he may be strengthened by the gift of your sevenfold grace to carry out faithfully the work of the ministry. May he excel in every virtue: in love that is sincere, in concern for the sick and the poor, in unassuming authority, in self-discipline, and in holiness of life. May his conduct exemplify your commandments and lead your people to imitate his purity of life. May he remain strong and steadfast in Christ, giving to the world the witness of a pure conscience? May he in this life imitate your Son, who came, not to be served by to serve, and one day reign with him in heaven. We ask this through our Lord Jesus Christ, your Son."

– For the ordination of a priest:
"Almighty Father, grant to this servant of yours the dignity of the priesthood. Renew within him the Spirit of holiness. As a coworker with the order of bishops may he be faithful to the ministry that he receives from you, Lord God, and be to others a model of right conduct. May he be faithful in working with the order of bishops, so that the Gospel may reach the ends of the earth, and the family of nations, made one in Christ, may become God's one, holy people. We ask this through our Lord Jesus Christ, your Son."

– For the ordination of a bishop:
"Father, you know all hearts. You have chosen your servant for the office of bishop. May he be a shepherd to your holy flock, and a high priest blameless in your sight, ministering to you night and day; may he always gain the blessing of your favor and offer the gifts of your holy Church. Through the Spirit who gives the grace of high priesthood grant him the power to forgive sins as you have commanded to assign ministries as you have decreed and to loose from every bond by the authority which you gave to your Apostles. May he be pleasing to you by his gentleness and purity of heart, presenting a fragrant offering to you, through Jesus Christ, your Son."

13E.2 Essential moment of Anointing of the Sick

The essential moment is when the priest anoints the sick on their forehead, saying:

"Through this holy anointing may the Lord in his love and mercy help you with the grace of the Holy Spirit."

When anointing the palms of the sick person's hands he says:

"May the Lord who frees you from sin, save you and raise you up."

13E.3 Welcome: Unfortunately … fortunately

1   Decide if and how you wish to split up the group. Sit in a circle.
2. Explain that you are going to tell a story together. You can suggest the opening phrase: "Unfortunately there is a lion in the sacristy."
3. Now the person on your left formulates the next phrase: "Fortunately it has no teeth." And the person on their left continues: "Unfortunately it has big claws …" And so on to tell a story.
4. After a warm up round, do the same for the theme of illness and the support the Church can give. Propose a new starting phrase: "Unfortunately many people in our community are sick. Fortunately we can help them in various ways. Unfortunately we cannot take away physical suffering. Fortunately the sacraments can help …"
5. If there is time, you can also introduce the theme of ordination: "Unfortunately there are not many priests …"

13E.4 Introductory dialogue: Common priesthood and ordained ministers

- Explain that Baptism makes a Christian share in the common priesthood of all the faithful. We are all called to present Jesus to the world through our way of living, good deeds, and words about the Gospel (SEE #TwGOD 3.42). What kind of tasks would this common priesthood encompass? Take a large sheet and write down all the ideas of the group.
- Continue explaining that certain men are chosen by God to serve as ordained ministers. There are three degrees of the Sacrament of Ordination or Holy Orders: the deacon, the priest, and the bishop (SEE #TwGOD 3.41). Do the participants know what their tasks are? Write these on the sheet. Some tasks will already have been mentioned as part of the common priesthood of all faithful.
- Examples of tasks are to proclaim the Gospel, celebrate Mass and the other sacraments, be a pastor, represent Christ, build the community, lead and teach the faithful, serve the poor, evangelize, imitate Christ …
- Speak together about the parallels and differences between the common priesthood of all faithful and Holy Orders. What makes the task of ordained ministers so special?
- (A question that may come up is about the ordination of women. All recent popes have been very clear that this is not possible [SEE #TwGOD 3.41]. Care should be taken that this issue will not dominate the conversation. The role of women in the Church is an important subject indeed – with great room for improvement – but this is not the moment. You could discuss it during one of the meetings on your group's question [SEE #TwGOD 2.16, MEETING 13D]).

- Explain that everyone who is seriously ill or old can ask to receive the Sacrament of the Anointing of the Sick. This is administered by a priest (or bishop) through prayer and anointing the sick person with holy oil. The sacrament can be celebrated at home or at the hospital without the sick person having to leave their bed, or during a liturgy in the church with the community present.
- Distribute the essential words of the sacrament (SEE WORKSHEET 13E.2) and ask participants to read James 5:14-16. Now look for parallels or differences between these words and the essential words of the sacrament. Speak about this together.
- Say that the text does not promise that the sick will be healed physically, but it does say that they will be saved. This sacrament does not replace medical care in any way. Jesus himself said that sick people need a doctor (LK 5:31). So what does the sacrament do, do you think?
- God's grace, received in the Anointing of the Sick, helps to find the necessary spiritual strength to bear suffering and pain. It also helps to heal the soul. You can absolutely pray for physical healing too, but always with the attitude that not your will but God's Will be done (SEE MEETING 9).
- Point out to the participants that illness is never a punishment for sin (although some sinful behaviour can lead to illness). So why does the Bible text speak about the forgiveness of sin through the sacrament?
- No one is without sin (ROM 3:10), and sin makes it more difficult to relate to God and receive his grace (SEE MEETING 13F). Especially when life is difficult, like when we are sick, we need God's grace most. Ideally, the sick person will first receive the other sacrament of healing, the Sacrament of Reconciliation. Also the Anointing of the Sick forgives sins, which underlines the importance of freeing the sick person of any obstacle that impedes reaching out to God and receiving his grace.

13E.6 Round Table 3: The sacrament of death or life?

- Some people have the idea that you should only call a priest to your sickbed when you are terminally ill. However, this is not correct. The Sacrament of the Anointing of the Sick can be received at any age after infancy, and can be repeated if necessary. So why would this sacrament so often be associated with death?
- We have seen before how suffering gets a certain meaning when lived in the light of faith together with Jesus who suffered for us (SEE MEETING 6). While we can do everything to make the suffering as bearable as possible, suffering in life is unavoidable, especially for the sick. But they are not alone: Jesus is always with those who are suffering (MT 28:20). He wants to give them strength right now, to bear their pain in faith, and also remind them that life in this world is not everything: a better life still is waiting in heaven. Can you imagine that this knowledge would strengthen you if you were seriously ill?
- Visiting the sick is one of the corporal works of mercy (SEE #TwGOD APP > 🧍 > 🏠 > ⏺). It is an important Christian duty to care for the sick, pray for their well-being and healing (spiritually and physically), and to comfort them in whatever way possible. The Sacrament of the Anointing of the Sick should be seen as part of this task of the community to care for the sick.

Liturgy 13E: The liturgy of Holy Orders

There are three degrees, or grades of the Sacrament of Holy Orders: the ordination to the diaconate, priesthood, and episcopate (SEE #TwGOD 3.41). These are administered consecutively, usually with a longer time between the ordinations. So a bishop is ordained three times during his life: to become deacon, priest, and finally bishop. Deacons and priests are ordained to assist the bishop in his ministry.

By their ordination, a very special task is conferred on these men: to function as a bridge between God and his faithful. They are very much in need of your prayers, for in spite of the beautiful ordination rite and their new sacramental status, they remain fallible humans, subject to all earthly temptations.

The celebration

The ordination rite takes place during Mass. Speaking generally, the ritual is similar for the ordination of deacons, priests, and bishops. What differs is the words of the prayer of ordination, the vestments, and the symbols of office. Also, deacons are not anointed.

The liturgy

- After the Gospel, the Holy Spirit is invoked by singing *Veni, Creator Spiritus* ("Come, Holy Spirit"). The candidate is called to come forward, is presented, and asked to promise to serve God and the Church with dedication and obedience, according to the ordination he will receive. At a bishop's ordination, the letter of appointment by the pope is shown and read.
- After the homily, the candidate prostrates himself before the altar as a sign that he surrenders his life to God and the Church, and supplicates God's grace over his ministry. All the congregation prays for him, invoking the prayer of the saints in the litany.

- In silence, the celebrant lays hands on the candidate. At a priestly ordination, each of the priests present also lays on hands after the bishop. At an episcopal ordination, only the bishops present do the same.
- The celebrant prays the prayer of ordination (SEE WORKSHEET 13E.1). At a bishop's ordination, the book of the Gospels is placed over the head of the candidate, as a sign that he is to preach the Word of God.
- Priests and bishops are anointed with chrism, holy oil: a priest is anointed on the inside of his hands, and a bishop on his head.
- The newly ordained receives the symbols of his office. A deacon is vested with stole and dalmatic, and receives the book of the Gospels. A priest is vested with stole and chasuble, and receives the gifts of bread and wine. A bishop receives the book of the Gospels, his ring, his mitre, and his pastoral staff.
- The newly ordained is now welcomed in their midst by his colleagues in the diaconate, priesthood, or episcopate.
- The newly ordained bishop processes through the church to bless the faithful. After Mass, a newly ordained priest may give his first blessing to individual faithful. Traditionally they kneel to receive this blessing and then kiss the palms of his hands that were anointed to be instruments in bringing God's grace through the sacraments.

The celebrant

The liturgy of Holy Orders is always celebrated by a bishop. Bishops are the successors of the Apostles, which is why we speak of "apostolic succession" (SEE #TWGOD 2.15). Like the Apostles did, bishops can pass their ministry on to other men through the sacrament of ordination. The bishop who ordains a bishop is assisted by two other bishops, called co-consecrators.

Liturgy of Holy Orders

Opening
- Welcome & penitential preparation
- Opening prayer

Liturgy of the Word
- Reading(s)
- Psalm
- Gospel

Liturgy of Ordination
- Imploring of the Holy Spirit
- Calling, presentation, and election of the candidate(s)
- Homily
- Promises of the candidate
- Litany of the saints
- Laying on of hands
- Prayer of ordination
- Investiture with liturgical dress
- Anointing with holy oil (priests, bishops)
- Presentation of symbols of the office
- Kiss of peace
- General intercessions

Liturgy of the Eucharist
- Prayer over the gifts
- Preface & Eucharistic prayer
- Rite of Communion
- Prayer after Communion

Conclusion
- Blessing & dismissal

TO PREPARE
- Rite of Ordination
- Choice of readings
- Vestments and symbols of office

Liturgy 13E: The liturgy of Anointing of the Sick

Anyone who is seriously ill has to undergo an important medical intervention, or faces a life-limiting condition can ask to receive this sacrament. This sacrament is sometimes called "extreme unction" or "last rites," as it is often received in the final stage of life (SEE #TwGOD 1.40). However, it is not at all limited to the dying, and in accordance with the custom of the Apostles (JAS 5:14-15). No need to hesitate to come back at a later stage: Anointing of the Sick can be received multiple times in life. In preparation, the sick are invited to receive the Sacrament of Reconciliation.

The celebration

Ideally, the sacrament is administered during Mass, with the community present so they can pray for the sick. Often, this is not possible because of the infirmity of the sick person. In this case, the celebration of the Eucharist is omitted (SEE BOX). For the anointing, the priest uses the oil of the sick, which was blessed specifically by the bishop on Maundy Thursday (SEE #TwGOD 3.30). In an emergency, he can bless any vegetable oil.

In a life-threatening emergency, the celebration can be reduced to a single anointing with the essential words (SEE WORKSHEET 13E.2). Note that the sacraments are only for the living: after death, the deceased are commended into the hands of their merciful God. If there is time, and depending on the condition of the sick, the priest can administer the "last rites." The sick person can first receive the Sacrament of Reconciliation. If they are not yet confirmed they can receive the Sacrament of Confirmation. The celebrant can confer the apostolic pardon for the dying, and absolve them of irregularities. The rite of the Sacrament of the Sick follows (SEE BELOW). The proper sacrament for

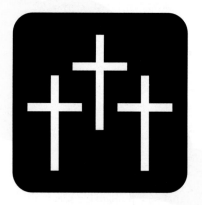

the dying is the last Communion, called viaticum after the Latin word that means something like "food for the road."

There is no special place in church architecture dedicated to this sacrament, which often is received at home or in the hospital. However, in many churches the three holy oils are preserved in a special place, recognizable in the architecture.

The liturgy

- The liturgy of the Anointing of the Sick starts after the reading(s) and the homily. The celebrant invites the faithful to pray for the sick person in a litany of prayers.
- The celebrant lays his hands on the head of the sick and prays in silence.
- The celebrant leads the faithful in a prayer of thanksgiving for the oil. If the oil is not yet blessed, he blesses it with a short formula of blessing.
- The celebrant anoints the sick on their forehead and on their hands saying the essential words (SEE WORKSHEET 14E.2).
- Then the celebrant prays a prayer for the sick, asking God to strengthen and comfort the sick person in the face of hardships, for healing if that is given, and for faithful consolation when preparing for death.
- The general intercessions may be omitted if the liturgy was started with a litany of prayers, or take the form of a continuation of this litany.

The celebrant

The celebrant is always a priest or bishop, just as for the Sacraments of the Eucharist and Reconciliation. These are moments where God directly intervenes through the ministry that was conferred to the priest. If no priest or bishop is available, a deacon or one of the faithful can pray with and for the dying person.

Liturgy of the Anointing of the Sick

Opening
- Welcome & penitential preparation
- Opening prayer

Liturgy of the Word
- Reading(s)
- Psalm
- Gospel
- Homily

Liturgy of Anointing of the Sick
- Litany
- Laying on of hands
- Prayer over the oil
- Anointing with holy oil
- Prayer after anointing
- (General intercessions)

Liturgy of the Eucharist
- Prayer over the gifts
- Preface & Eucharistic prayer
- Rite of Communion
- Prayer after Communion

Conclusion
- Blessing & dismissal

TO PREPARE
- Rite of the Anointing of the Sick
- Choice of readings
- Intentions for the general intercessions

Procedure for Meeting 13F Reconciliation

Relate

00.00 Opening prayer
- Choose a prayer from Appendix 5 or use the *Tweeting with GOD* app.

00.02 Welcome: Raise your card
- Follow the indications on Worksheet 13F.3.

00.15 The previous meeting
- Engage in a simple and quick recap. What touched the participants most in the previous meeting? Are there new questions or ideas? How did they fare with the dual challenge?
  - Are there doubts about the Questions in the *Tweeting with GOD* book?
  - How did it go with your visit to the sick and/or sending them a card?
- (The participants who prepared today's Questions can briefly present the theme).

Think

00.20 Introduction: God & our missteps
- Start by saying that our faith is based on a relationship with God. In every relationship it is important to say "sorry," to ask forgiveness. If we do not do this, our relationship with the other becomes difficult because there are unspoken and unresolved things between us. Asking forgiveness and being forgiven can resolve this situation. "How do you ask forgiveness of the other if you did something wrong?" Speak about this.
- Explain that it is the same in our relationship with God. He never did anything wrong, but we make many missteps and commit sins, involving him and the people around us. In fact, when we hurt others or ourselves, it also hurts God! To maintain our good relationship with him, it is important to ask him to forgive our missteps, our sins. How can we ask God for forgiveness? Speak about this briefly without taking it much further for now.

00.25 Round Table 1: The prodigal son
- Follow the directions of Worksheet 13F.4.

00.55 Break [END FIRST & START SECOND SESSION (SEE GS2)]

01.00 Today's hero: Saint John Nepomuk
- Watch the video of Saint John Nepomuk via *Online with Saints*.
- Ask: "What does the life story of Saint John Nepomuk teach us about the Sacrament of Reconciliation?"

01.10 Round Table 2: Forgiveness in my life
- Follow the directions of Worksheet 13F.6.

01.25 Round Table 3: The Sacrament of Reconciliation
- Watch the video of #TwGOD Question 3.38 together: "Why confess to a priest instead of directly to God?" Discuss difficult points.
- Explain: "The forgiveness you receive from God is a great gift: it is an opportunity to get back on the right path. To receive God's forgiveness is an experience that completely frees you of your sins and that helps you in your life of faith. Has one of you already experienced God's forgiveness in Confession?" If so, you can ask: "Without telling us your sins, what can you say of the experience of forgiveness in the Sacrament of Reconciliation?" Alternatively, the moderator can share their experience (SEE APPENDIX 2).
- "To prepare yourself for the Sacrament of Reconciliation, it is good to consider how you have lived with God, other people, and yourself over the past

time. We call this an examination of conscience (SEE WORKSHEET 13F.2)."

- Say in conclusion: "The priest is bound to keep your sins secret: the 'seal of Confession' ensures that he cannot repeat what you have said. Like God, he is not so much interested in your sins (he too is a sinner), but he wants to forgive you in the name of God!"

Pray

01.40 Synthesis and actualization

- Explain that asking forgiveness is important in any relationship, so also in our relationship with God. At the same time, it is also our duty to forgive those who ask for pardon. During the next meeting we will have the opportunity to pray together and receive God's forgiveness in the Sacrament of Reconciliation: "Maybe you have never received this sacrament. Do not be afraid! It is a very beautiful experience, and it is not necessary to know all the procedure in advance: the priest will guide you step by step."
- "To prepare yourself for asking God's forgiveness, look back over your life (since baptism/your last confession) and remember your most important sins. Optionally, you can write them down. Try to see the main line, for you will never be able to mention all the details, and your confession would be too long. To help you prepare, we give you a paper to guide you through your examination of conscience (SEE WORKSHEET 13F.2)."
- Conclude with the question: "How can what I have learned nourish my personal faith and relationship with Jesus? How can I put this into action?" Speak briefly about this.

01.45 Closing prayer

- Go (if possible) to the chapel or church. Light the candles and sing a song.

- Then read a text of Pope Francis on the prodigal son (SEE WORKSHEET 13F.7). The participants were very active during the meeting, now they can let themselves be guided.
- Read slowly. It is not necessary to finish the text. Simply stay a few moments in silence after each paragraph.
- If you deem this useful, you can add a time for intercessions to ask for the inspiration of the Holy Spirit to better recognize our sins as we prepare for Confession next time.
- Conclude with an Our Father and a Hail Mary.

01.58 Conclusion in the meeting room

- Remind participants of the date for the next meeting and present the dual challenge:
  - Read these Questions in the *Tweeting with GOD* book: 3.38 & 3.39.
  - Participants look back over their life so far, and prepare for Confession following the steps for the examination of conscience (SEE WORKSHEET 13F.2).

TO PREPARE
- Bibles
- Video equipment (internet)
- *Tweeting with GOD* book and app
- *Online with Saints* app
- Red, yellow, green cards (DL)
- Puzzle for Round Table 1 (DL)

Worksheet 13F

13F.1 Essential moment of Reconciliation

The person who wants to ask God's forgiveness for their sins, the penitent, prepares themselves by an examination of conscience (SEE WORKSHEET 13F.2). There are two essential parts, indicated in bold:

1 **Confessions of their sins by the penitent with a contrite heart,** which means that they are very sorry for what they did wrong. The penitent makes an act of contrition, saying, for example: "O my God, I am heartily sorry for having offended you, and I detest all my sins, because of your just punishments, but most of all because they offend you, my God, who are all good and deserving of all my love. I firmly resolve, with the help of your grace, to confess my sins, to do penance, and to amend my life."

2. The forgiveness of God through the words of the priest then follows: **"God, the Father of mercies, through the death and the resurrection of his Son has reconciled the world to himself and sent the Holy Spirit among us for the forgiveness of sins; through the ministry of the Church may God give you pardon and peace, and I absolve you from your sins in the name of the Father, and of the Son and of the Holy Spirit."**

The priest may conclude: "May the Passion of our Lord Jesus Christ, the intercession of the Blessed Virgin Mary, and of all the saints, whatever good you do and suffering you endure, heal your sins, help you to grow in holiness, and reward you with eternal life. Go in peace."

13F.2 Preparation for Confession: Examination of conscience

My relationship with God
- Have I taken time to pray? How? Did I pray because I wanted to or because I felt obliged? Have I prayed regularly?
- What have I done to learn something about God in order to advance in my relationship with him? Was it enough?
- Have I regularly attended Mass and community prayer? With what attitude?
- Have I shown respect for God in my life? In my manner of speaking and my way of acting?
- How have I treated God's creation? Have I wasted things? Have I done enough to reduce my ecological footprint (for example by taking public transport or by paying attention to my waste)?

My relationship with others
- How have I treated my family and friends? Have I helped them when needed? Have I told the others where I went and did I get back on time for our community life? Have I brought peace or did I contribute to unrest? Have I participated in bullying at work or at school? Have I asked forgiveness for my mistakes? Have I forgiven those who hurt me?

- How did I behave at school? How have I treated my teachers? Have I paid attention in class? Have I wasted my time? Have I done my homework conscientiously?
- How did I behave at work? How have I treated my colleagues? Was I always ready to help them? Have I wasted the time of my employer?
- How have I treated people I did not know? Have I assisted those who needed help?
- Was I always cordial and courteous? Have I kept my promises? Have I cheated or did I lie? Have I spoken ill of someone?
- Have I shared my goods and talents with those in need? Have I given my time and energy to others?
- Have I used my friends or my family for my own benefit? Have I made fun of them? Have I made an effort to understand their difficulties and our differences?
- Have I acted without asking anything in return? Have I acted quietly, without asking for attention for what I did or gave?

My relationship with myself
- Am I happy to be who I am? Have I seen myself as a creation of God?
- Have I mainly focused on what is negative in me? Have I paid too much attention to my appearance and how others see me? Have I spent too much time or money on myself, on fashion, electronics, or other things?
- Did I want to be popular and seen in a positive light? Was I too proud or too content with myself?
- Have I taken care of my physical, emotional, and spiritual well-being? Have I taken enough rest?
- How did I make my choices? Consciously or because everyone else did it? Or have I avoided making a choice because it was the easiest way? Have I asked God's help to make good choices?
- How have I treated my body? Have I maintained my purity? Did I disrespect my sexuality? Have I restrained myself in a healthy and spiritual way? Have I hurt my body voluntarily? Have I used drugs, abused sugar, tobacco, alcohol? Have I exercized enough, without exaggeration?
- Have I taken care of my personal development and my education, diligently and without exaggerating? Have I finished what I had to do?

Conclusion
- Now think of the most important things that you want to ask forgiveness for.
- Do you want God to become part of your life again? Ask him!
- What particular grace do you want to ask from God to help you improve yourself in order to live closer to him in daily life?

13F.3 Welcome: Raise your card

1. Explain the rules: "In a moment I will read out a statement, and give a little time to think. Then you can express your opinion. For this purpose, you will receive three cards. Raise the red card if you disagree with the statement, the green card if you agree, and the yellow card if you are neutral. You can then share your opinion in small groups with the people around you."

2. Let's start with a practice statement: "Reading books is bad for your eyes."
3. After a brief pause invite participants to raise their cards to express their opinion.
4. Take a few minutes to discuss with the people around you why you raised this card.
5. At the right moment you say: "Hands up if you wish to share your opinion with us all."
6. Thank those who spoke to the group and move on to the next statement:
   - In every relationship it is important to say "sorry" from time to time.
   - I have difficulty asking forgiveness for my faults, to say "sorry."
   - It is easier to forgive than to ask forgiveness.
   - The Church helps us to become better people by inviting us to say "sorry" with all our heart.
   - Jesus wants us to be sorry for our sins.
   - Forgiving and asking forgiveness help me to grow and be happy.

13F.4 Round Table 1: The prodigal son

- Prepare a copy of the puzzle of the stained-glass window for each group, depicting the prodigal son in Sens Cathedral (SEE WORKSHEET 13F.5). Cut the pieces and place each puzzle in an envelope.
- Read the biblical text Luke 15:11-32 together. Do not discuss the text at this point.
- Make small groups (SEE APPENDIX 3.1 & 3.2) and give each group a puzzle. Ask the groups to put the story told by the pieces of the puzzle in order.
- When they have finished, distribute the key and invite the groups to correct their solution of the puzzle if necessary.
- Then ask the groups to talk about the scenes they put in order: "What is the essential message of the story? Are there aspects that you do not understand?"
- Invite the participants back together in the large group and ask what questions remain.
- Then say that the two brothers show two ways of looking at sin and forgiveness. "What are these two ways?"
- You will find that the prodigal son is a public sinner who comes to see his wrong, while the eldest son is also selfish and sinful, but he does not recognize this and does not ask for forgiveness. "Do you recognize yourself in the attitude of one of the brothers? There is something of each brother in all of us. How can the sin and evil we commit block us on our path?" Speak about this briefly.
- The monk who designed this window saw a clear parallel between the father in the parable and our forgiving God who welcomes his lost children at all time. Thanks be to God, we can receive his forgiveness in the Sacrament of Reconciliation. "Look at the puzzle: do you perceive what the author wanted to express?" Discuss together.
- Jesus told the story of the prodigal son to show God's goodness: he is the good father who is always waiting for us. He hopes at every moment that we will decide to change what is wrong in our lives and come back to him. He knows that after receiving his forgiveness we will sin again, but he is always ready to forgive without counting! "Can you imagine someone who never stops forgiving?"

Key: Correct order of the stained-glass pieces of the prodigal son

11. The father speaks with the prodigal son's brother

12. Also the other brother comes home

10. They celebrate in joy

9. The prodigal son's brother speaks to a servant

7. The father embraces his son

8. The fattened calf is sacrificed

6. The prodigal son bound by sin

5. The prodigal son herds the pigs

3. The prodigal son is led astray by three prostitutes

4. The prodigal son is crowned by prostitutes

2. The father shares his inheritance between his sons

1. Father, give me the share of the property that falls to me

- Ask: "Did you ever forgive someone with all your heart? Are there things you would not be able to forgive?"
- And: "In your relationship with others, do you see a difference between less serious and more serious missteps?" Speak about this.
- People who are always together, like a married couple, have the experience that they need to continually forgive each other: without forgiveness their relationship cannot prosper!
- There is the couple's everyday forgiveness for less serious offences. Without asking specifically for forgiveness, they express their forgiveness with the final "good night" before bed. Among friends this may be a warm "cheers": when drinking a glass together they forgive without words. "What do you think of this way to forgive?"
- This experience of daily pardon is like the forgiveness we receive from God when praying "I confess ..." at the beginning of Mass, or when performing an act of love for someone else. Speak about this: do participants understand this?
- We call these daily sins "venial sins": they hurt our relationship with God, but do not cut off all communication with him. Still, they need to be forgiven, or else they clutter and hinder our relationship with God more and more.
- The same couple will also experience that there are wrongs that cannot simply disappear like that. These missteps cannot be forgiven in passing. Especially when it comes to fidelity in a relationship, or real selfishness at the cost of the other. The couple will have to sit down and talk together before asking and receiving forgiveness from each other. It is the same thing between friends: only after an explicit "I forgive you" can the friendship continue to grow. Do you agree?
- With God, it is the same: there are times when we must ask for his forgiveness before being able to continue our journey with him. We call these most serious sins "mortal sins" because they "kill" our relationship with God. They cut us off from God until we turn back to him and ask to receive his forgiveness. We do so concretely through the Sacrament of Reconciliation, Confession (SEE MEETING 14). God is always waiting for us. We can be absolutely certain that God wants to forgive us at every moment, but he leaves us free: It is up to us to take the step of asking for forgiveness in order to receive it.

- The Parable of the Merciful Father ... tells of a father and his two sons, and it helps us understand the infinite mercy of God. We shall begin at the end, that is, the joy in the heart of the father. ... Jesus does not describe a father who is offended and resentful. ... On the contrary, the father embraces him, awaits him with love. ...

- Certainly, the son knows he erred and acknowledges it: "I have sinned."... These words crumble before the father's forgiveness. The embrace and the kiss of his father makes him understand that he was always considered a son, in spite of everything.

- This teaching of Jesus is very important: our condition as children of God is the fruit of the love of the Father's heart; it does not depend on our merits or on our actions, and thus no one can take it away, not even the devil! No one can take this dignity away.

- Jesus' words encourage us never to despair. I think ... of those who have made mistakes and cannot manage to envision the future, of those who hunger for mercy and forgiveness and believe they don't deserve it. ... In any situation of life, I must not forget that I will never cease to be a child of God, to be a son of the Father who loves me and awaits my return. Even in the worst situation of life, God waits for me, God wants to embrace me, God expects me.

- In the parable there is another son, the older one; he too needs to discover the mercy of the father. ... His words lack tenderness. ... We see the contempt: he never says "father," never says "brother," he thinks only about himself. ... The poor father! One son went away, and the other was never close to him! The suffering of the father is like the suffering of God, the suffering of Jesus when we distance ourselves from him, either because we go far away or because we are nearby without being close.

- The elder son needs mercy too. The righteous, those who believe they are righteous, are also in need of mercy. This son represents us when we wonder whether it is worth all the trouble if we get nothing in return. ... There is no "bargaining" with God, but rather following in the footsteps of Jesus who gave himself on the Cross without measure. ...

- The sons can decide whether to join in the joy of the father or to reject it. They must ask themselves what they really want and what their vision is for their life. The parable is left open-ended: we do not know what the older son decided to do. And this is an incentive for us. This Gospel passage teaches us that we all need to enter the House of the Father and to share in his joy, in his feast of mercy and of brotherhood. Brothers and sisters, let us open our hearts, in order to be "merciful like the Father"!

[POPE FRANCIS, GENERAL AUDIENCE, 11 MAY, 2016]

Liturgy 13F: The liturgy of Reconciliation

The Sacrament can be received anywhere: in most informal circumstances like on a bus during a pilgrimage, or during a walk in the mountains. You just need a priest. In the architecture of most churches a special place or separate room is dedicated to confession, the confessional. Traditionally it has two entrances, for the priest and the penitent, with a grill between them to ensure the anonymity of the penitent.

The celebration

There is no need whatsoever to be afraid of the ritual: the priest is very used to helping you through every step of the liturgy (SEE BOX). It is possible to receive this sacrament during a liturgy of prayer and reconciliation (SEE MEETING 14). Even then, the confession of your sins is always in private, and the priest will never speak of what passes between you.

The liturgy: How to confess?

- You can prepare for the Sacrament of Reconciliation by asking for God's help to know your sins. Then you can look at what you did wrong and at what you failed to do. Thus you examine your conscience, for example by considering each of the Ten Commandments (SEE WORKSHEET 13F.2). Once you know your sins you can follow these next steps:

- Go to a priest and say: "Bless me, Father, for I have sinned. My last confession was (number of weeks, months, or years) ago."

- Tell the priest all of the sins you have committed since your last confession. Be brief but complete and clear as to what you have done wrong and how often.

- Answer possible questions and listen as the priest gives you advice and a penance. This penance is a sign of our desire to make up for the wrong we did, knowing that in the end it was

Jesus who made up for it on the cross once and for all (SEE MEETING 8; #TWGOD 3.38).

- When asked by the priest, say an act of contrition to show that you really repent of your sins. You can use a standard prayer (SEE WORKSHEET 13F.1) or tell Jesus in your own words that you are sorry for your sins, intend not to commit them again, and seek his grace to improve your life.
- The priest will stretch out his hands and give you absolution (SEE WORKSHEET 13F.1). Thereby God forgives you all the sins you confessed. After that, your sins no longer stand in the way of you and Jesus, who tells you: "Go, and do not sin again" (JN 8:11).
- The priest then says, for example: "Give thanks to the Lord, for he is good." You reply: "His mercy endures forever" (OR SEE WORKSHEET 13.1).
- Take a moment to pray, thanking God for his mercy. Perform your penance as soon as possible.

[CF. #TWGOD 3.39]

The celebrant

The celebrant of the Sacrament of Reconciliation is always a priest (or a bishop). The task to forgive sins was given directly by Jesus to the Apostles: "Receive the Holy Spirit. If you forgive the sins of any, they are forgiven them; if you retain the sins of any, they are retained" (JN 20:22-23).

Liturgy of Reconciliation

Opening
- Welcome and invitation to trust in God

(Optional reading of the Word of God)

Confession of sins
- By the penitent in their own way
- The priest may ask some questions
- Words of counsel by the priest
- Communication of the penance
- Act of penance by the penitent

Absolution
- By the priest with hand extend

Conclusion
- Praise of God
- Dismissal

TO PREPARE

- Examination of conscience (DL)
- A priest and a quiet place

Meeting 14: PRAY – How can I turn to God? How can I ask for forgiveness?

The purpose of this meeting is to dedicate time to prayer. Speaking about faith helps to advance on the path to God, but the relationship with God should also be experienced, especially in prayer (SEE #TwGOD 3.2). When we approach God and contemplate his greatness and love, we see more easily that we are not perfect and need his forgiveness (SEE MEETING 13F). To help them grow in faith [and prepare for the great moment of receiving the Sacraments], the participants are invited to purify themselves internally and to ask forgiveness for their sins. This meeting is ideal for this.

The Sacrament of Reconciliation is not old-fashioned! On the contrary: everyone needs to be freed from whatever burdens them in order to live in freedom and happiness. We need God's forgiveness if we want to enter into a relationship with him! You could say that the Sacrament of Reconciliation clears out our channels of communication with God. This is the moment to throw out every obstacle caused by sin (SEE #TwGOD 3.38). God is always ready to forgive, but asking for forgiveness in the Sacrament of Reconciliation may seem daunting. The profound and prayerful atmosphere created at this meeting will hopefully help.

The meeting

Creating a warm atmosphere in the church or chapel will help participants find the courage they need to come forwards and ask for forgiveness. Dim the lights and make sure it is neither too cold nor hot. Music is also important: someone could play and sing quiet songs of worship, or you can prepare a playlist of recordings. Background music also helps the participants be more confident that no one but the priest will hear their confession. Place a large cross near the altar (if possible, well lit), and a basin with holy water. Prepare pairs of chairs for Reconciliation, one for the priest and the other for the penitent, next to an icon and candles. Get a corner ready for writing letters.

Prayer

During all your material preparations, do not forget the importance of praying for the participants and for the success of the meeting.

You can distribute a sheet with the steps for the examination of conscience to help prepare for the Sacrament of Reconciliation (SEE WORKSHEET 13F.2). The moderator will preferably be among the first to confess - not only to set an example but especially because they too need God's forgiveness. The aim is to help the participants to overcome possible fear

Prayer and reconciliation

Objective of this meeting:
This is the perfect moment to pray together and to receive the Sacrament of Reconciliation.

Related Questions:
3.38, 3.39, 4.12, 4.13

and any hesitations as far as possible to encourage free access to the Sacrament of Reconciliation. There is no need for anyone to be perfect just now: the most important thing is to come to the sacrament.

It would be ideal if it is possible to expose the Blessed Sacrament. Jesus, truly present (SEE MEETING 13C), will help particularly to pray and be honest to him. A short introductory reminder on adoration may be useful, even if the participants have already experienced this (SEE MEETING 8; #TWGOD 3.14).

Additional suggestions

- If you cannot access a church or chapel, you can prepare the meeting room for the occasion, for example with a large cross, icon, candles ...
- You can show the participants and the priest the essential texts for Reconciliation in the *Tweeting with GOD* app (SEE #TWGOD APP > ⚑ > ⛪ > ☺).
- You could prepare small papers with the names of the participants: each takes a paper and commits themselves to pray for that person today in particular. Another idea is to ask the participants to write a prayer intention on straps of paper, which are then distributed: everyone pray for the intention they receive. You could even propose to continue to pray for the same person or intention during the weeks and months ahead.

....

The gist of it

- **Opening prayer**
- **Scripture reading and testimony**
- **Common prayer for forgiveness**
  - Introduction to the Sacrament of Reconciliation
- **Individual prayer**
  - Receive the Sacrament of Reconciliation
  - Pray in silence
  - Write a letter to God or a friend
  - Light a candle
  - Bring your prayers to the altar
- **Praying together in conclusion**
- **(Speaking together)**

Procedure for Meeting 14

Preparation

- Prepare a large cross, if possible close to the altar and well lit. Place a basin with holy water near to it.
- Before the cross, place a carpet with kneelers.
- Roll out banners of aluminium foil before the cross, on which small candles can be placed. Add also a basket or a box to gather the letters.
- Place paper, pens, envelopes (on a table) in a corner of the church.
- Also lay out reading material, like some Bibles and spiritual books.
- Prepare everything for the exposition of the Blessed Sacrament.
- Prepare the music group or playlist of recordings.
- Light the candles in the church or chapel, also on the altar, in front of the cross and the statue of Our Lady. If possible, dim the lights to create a warm atmosphere.

Introduction

00.00 Opening

- Start with a quiet, meditative song.
- Make the sign of the cross and introduce the prayer: "We will take time to pray now. After a first part all together, we propose various activities you can participate in. We invite you to participate with all your heart and take this opportunity to meet God."

00.02 Scripture reading and testimony

- Read a Bible text (E.G. IS 61:1- 4, LK 15:11-32, JN 3:16-17, 2 COR 5:18-21, OR EPH 1:3-10).
- Someone can give a testimony about prayer (SEE APPENDIX 2).

00.15 Common prayer of forgiveness

- Pray, for example: "As the prayer of the Our Father teaches us, let us now ask all together for God's forgiveness, to prepare ourselves to personally ask for forgiveness later:
  - Infinitely good Father, we have sinned against you. We ask you to forgive us for all our wrong-doings. *R/. Lord, have mercy.*
  - Infinitely merciful Father, you love us and have created us good. Yet we have done wrong – forgive us. *R/.*
  - Good Father, you want nothing more than that sinners return to you. Help us to always know your love better, and to receive your forgiveness. *R/.*
  - Jesus, we are preparing ourselves to receive the Sacrament of Reconciliation. Help us and forgive us our trespasses. *R/.*
  - Together we pray the Our Father ..."
- Introduce the Sacrament of Reconciliation: "Ultimately, life revolves around our relationship with Jesus (SEE #TWGOD 3.1 & 4.1). Like in any relationship, it is important to be honest, even about what went wrong – and to ask forgiveness for your sins. To make this possible, Jesus gave us the Sacrament of Reconciliation (also called Confession). He listens to you and forgives your sins through the priest (SEE #TWGOD 3.38-3.39). We warmly invite you to take advantage of the opportunity to receive the forgiveness of God right now. Fear not: the priest will help you step by step."
- Someone can share their experience with the Sacrament of Reconciliation, showing that it is an experience of love, mercy and encountering God (SEE APPENDIX 2). There is no reason to be afraid!
- Leave some time for silence and meditative singing during which participants can pray and meditate on what has been said.

00.25 Individual prayer

- Sing a song during which the Blessed Sacrament is exposed.
- Explain that during this prayer time we propose various activities: "You can choose. We invite you to maintain the silence to give everyone the opportunity to make most of this time. You can ...
  - sit at the feet of the cross or another significant place in the church and spend time with God in prayer;
  - make the sign of the cross with holy water, as a reminder that in Baptism you have become a child of God;
  - visit Jesus present in the Blessed Sacrament and talk to him about anything you want to say (SEE #TwGOD 3.14);
  - go to the priest to receive forgiveness in the Sacrament of Reconciliation. He will guide you through the consecutive steps;
  - light the candle you will receive from the priest and place it before the altar and the cross, both symbols of Jesus, who sacrificed his life for you (it is a good time to do the penance the priest has given you (SEE #TwGOD 3.38)).
  - write a letter to God or to a friend to ask for forgiveness, then place the letter in the basket before the large cross. Letters to God will be destroyed; letters to others will be mailed. (Obviously, this is not the time to do all your private correspondence!)"
  - write down your prayer intentions and place these in the basket in front of the cross.
- Stimulate the participants to make the most of this time of prayer and forgiveness to grow further in faith and in their relationship with God.
- Animate this prayer time with meditative music and songs.
- If necessary, somewhere halfway you could suggest once more that the participants take advantage of the presence of the priest for the Sacrament of Reconciliation – without putting pressure: everyone should feel invited but free to answer.

01.40 Praying together

- To finish, all come together. A participant lights a candle before the statue of Our Lady and all pray the Hail Mary.
- Conclude the prayer time with the Our Father or another prayer which most participants know. Sing a song in thanksgiving.

Conclusion

01.45 Optionally speak together

- Prepare something to eat and drink in a separate room.
- Those who wish can now exchange informally about their experiences of prayer: "How was it? What have you learned? Did it bring you closer to God? Could you pray? What was difficult? What did you like?"
- Remind participants of the date for the next meeting and the dual challenge of last meeting.

TO PREPARE
- Large cross, holy water
- Paper, pencils, envelopes, basket
- Possibility to confess, candles
- Blessed Sacrament
- Music
- Bible, other reading materials
- *Tweeting with GOD* book & app

Meeting 15: Your group's questions 3

This meeting about your group's questions forms an integral part of the course schedule. We have explained earlier how to approach this meeting (SEE GS8). If you need help to encourage the participants to ask questions, you can look back to the introductory pages (SEE GS9).

Sample procedure for Meeting 15

Relate

00.00 Opening prayer
- Choose a prayer from Appendix 5 or use the *Tweeting with GOD* app.

00.02 Welcome
- Decide on a warm up activity (SEE APPENDIX 3.7).

00.15 The previous meeting
- Engage in a simple and quick recap. What touched the participants most in the previous meeting? Are there new questions or ideas? How did they fare with the dual challenge?
  - Are there doubts about the Questions in the *Tweeting with GOD* book?
  - How was it to prepare for Confession and receive the Sacrament of Reconciliation?
- (The participants who prepared today's Questions can briefly present the theme).

Think

00.20 Round Table 1: First question
- Watch that all participants who wish to have the possibility of asking questions and presenting their view on the matter.

00.45 Today's hero: Choose from the app

- Choose the video of a saint that may help with the dialogue on today's theme.

00.55 Break [*END FIRST & START SECOND SESSION (SEE GS2)*]

01.00 Round Table 2: Second question / a new angle on the first question
- Make sure that the questions are discussed in depth. This might be a good moment for dialogue in small groups.

01.25 Round Table 3: Deepening the theme
- You can check among the questions on the website tweetingwithgod.com whether a video is available about today's theme.

Pray & Act

01.40 Synthesis & actualization
- Check whether there are any remaining questions, which you can briefly address at this point, or defer to another meeting.
- Conclude with the question: "How can what I have learned nourish my personal faith and relationship with Jesus? How can I put this into action?" Speak briefly about this.

01.45 Closing prayer
- Go (if possible) to the chapel or church. Light the candles and sing a song.

- Open the prayer, for example: "Lord Jesus, thank you for today's dialogue. We have been able to grow in our understanding of the theme, and we hope that this will bring us closer to you. Help us recognize your presence in our lives, and inspire us with your Holy Spirit to keep searching for the truth."
- You can repeat a prayer method from one of the previous meetings, or add a time of intercession with the group, for example.
- Conclude with an Our Father and a Hail Mary.

01.58 Conclusion in the meeting room
- Remind participants of the date for the next meeting, asking them to bring a rosary if they can find or buy one. Present the dual challenge:
  - Read the related Questions in the *Tweeting with GOD* book.
  - Define together what you will do for the second challenge.

TO PREPARE
- Bibles
- Video equipment (internet)
- *Tweeting with GOD* book & app
- *Online with Saints* app

The gist of it

- **Pray, relate, recap**
- **Round Table 1: First question**
  - Paying attention that all who wish can contribute
- **Today's hero: Choose from the app**

....

- **Round Table 2: Second question / a new angle on the first question**
  - Maybe work with small groups.
  - Make sure that the questions are discussed in depth
- **Round Table 3: Deepening the theme**
  - Check whether a video about the theme is available
  - Attention that everyone gets to say what they want to
- **Synthesis & actualization**
- **Closing prayer**
  - Ask the help of the Holy Spirit to find answers
- **Dual challenge**
  - Read the #TwGOD Questions related to the theme(s) covered
  - Define the second challenge together

Meeting 16: Sanctity – What do Mary and the saints have to do with my relationship with God?

The purpose of this meeting is to recognize how the saints have gone on a journey of life and faith before us: we are not alone on our path to God. They pray for us in heaven and we can ask them to pray with us. We are all called to become saints. Since everyone is different and has their own path with God, this is not about "copying" the life of a saint, but about being inspired to find our own way towards sanctity.

One might think that the saints never had any problems in their faith, nor any serious temptation in their lives. The opposite is true. Many of them were anything but "virtuous" in their youth. Like us, they were tempted towards sin, committed often many errors, and frequently did not understand much of life and faith. Others were very young when they were ready to die with conviction and courage, rather than to deny their love for God. The saints are models through their personal lives. They often brought about change through their well-founded criticism of society or members of the Church. More fundamentally, each of them served the Church by their love for the crucified and resurrected Christ.

The meeting

After taking a selfie with a saint, the meeting starts by helping the participants to see the differences between stars, superheroes, and the saints.

Then we'll look at the example of Our Lady and the saints. That is the beginning of discovering the importance of the lives of the saints for us, not just as examples to follow, but also because of their presence with God and their prayer for us. Why we should ask the saints to pray for us is the subject of the next session. The aim is especially to show how close the saints are to us, and how they show that we too can get to heaven.

Prayer

In the concluding prayer, you can pray a decade of the Rosary together. It will most probably be necessary to explain the Rosary and how to pray it (SEE #TWGOD 3.12). In addition, you can pray a Litany of the Saints in which you can insert all the saints of the parish, the names of participants ... (SEE WORKSHEET 16.1).

Mary, the saints, and me

Objective of this meeting:
You are not alone: those in heaven accompany us, they pray with us and for us!

Related Questions:
1.38, 1.39, 1.40, 4.15, 4.16

Dual challenge:
- Read these Questions in the *Tweeting with GOD* book: 1.38 & 4.15.
- Pray a decade (or more) of the Rosary at home with the help of the *Tweeting with GOD* app.

Additional suggestions

- The YouTube channel of *Tweeting with GOD* offers various videos on questions related to the devotion to Mary and the saints. On the YouTube channel *Online with Saints*, you find many videos in which the saints speak about their lives.
- You could bring some icons or statues of the saints and refer to these during the dialogue.
- If the group is creative you could suggest they learn how to make a rosary bracelet or a full rosary using a single string. The participants can finish the rosary at home. At a future meeting, everyone can bring their rosary so that a priest can bless them.
- You can look for the saints related to the names of participants and invite them to get to know their patron saint better.
- Together, you can prepare your own litany of the saints, adding the saints that you want to the Litany of the Saints in the Roman Missal (SEE WORKSHEET 16.2).
- Given the lack of time, we are not talking about patron saints. If you want to add an extra meeting about the saints, you could then talk about patron saints. The *Online with Saints* app indicates for every saint whom and what they are patron of.

The gist of it

- **Pray, relate, recap**
- **Round Table 1: Role models**
  - Activity: How is holiness expressed in daily life?
  - Can we distinguish specific Christian qualities in the saints?
- **Today's hero: The Virgin Mary**

....

- **Round Table 2: The lives of the saints**
  - Small groups: Study a saint in *Online with Saints*
  - Plenary: Present the saint's life
  - What can we learn from these saints? Do you want to become a saint?
- **Round Table 3: Praying to Mary and the Saints**
  - Video: Should I pray to the saints? (#TwGOD 4.16)
- **Synthesis & actualization**
- **Closing prayer**
  - Explain and pray a decade of the Rosary
  - Pray the Litany of the Saints
- **Dual challenge**
  - Read the #TwGOD Questions
  - Pray a decade of the Rosary

Procedure for Meeting 16

Relate

00.00 Opening prayer
- Choose a prayer from Appendix 5 or use the *Tweeting with GOD* app.

00.02 Welcome: Selfie with a saint
- Follow the indications on Worksheet 16.1.

00.15 The previous meeting
- Engage in a simple and quick recap. What touched the participants most in the previous meeting? Are there new questions or ideas? How did they fare with the dual challenge?
    - Are there doubts about the Questions in the *Tweeting with GOD* book?
    - How was it to prepare your confession and receive God's forgiveness?
- (The participants who prepared today's Questions can briefly present the theme).

Think

00.20 Round Table 1: Role models
- Follow the indications on Worksheet 16.2.

0.45 Today's hero: The Virgin Mary
- Watch the video on Mary via *Online with Saints*.
- Is Mary is different from the other saints? How is she different or the same? Answers may include: She is the mother of God, chosen by God himself. She was holy since her conception. When God called her, she gave him her unconditional "yes" (Lk 1:38). She knows Jesus more intimately than anyone else. At the wedding in Cana, she shows how Jesus listens to her: even though it seems he did not want to perform a miracle, he does so at Mary's request (Jn 2:1-11).

- Note that there will possibly be participants who may have a difficult or painful relationship with their mother. You could help them see how Mary is not only mother, but also friend, confidante … Contrary to the mothers of this earth, she is without fault and loves every person with a pure love.
- Conclude that there are several reasons why Mary is first among the saints. She can carry our prayers to God. Today we can ask her to pray for us in a particular way.

00.55 Break [END FIRST & START SECOND SESSION (SEE GS2)]

01.00 Round Table 2: The lives of the saints
- Explain that the saints are examples and models for us: they lived their lives as true Christians and show that it is possible for us to do the same. Ask them to open the *Online with Saints* app. Divide the participants into three groups: each group can choose a saint and take 10 minutes to study their life together.
- Then each group presents "their" saint to the entire group in 2 minutes. Some questions to help prepare the presentation: Was there a key moment in their lives? What did they do? Why are they holy?
- After the three presentations, think together about these questions: "What can I learn from these saints? What about these saints' lives can apply to my life right now? Do I have to do the same?"
- Say that we are all called to become saints: "God wants your joy to be perfect, a joy that you will find only in seeking to live in holiness. You can do this by trying to be the best version of yourself. Saint John Paul II said to young people: 'Do not be afraid to be the saints of the new era'. What does that mean for you?" Discuss together.
- Conclude saying that most saints were not holy from the moment of their birth: "They grew in their

relationship with God in very different ways. We have seen three examples and can learn something from each of them. Note that the idea is not to copy the life of a saint exactly: everyone has their personal vocation. You can let yourself be inspired by looking how a saint brought Jesus' message into practice in their time, just as you are called to do in this time."

01.20 Round Table 3: Praying to Mary and the saints

- Explain: "The great desire of God is that we will live forever! After we die on earth, he hopes to welcome us with him in heaven. The saints are already there, and they celebrate the presence of God: therefore, heaven is a great feast. The saints are always close to God, and they can bring your prayer before him. So you can ask the saints to pray for you! Have you ever done this?"
- Watch the video of #TwGOD Question 4.16 together: "Should I pray to the saints?"
- Why would it be "useful" for you to ask a saint to pray for you? Do you have some favorite saints that can carry your requests to God?

Pray & Act

01.35 Synthesis and actualization

- Say in conclusion: "The saints were people like you and me. Their faith, endurance, and trust in God helped them to become saints. You too are called to become a saint. With the help of God you can do it!"
- Conclude with the question: "How can what I have learned nourish my personal faith and relationship with Jesus? How can I put this into action?" Speak briefly about this.

01.40 Closing prayer

- Go (if possible) to the chapel or church. Light the candles and sing a song, for example a Marian song.

- As an introduction, briefly explain what the Rosary is, and how to pray it (SEE #TwGOD 3.12). Remind participants that we are seeking the intercession of the saints, so that they can pray for us in heaven, and continue to do so when we stop praying. For the prayer of the Rosary, see the *Tweeting with GOD* app (#TwGOD APP > 🙏 > ⛪ > 🕐).
- Pray a decade of the Rosary.
- Ask the saints to pray for you by praying the Litany of the Saints (SEE WORKSHEET 16.3).
- Finish by praying the Our Father together.

01.58 Conclusion in the meeting room

- Remind participants of the date for the next meeting and present the dual challenge:
  - Read these Questions in the *Tweeting with GOD* book: 1.38 & 4.15.
  - Pray a decade (or more) of the Rosary at home with the help of the *Tweeting with GOD* app.

TO PREPARE	– Video equipment (internet) – *Tweeting with GOD* book & app – *Online with Saints* app – Pictures for Round Table 1 (DL) – Rosary – Litany of the Saints (DL)

Worksheet 16

16.1 Welcome: Selfie with a saint

- Ask participants to take out their phones and open the *Online with Saints* app.
- Invite them to find a partner for this activity.
- Search together in the "All Saints" section whether your patron saint is already present in the app. If so, open the profile of that saint. If not, choose a saint, and open their profile.
- Click on the selfie icon and make a selfie of the two of you together with the saint. Have a chat about that saint.
- Now go find someone else to take a selfie in the same way.

16.2 Round Table 1: Role models

- The purpose of this activity is to show that holiness is expressed in daily life. The saints are not stars, super-heroes, or exceptions: They are like us!
- Place about 25 pictures of people on the table. Each belongs to one of three categories: 1. Pictures of stars of this moment, like musicians, sports stars, actresses, actors ... 2. Illustrations of daily role models who are everyday superheroes like mom, dad, granny, coach, teacher, scout leader ... 3. Images of saints (for example, Mary, Francis of Assisi, Monica, Dominic Savio, Martin of Tours, Teresa of Calcutta, Blessed Luigi and Maria Quattrocchi, Carlo Acutis ...).
- *Dialogue 1.* Invite everyone to choose a picture and explain why they chose it. The answers will probably mostly be based on taste, beauty, and importance. Then ask about the qualities of that person. Speak together about their (non-)qualities.
- *Dialogue 2.* Invite everyone to choose a picture again, this time based on the human qualities of this person. Ask why they chose this photo. The answers will probably go deeper than in the first round. Ask again about the qualities they attribute to that person. Talk about their (non-)qualities.
- *Dialogue 3.* Invite participants to take a good look at the photos on the table. These can be divided into three categories: "Can you recognize these categories?" (stars, daily superheroes, saints). Ask: "What are the differences between the qualities attributed to these people? What makes someone a saint?" Then ask: "Who is the patron saint of our parish? What did he or she do? Why are they a saint?"
- *Conclusion.* Ask: "Do you want to be a football star, rock star, famous dancer (category 1), or rather an example for others (category 2), or a saint (category 3)? What will that choice demand of you?" Give examples for each category. Should I behave differently in the various categories? Does me being a Christian change this? Talk about these questions.
- The goal is to discover if there are basic qualities that apply to everyone, and always, and that all are called to proceed on their path towards holiness. We will find these qualities in the saints. Do the participants also want to have these qualities for themselves and their family?

16.3 The litany of the Saints (Roman Missal)

Lord have mercy.
Christ have mercy.
Lord have mercy.

Lord have mercy.
Christ have mercy.
Lord have mercy.

Holy Mary, Mother of God,	pray for us.	Saint Agnes,	pray for us.
Saint Michael,	pray for us.	Saint Gregory,	pray for us.
Holy Angels of God,	pray for us.	Saint Augustine,	pray for us.
Saint John the Baptist,	pray for us.	Saint Athanasius,	pray for us.
Saint Joseph,	pray for us.	Saint Basil,	pray for us.
Saint Peter and Saint Paul	pray for us.	Saint Martin,	pray for us.
Saint Andrew,	pray for us.	Saint Benedict,	pray for us.
Saint John,	pray for us.	Saint Francis and Saint Dominic,	pray for us.
Saint Mary Magdalene,	pray for us.	Saint Francis Xavier,	pray for us.
Saint Stephen,	pray for us.	Saint John Vianney,	pray for us.
Saint Ignatius of Antioch,	pray for us.	Saint Catherine of Siena,	pray for us.
Saint Lawrence,	pray for us.	Saint Teresa of Jesus,	pray for us.
Saint Perpetua and Saint Felicity,	pray for us.	All holy men and women, Saints of God,	pray for us.

Lord, be merciful,
From all evil,
From all sin,
From everlasting death,
By your Incarnation,
By your Death and Resurrection,
By the out-pouring of the Holy Spirit,

Lord, deliver us, we pray.
Lord, deliver us, we pray.
Lord, deliver us, we pray.
Lord, deliver us, we pray.
Lord, deliver us, we pray.
Lord, deliver us, we pray.
Lord, deliver us, we pray.

Be merciful to us sinners,
Jesus, Son of the living God,

Lord, we ask you, hear our prayer.
Lord, we ask you, hear our prayer.

Christ, hear us,
Christ, graciously hear us,

Christ, hear us.
Christ, graciously hear us.

Meeting 17: Christian life – How is our faith summarized in the Creed and the Commandments?

The purpose of this meeting is to come to a first synthesis of the Catholic faith. The Apostles' Creed contains the basic teaching of all our faith. This text dates from the first centuries of Christianity and was used to

announce and explain the faith in the love of our God to the various communities. The text of the Creed initiates a dialogue about what is the center of faith. The idea is to take stock of all that has preceded, and to help participants come to a personal synthesis of their faith in God, discovering also the issues that remain unresolved (and demand further study).

Our faith is not primarily doctrine, but first of all life in God. The Ten Commandments want to help us live well with God and those around us, while the precepts of the Church help our Christian life in community. During this meeting, there is not enough time to study the Commandments in detail. The idea is merely to discover how the Church offers them as guides for our daily lives. Ideally, the Apostles' Creed and the Ten Commandments should provoke new questions and stimulate the participants to persevere in their search for answers. You might even offer to continue the meetings in a new form (SEE FOLLOW-UP). In any case, participants can find many answers by themselves in the *Tweeting with GOD* app and book.

The meeting

We work very concretely with the Apostles' Creed, offering participants the chance to react on articles of the faith. The aim is to initiate a deep dialogue on the key elements of the faith. Obviously, it is impossible to talk about everything in the available time. But the exercise will hopefully help the participants realize how the course has introduced them to the central elements of faith. Now they can ask themselves how to continue on the path of personal faith they started.

The doctrinal expressions of faith are here to help understand and deepen our relationship with God. Like every relationship, the relationship with God is experienced in everyday life. As an early "parting gift," we want to hand the participants the Commandments of God and the precepts of the Church – not as a system of rigid rules but as an inspiration on their path of life, to help them live increasingly for God and less for themselves.

Creed and Commandments

Objective of this meeting:
Synthesis of all that was discussed and experienced so far on the basis of the Creed, taking the Ten Commandments as a guide for daily life.

Related Questions:
1.19, 1.24, 1.27, 1.31, 1.33, 2.12, 2.20, 2.23, 4.9, 4.10

Dual challenge:
- Read these Questions in the *Tweeting with GOD* book: 4.9 & 4.10.
- Review your resolutions for continuing on your faith journey and put them into practice.

Prayer

Thanksgiving – giving thanks to the Lord – will be central to the prayer of this meeting. We will conclude by imploring God's blessing for the further journey in faith of the participants. It is a good moment for them to write down some intentions or resolutions for their life of faith.

Additional suggestions

- You could go back to the table of contents of the meetings and see how everything said and done fits with the Apostles' Creed (SEE GS3).
- If possible, a minister can give a personal blessing to each of the participants (with the Blessed Sacrament).
- The *Tweeting with GOD* app contains the formulas of Catholic doctrine, which function as reminders of many aspects of the faith (SEE #TwGOD APP > 🧎 > ⛪ > ⊙).
- So that participants may know the initiatives of the local community that may help as a follow-up to this course, you can invite some representatives to present these initiatives (SEE FOLLOW-UP).
- If you want to give participants a souvenir of this journey together, you could prepare cards with the Creed on one side and the Commandments on the other as a reminder of their path together.

The gist of it

- Pray, relate, recap
- Round Table 1: The Apostles' Creed
  - Activity: What articles of the Creed do you like or find difficult?
- Today's hero: Blessed Pier Giorgio Frassati

....

- Round Table 2: The Commandments
  - What can help to live as a Christian every day?
  - How can Mt 19:16-26 help to find an answer?
  - Video: Are the Ten Commandments still relevant? (#TwGOD 4.9)
- Round Table 3: Follow up
  - How can you continue to grow in faith even after this course?
  - What local initiatives can help?
- Synthesis & actualization
- Closing prayer
  - Write down some concrete resolutions for continuing your journey of faith
- Dual challenge
  - Read the #TwGOD Questions
  - Put your resolutions into practice

Procedure for Meeting 17

Relate

00.00 Opening prayer
- Choose a prayer from Appendix 5 or use the *Tweeting with GOD* app.

00.02 Welcome: Scripture charades NT
- Follow the indications on Worksheet 17.1.

00.10 The previous meeting
- Engage in a simple and quick recap. What touched the participants most in the previous meeting? Are there new questions or ideas? How did they fare with the dual challenge?
  - Are there doubts about the Questions in the *Tweeting with GOD* book?
  - How was it to pray a decade of the Rosary?
- (The participants who prepared today's Questions can briefly present the theme).

Think

00.15 Round Table 1: The Apostles' Creed
- In preparation, write the 12 Articles of Faith on a large sheet of paper, which you now place at the center.
- Start by saying that in this meeting you would like to take a look at the content of the Apostles' Creed and see how this is linked to all that was said and experienced so far during our preparation course. This is a moment of synthesis, and especially a time to see where everyone stands personally in their faith. Take a good look at the 12 Articles of Faith and think about it for a few minutes in silence.
- Ask: "In these 12 Articles, do you recognize elements from our meetings? Which ones?" Speak about this and stimulate everyone to share their thoughts.

- Then ask: "In what way can we say that the Apostles' Creed is a synthesis of all our faith?" Speak about this.
- "Take a marker and put a green dot next to the article you like best." Speak about why they chose this article.
- "Now put a red dot next to the item you find most difficult or do not understand." Discuss these articles and see whether participants can explain some difficult or challenging points to each other.
- "The first words are 'I believe', or 'Credo' in Latin. It is impossible to understand all aspects of God with our intelligence. His greatness is ever beyond us! This is why it is very normal that there are things you do not understand. Do you think it is necessary to understand everything to be able to believe?"
- Conclude: "Even if God always surpasses us, we can discover and know much about him. Think back for a moment: What was new for you? What notion touched you most deeply? Think about it in silence." After a few minutes, ask those who wish to share their thoughts.

00.45 Today's hero: Blessed Pier Giorgio Frassati
- Watch the video of Blessed Pier Giorgio Frassati via *Online with Saints*.
- Ask: "What does his life story tell you?" And: "Does he inspire you to do something similar?"

00.55 Break [END FIRST & START SECOND SESSION (SEE GS2)]

01.00 Round Table 2: The Commandments
- Follow the indications on Worksheet 17.2.

01.20 Round Table 3: Follow-up
- This is a good time to present future prospects and opportunities to continue to grow in faith (SEE FOLLOW-UP).

- Ask the participants how they think they can continue to grow in faith after this course. Speak about this together.
- You could possibly invite some representatives to present concrete prospects and opportunities offered in your local community.
- Warmly invite everyone to continue to grow in faith and join in a group or initiative to continue to deepen their personal faith.

Pray & Act

01.35 Synthesis & actualization
- Explain that there are many things to know and study about our Catholic faith. Two thousand years of Christian history have given us a lot of reflections and texts but the most important thing is a living relationship with the Lord. Starting from that relationship, we have deepened many central elements of the Christian faith and we thought a lot about the logic of our faith. Together we prayed, helped our neighbor and celebrated God's love. Thus we were helped to grow in our faith (and prepare for receiving one or more sacraments). "What do you retain especially from all this?"
- Then ask: "What is still missing?" The answers may lead to dialogue on very different themes, but this is not the time to fully explore these thoughts. The question merely intends to help the participants see that not everything is clear yet, and some work still remains to be done after this course.
- Conclude with the question: "How can what I have learned nourish my personal faith and relationship with Jesus? How can I put this into action?" Speak briefly about this.

01.45 Closing prayer
- Follow the indications on Worksheet 17.4.

01.58 Conclusion in the meeting room
- Distribute the cards of the Creed and the Ten Commandments (SEE WORKSHEET 17.3). Remind participants of the date for the next meeting and present the dual challenge:
  - Read these Questions in the *Tweeting with GOD* book: 4.9 & 4.10.
  - Review your resolutions for continuing on your faith journey and bring them into practice.

TO PREPARE
- Bibles
- Video equipment (internet)
- *Tweeting with GOD* book & app
- *Online with Saints* app
- Sheets Scripture Charades NT (DL)
- Large sheet, green & red markers
- Cards with Creed & Commandments (DL)

Worksheet 17

17.1 Welcome: Scripture Charades NT

Prepare a series of little papers with titles of Bible stories (see below). Consider whether your group will know most of these stories. If not, prepare a list with all these titles and hang it on the wall so the group can see them as a help in guessing.

Explain that this activity is called Scripture Charades: "One of you gets up front and receives a note with the title of a Bible story written on it. You get 60 seconds to act this out with the group guessing. After 60 seconds, read aloud the brief summary for each of the Bible stories that were guessed. Then someone else gets 60 seconds to act out as many Bible stories as possible. The one who gets the most correct guesses wins."

Titles of bible stories
- *Jesus' birth* (Lk 2:1-7). How Jesus was born in the grotto in Bethlehem, for there was no place in the inn.
- *Visit of three wise men* (Mt 2:1-12). How three magi from afar followed a star that brought them to Jesus.
- *John the Baptist* (Mt 3:1-12). How John called people to turn back to God and prepare for Jesus' coming.
- *Jesus' baptism* (Mk 1:9-12). How John baptized Jesus and God's voice said that Jesus is his beloved Son.
- *Jesus is tempted in the wilderness* (Lk 4:1-13). How the devil tried in vain to tempt Jesus into sin.
- *Jesus calls the first Apostles* (Mk 1:16-20). How Jesus called fishermen to follow him, and they left everything behind.
- *Jesus changes water into wine* (Jn 2:1-11). How Jesus performed his first miracle at a wedding in Cana.
- *Jesus calms the storm* (Mt 8:23-27). How Jesus saved the frightened Apostles in a boat on the rough lake.
- *Jesus walks on water* (Mt 14:22-33). How Jesus came walking over the lake to the boat of the Apostles.
- *The good Samaritan* (Lk 10.25-37). Jesus' parable about a non-Jew who saved a Jew ignored by others.
- *Jesus feeds five thousand* (Mk 6:31-44). How Jesus fed a great crowd with a few loaves of bread and some fish.
- *The sermon on the mount* (Mt 5:1-7:29). Jesus gave a long list of teachings, sitting on a mountain.
- *Jesus raises Lazarus from the dead* (Jn 11:1-44). Jesus cried and then brought his good friend back to life.
- *The prodigal son* (Lk 15:11-32). Jesus' parable of how our merciful Father always expects us to return to him.
- *Jesus washes the Apostle's feet* (Jn 13:1-30). How Jesus showed that we are never too important to serve.
- *The Last Supper* (Mk 14:12-26). How Jesus took bread and wine, saying, "this is my Body, this is my Blood."
- *Peter denies Jesus* (Lk 22:54-62). How Peter discovered that even he could not remain faithful to Jesus.
- *Jesus is crucified* (Mk 15:20-41). How Jesus had to carry his own cross, was nailed to the cross, and died.
- *Jesus is buried* (Mt 27:57-66). How the body of Jesus, who was truly dead, was buried in a grave.
- *Jesus rises from the dead* (Mt 28:1-20). How Jesus became alive again on the third day of his death.
- *Jesus on the road to Emmaus* (Lk 24:13-35). How the risen Jesus met his disciples and gave them new hope.
- *Jesus Ascends to heaven* (Acts 1:4-11). How Jesus told the disciples to preach the Gospel and went to God.
- *Pentecost* (Acts 2:1-13). How the Holy Spirit came down on the Apostles, who preached with enthusiasm.

- Explain: "Even if you have learned a lot during our meetings, this does not mean that your faith journey is complete. On the contrary, you are at the beginning and there is still much to learn and do. We hope that you can continue on your path, in the belief that God is always close with his Spirit of love and grace. But how to live as a Christian in everyday life? What could help you with this?" Speak about it.
- The desire to live well belongs to every time and place. Look at Jesus' response to a young man who loved life so much that he wanted to live forever. Read Matthew 19:16-26 and speak about this.
- Watch the video of #TwGOD Question 4.9 together: "Are the Ten Commandments still relevant?"
- Ask: "Do you think the Commandments can help you in your life? How?" Speak about this.
- Look up the Ten Commandments in the *Tweeting with GOD* app (SEE #TwGOD APP > > >). Further down, you will also find the five precepts of the Church.
- This is good moment to briefly speak about each Commandment as far as time allows. You can find a summary in the *Tweeting with GOD* book (SEE #TwGOD 4.9).

The Apostles' Creed
1. I believe in God, the Father almighty, Creator of heaven and earth,
2. and in Jesus Christ, his only Son, our Lord,
3. who was conceived by the Holy Spirit, born of the Virgin Mary,
4. suffered under Pontius Pilate, was crucified, died and was buried;
5. he descended into hell; on the third day he arose again from the dead;
6. he ascended into heaven, and is seated at the right hand of God the Father almighty;
7. from there he will come to judge the living and the dead.
8. I believe in the Holy Spirit,
9. the holy catholic Church, the communion of saints,
10. the forgiveness of sins,
11. the resurrection of the body,
12. and life everlasting. Amen.

(SEE #TwGOD 1.33)

The Ten Commandments
1. I am the Lord your God: you shall have no other Gods before me.
2. You shall not take the name of the Lord your God in vain
3. Remember the sabbath day, to keep it holy.
4. Honor your father and your mother.
5. You shall not kill.
6. You shall not commit adultery.
7. You shall not steal.
8. You shall not bear false witness against your neighbor.
9. You shall not covet your neighbor's wife.
10. You shall not covet your neighbor's goods.

(SEE #TwGOD 4.9)

Don't forget (How) to grow in faith! A course that explored the Catholic faith, searched for answers to questions, and prepared for the Sacraments

17.4 Closing prayer

- Go (if possible) to the chapel or church. Light the candles and sing a song.

- Pray, for example: "Lord, here we are together to meet you. Thank you for all we have been able to receive …"
- Each participant receives a sheet and a pencil. Explain that you will take a moment of silence. "Write down some concrete resolutions: How do I wish to keep moving forward on my journey of faith? You could, for example, decide to pray alone for 3 minutes every morning, read a theme from *Tweeting with GOD* every Monday night, look up the Sunday Gospel every Saturday, recite a Hail Mary before getting angry, smile at that one person you do not like …"
- After the silence pray, for example: "Thank you, Lord, for all your kindness and all the talents you gave us! Help us continue to advance on the path of life with you. We ask you to bless each of us! Help us with your grace and love to become better Christians every day. Mary, our Mother, pray for us!"
- Conclude with an Our Father and a Hail Mary.

Meeting 18: CELEBRATE – Can a good Catholic party?

In our earthly life it is important to celebrate our successes and it is even more important to celebrate the successes of God! That is what we wish to reflect on and do during this meeting. The participants have come a long way in deepening the faith together, and maybe even received one or more sacraments! The conversation will help to see the importance of celebrating and how to do this in a good way. The greatest celebration of all is the Eucharist, which will be discussed before concluding the meeting with a party. The party is not only fraternal and material: we wish to celebrate with God. Look for example at the party prepared by the father of the prodigal son (Lk 15:22-24.32). And at the wedding at Cana, when they ran out of wine, Jesus gave wine in abundance (Jn 2:1-10). It is therefore "very Catholic" to party and celebrate the graces received from God!

The meeting

In a first Round Table, we will speak about the subject of partying, looking for ways in which a Catholic can celebrate. Attention will be given to inappropriate ways of celebrating, but we hope that participants have by now developed a common sense for what is right and wrong, so that it is not necessary to linger too long on what is to be avoided. Rather, the focus can be on the importance of celebrating together.

The second Round Table will focus on the celebration of the Eucharist, the greatest celebration of all. It is the source and summit of our Christian life, which is why this topic is part of the meeting on partying and celebration.

The final party of the meeting can run very simply. Try to create a festive atmosphere in the meeting room with some music, soft light, and something to eat and drink. You can freely spend time together in joy and thanksgiving.

Prayer

Before (or after) the party take time for prayer. Invite the participants for a prayer of praise and thanksgiving. If you want to extend the thanksgiving part, you could read the Bible text Ephesians 1:3-14. Take a moment of silence and then exchange briefly on what the participants were touched by in this text. Conclude with Ephesians 1:15-19 text and a moment of silence. Then conclude the prayer.

Party, Eucharist, and thanksgiving

Objective of this meeting:
Think about what makes a good Catholic party, the celebration of the Eucharist, and partying in thanksgiving.

Related Questions:
3.29, 3.44, 3.45, 3.46, 3.47, 3.48, 3.49, 3.50, 4.10

Additional suggestions

- You could play some games. For example, sitting in a circle you could pass around a present with several layers of paper until the music stops. Whoever holds the present in hand can remove a layer, before passing it to the next person; who removes away the last layer has won. Or repeat one of the activities of previous meetings that the participants enjoyed.
- You could also decide to conclude with a Eucharistic celebration before the party. The participants can do all the preparation, the singing, the reading, the general intercessions, the serving ...

The gist of it

- **Pray, relate, recap**
- **Round Table 1: Partying**
  How can Catholics party? Did Jesus go to parties?
  – Is moderation a virtue? What is the difference from being boring
- **Today's hero: Saint Vitus**
- **Round Table 2: Celebration of the Eucharist**
  – Why do we speak of the "celebration" of the Eucharist? What is the difference from partying?
  – Why is the first precept of the Church linked to Mass?
- **Synthesis & actualization**
- **Closing prayer**
  – Keep it simple and short

....

- **Celebrate: party time!**

Procedure for Meeting 18

Relate

00.00 Opening prayer
- Choose a prayer from Appendix 5 or use the *Tweeting with GOD* app.

00.02 Welcome: Scissors, Paper, Rock
- Follow the indications on Worksheet 18.1.

00.10 The previous meeting
- Engage in a simple and quick recap. What touched the participants most in the previous meeting? Are there new questions or ideas? How did they fare with the dual challenge?
  - Are there doubts about the Questions in the *Tweeting with GOD* book?
  - Do you think that your resolutions from the last meeting are feasible? (If not, take a little time to adapt these now.)
- (The participants who prepared today's Questions can briefly present the theme.)

Think

00.15 Round Table 1: Partying
- Ask: "Do you like to party? What is your favorite way to party and celebrate?"
- Then ask: "Do you think that Catholics who take their faith seriously should party?" And: "If so, is there a specific Catholic way to party?" Speak about this together.
- Remind participants that Jesus performed his first miracle at a wedding party (SEE MEETING 13D). Read in the Bible from John 2:1-11 and speak together about what this means for our view of partying. You can also refer back to the celebration called for by the father of the prodigal son (LK 15:22-24.32; SEE MEETING 13F).

- Partying and celebrating are universal ways in which we express our joy together as people. There are many ways to party, and many of these are perfectly okay for Catholics. Where do you think we have to draw a line? What elements of common partying are not in accordance with a Christian lifestyle? Participants probably will come up with drugs, sex, certain types of music, excessive drinking, etc.
- It would seem that many things that happen at modern parties are not for Catholics. Does this make a Catholic party automatically boring? How can you have a great party as a Christian? Speak together about the best ways of having a great time together, whilst avoiding excesses.
- Moderation is a great Christian virtue. It means that you can choose to let yourself go at a party, but always up to a certain limit. You remain in charge, because you have received a responsibility from God for yourself and others. How is moderation different from being boring?
- Conclude that it is very Catholic to party and to celebrate the graces we received from God. Jesus too visited parties. There are many ways to truly party and still remain faithful to your dedication to God. We even have the ancient custom of carnival, where we party before starting the great fast of Lent.

00.25 Today's hero: Saint Vitus
- Watch the video of Saint Vitus via *Online with Saints*.
- Ask: "What does Vitus tell us about partying and dancing?" And: "Does he inspire you to do something similar?"

00.35 Round Table 2: The celebration of the Eucharist
- Explain that we often speak of the "Celebration of the Eucharist": "Why do you think we speak of "celebration" in this context? Is this celebration

very different from the partying we spoke about before? What are the parallels and differences you can talk about?"

- Remind participants that the Eucharist is called the source and summit of Christian life (CCC 1324; SEE MEETING 13C): "What do you think is meant by this? Why can we say that the Eucharist is both the source and summit of our lives as Christians?" Speak about this.
- The word "Eucharist" means "Thanksgiving": "Why do you think this sacrament has this name? What can we be thankful for in this context?"
- Continue: "The five precepts of the Church intend to help you in your daily life as a Christian (SEE MEETING 17; #TwGOD APP > 🙏 > ⛪ > ◎). The first of these precepts is that Catholics are asked to participate in the weekly Sunday Eucharist. This in itself demonstrates how important the Eucharist is for our daily life. How do you think that the Eucharist can help you?"
- Ask: "Do you go to Mass sometimes. Why or why not?" and then: "How could regular participation in the Mass help you in your life of faith?"
- Conclude by saying that on earth we cannot come closer to the real presence of Jesus than in the Eucharist. Here, Jesus is present with his body and blood, soul and divinity. This is such a great gift from the part of God, that we want to celebrate and be joyful. Jesus gave us hope, even after we die, and is with us at this very moment. That is worth a proper party!

Pray & Act

00.50 Synthesis & actualization

- Ask: "How can what I have learned nourish my personal faith and relationship with Jesus? How can I put this into action?" Speak briefly about this.
- Conclude by saying that we have seen during all our meetings how it is possible to grow in faith together. We pray that you will be able to ever move forward on your path with God. And that, especially in difficult times, you will know that you are loved by Jesus who is always close to those who invoke him. That is why we want to conclude our journey together with prayer.

00.53 Pray

- Pray, for example: "We thank you, Lord, for your blessings. We are here to praise you and thank you. Help us to live in the grace of our faith and to offer ourselves to you at every moment. Holy Spirit, help us to continue to move forward on the path of faith, to pray regularly, to celebrate at times, and to persevere in our life with you. Thank you, Lord, for today's dialogue and our party together!"
- (You may continue wish to continue with some intercessions and a time of thanksgiving).
- Conclude with the Our Father and the Hail Mary.

00.55 Break [END FIRST & START SECOND SESSION (SEE GS2)]

Celebrate

01.00 Party time!

- Create a great atmosphere, prepare some good things to eat and drink, get the music playing ... and party!

TO PREPARE
- Bibles
- Video equipment (internet)
- *Tweeting with GOD book & app*
- *Online with Saints app*
- A festive atmosphere
- Something to eat and drink
- Music

Worksheet 18

18.1 Welcome: Scissors, Paper, Rock

1. Explain that you are going to play Scissors, Paper, Rock. Does everyone know the rules?
2. If not, explain: "Make one of three shapes with your hand: for Scissors you hold out your index and middle finger forming a 'V', for Paper you hold out a flat hand, and for Rock you hold out a closed fist. If you both choose the same shape, replay the game immediately. Paper covers Rock (Paper wins), Scissors cut paper (Scissors win), Rock blunts Scissors (Rock wins)."
3. In just a moment, you will find a partner for this game. If you lose, you will become the winners' personal cheer squad as they move on to find another person to play the game with. Eventually we will have two big teams to have the final game.
4. Ask whether there are any questions and get started.

Follow-up after *How to grow in faith*

The end of our journey *How to grow in faith* is not really an end. It is rather the beginning of a new way of living as a Christian, for which the participants will need the Holy Spirit and his graces at every moment. The purpose of this entire course has been to help them grow in faith and prepare them for their further life as mature Christians. It is important to keep this direction in mind and gradually give them more responsibilities, suggesting concrete ways for them to join the life of a local community, whilst ensuring the well-being of everyone (SEE BOX).

A new beginning

The following three commitments on the part of the participants could help them continue to make progress on their path with God after *How to grow in faith*:

- A commitment to continuously deepening knowledge of the faith, reading the Bible and fundamental documents like the Catechism of the Catholic Church, and studying resources like *Tweeting with GOD*, *Online with Saints*, and manifold other reliable information.
- A commitment to regular personal prayer, and finding the Will of God, possibly helped by spiritual accompaniment. The only way to grow in your relationship with Jesus is by passing time with him.
- A commitment to the Church, the local community. Even if there is no active community or parish nearby, it is still of vital importance to find ways to live your faith with others.

Continuing

If (part of) your group is motivated to continue searching for answers to faith-related questions, you could use the same format as presented in this course. The general idea of such meetings would be the same as during the course but with greater freedom of choice of topics. The moderation can be done jointly by the group itself. The most important thing is the motivation of the participants. The *Tweeting with GOD Manual* and the *Specials* give many explanations and ideas on how to organize such meetings just by yourself (SEE WWW.TWEETINGWITHGOD.COM/HOWTO).

Possibilities

The possibilities for living your faith in the Church are manifold and a reflection of the Christian life of the community:

- Faith reflection group
- Caritas service
- Youth group, adult group ...
- Choir
- Altar servers
- Sacristans
- Prayer group
- Readers
- Extraordinary ministers
- Visiting the sick
- Music group
- Ushers
- Pilgrimage team
- Parish council
- Cleaning group
- Something new ...
- Etcetera

Practical suggestions

- You are trying to grow and deepen a relationship: seek God at every moment possible, and include him in your daily routine. For example, say a brief prayer of thanksgiving before you start eating, pray in the morning before the start of the daily buzz, pray in the evening when everything grows still, throw brief interjections to heaven saying thank you, I'm sorry, help me ...

- Christian life is not about programs and projects, but about a continuous journey with Jesus, alone and with others. Schedule moments for time with God in your weekly calendar. For example, write down appointments with God for personal prayer, for a moment of exchange about the faith with others, for Bible study, for visiting a lonely neighboor ...

- God has given the sacraments and the liturgy to strengthen and inspire you for your life as a Christian. Make sure to participate in the weekly Sunday Eucharist and the celebrations of the liturgical year: these are a great help for living your faith on a daily basis. Do not forget the importance of regularly asking forgiveness from God in the Sacrament of Reconciliation.

- Check with your local parish or community what opportunities for living and deepening the faith are on offer.

- If in your neighborhood there are not many possibilities for continuing to grow in faith, consider starting something with your course mates, or joining an (online) community for regular meetings of prayer, sharing, and deepening the faith. Try to meet regularly, even if only by videoconference.

- We all need a boost from time to time. Pilgrimages and retreats are great ways to regain weakened or lost enthusiasm, and to refocus on the importance of your personal relationship with Jesus. For example, visit a monastery or holy place for a day of recollection, book some days of retreat with a few friends or alone, sign up for a pilgrimage ...

- Above all, realize that you are not alone on this exciting journey of faith: Jesus tells you here and now: "Remember, I am with you always, to the end of the age" (MT 28:20).

Appendix 1: The Books of the Bible

Old Testament

GEN	Genesis	PROV	Proverbs
EX	Exodus	ECCL	Ecclesiastes
LEV	Leviticus	SONG	Song of Solomon
NUM	Numbers	WIS	Wisdom
DEUT	Deuteronomy	SIR	Sirach (Ecclesiasticus)
JOSH	Joshua	ISA	Isaiah
JUDG	Judges	JER	Jeremiah
RUTH	Ruth	LAM	Lamentations
1 SAM	1 Samuel	BAR	Baruch
2 SAM	2 Samuel	EZEK	Ezekiel
1 KINGS	1 Kings	DAN	Daniel
2 KINGS	2 Kings	HOS	Hosea
1 CHR	1 Chronicles	JOEL	Joel
2 CHR	2 Chronicles	AM	Amos
EZRA	Ezra	OB	Obadiah
NEH	Nehemiah	JON	Jonah
TOB	Tobit	MIC	Micah
JDT	Judith	NAH	Nahum
ESTH	Esther	HAB	Habakkuk
1 MACC	1 Maccabees	ZEPH	Zephaniah
2 MACC	2 Maccabees	HAG	Haggai
JOB	Job	ZECH	Zechariah
PS	Psalms	MAL	Malachi

New Testament

Mt	Matthew	1 Tim	1 Timothy
Mk	Mark	2 Tim	2 Timothy
Lk	Luke	Titus	Titus
Jn	John	Philem	Philemon
Acts	Acts of the Apostles	Heb	Hebrews
Rom	Romans	Jas	James
1 Cor	1 Corinthians	1 Pet	1 Peter
2 Cor	2 Corinthians	2 Pet	2 Peter
Gal	Galatians	1 Jn	1 John
Eph	Ephesians	2 Jn	2 John
Phil	Philippians	3 Jn	3 John
Col	Colossians	Jude	Jude
1 Thess	1 Thessalonians	Rev	Revelation (Apocalypse)
2 Thess	2 Thessalonians		

Appendix 2: How to share your testimony? Why evangelize?

The aim of sharing your faith experience in a testimony is to help others grow in their faith. Your faith story is not your own doing, but God's action. So be careful not to boast, and humbly admit that it is all God's gift to you. At the same time, there is no need for false humility: simply say things as you feel them and experienced them. There are a few points that may help you prepare for your testimony.

Jesus at the center
It is God himself, who invites us to testify of our relationship with Jesus:
- "Go home to your friends, and tell them how much the Lord has done for you, and what mercy he has shown you" (Mк 5:19).
- "I want you to know, that what has happened to me has actually helped to spread the gospel" (Phil 1:12).
- "I am not ashamed of the gospel; it is the power of God for salvation to everyone who has faith" (Rom 1:16).

And he promised the help of the Holy Spirit to those who have to give witness of their faith:
- "The Holy Spirit, whom the Father will send in my name, will teach you everything, and remind you of all that I have said to you" (Jn 14:26).
- "Do not worry beforehand about what you are to say; but say whatever is given you at that time, for it is not you who speak, but the Holy Spirit" (Mк 13:11).

Tips for sharing

- Start with a quiet prayer: you want to talk about Jesus, not about yourself in the first place. Ask the Holy Spirit to help you.
- Try to relate to your public: use examples and a language they will understand.
- Keep it short and to the point.
- You may wish to practice telling your story aloud to a friend (or to the mirror).
- Try to be honest and simple: admit mistakes without insisting on your sins, share graces received without claiming credit, and avoid giving the impression that faith is all easy.
- Avoid preaching! You want to share what happened to you to equals.
- Do not be afraid to show your enthusiasm for Jesus: people will mostly remember how you spoke, and less what you said.
- Avoid reading everything from paper, but do prepare yourself well: know what you want to say and how.
- Make jokes when you feel like it, without making your story ridiculous.
- You may be confident in your speaking, trusting that God will help you (Mк 13:11).

Sharing your testimony

Depending of the subject of your testimony, the public, and the time available, your testimony can cover three parts.

- Life before the specific encounter with Jesus you wish to speak about. How was it, what was good, what missed?
- The experience of the encounter with Jesus. This is the central part of your testimony. What happened (where, when, and how), what did you feel, what did it do to you?
- Life after the experience. How did it change your life? Where do you stand now? You could even add a few words on where you would like to go next.

Evangelization

Jesus told the disciples and all of us: "Go into all the world and proclaim the good news to the whole creation" (Mk 16:15). Mission and evangelization are based on God's love for everyone, and our love for our neighbor:. We want to share with them what we know is good for us!

As Pope Francis wrote: "We know well that with Jesus life becomes richer and that with him it is easier to find meaning in everything. This is why we evangelize. A true missionary, who never ceases to be a disciple, knows that Jesus walks with him, speaks to him, breathes with him, works with him. ... A person who is not convinced, enthusiastic, certain, and in love, will convince nobody" (Evangelii Gaudium, 266).

Faith is not something abstract, it is all about a relationship. Whenever you speak about God, you yourself are involved as well. And whenever you are sharing your testimony about your experience with him, you are sharing the Gospel as Jesus invited you to do.

It is good to think beforehand about what you would answer to some common questions from others like: "Why do you believe?" or "Why is this Jesus guy of 2,000 years ago still important to you?" Remember the words of Saint Peter: "Always be ready to make your defence to anyone who demands from you an accounting for the hope that is in you" (1 Pet 3:15).

Appendix 3: Interactive methods for your group

3.1 Forming groups using matching napkins

1. Get colored napkins in as many colors as the number of groups you would like to create. For example, if you want three groups, you will need three colors. Make sure the total number of napkins corresponds with the number of participants, and that you have roughly the same number of napkins of each color.
2. Use the napkins at the start of your activity, for example, to accompany a snack or drink. Tell the group to keep their napkins because they will need these later. (You can steer the creation of small groups a little without participants noticing. Is there a shy person whose friend always does the talking? Give each of them a different color napkin!)
3. When you're ready to break into small groups, ask participants to take their napkins. Ask them to find others in the room with the same color napkins as theirs. Then direct the small groups to areas where they can discuss together.
4. You can come up with all sorts of variations; for example, substitute napkins with cups, straws, name tags ...

> **TO PREPARE**
> – Napkins of different colours

3.2 Forming groups using the participants' shoes

1. Ask participants to take off one shoe and to lay it in a row. Do not tell them yet what the purpose is.
2. Divide the shoes into groups (decide beforehand how many groups you will have).
3. Now tell participants to put their shoes back on and join their sharing group.

3.3 Stimulating questions

1. Divide the participants into small groups of 5 to 7 people (see Appendix 3.1 & 3.2).
2. Invite the participants to work in silence. Optionally play some background music.
3. Explain the rules: "Everyone receives a sheet on which you write a question which is relevant for you. When all have written their question, you pass the sheet to your righthand neighbor, who seeks to answer in a few words in writing. Then that person passes the sheet to their righthand neighbor, so that they write an answer too. Stop whenever time is up."
4. At the end of this exercise, everyone receives the answers to their question.
5. To continue the exchange, you can then meet together, and talk about some selected questions and answers.

> **TO PREPARE**
> – Paper & pens
> – (Speaker for playing music)

3.4 Stimulating interaction

1. Participants are free to ask the group questions. The questioner can point out who will answer the question first.
2. To deepen the response and stimulate participation, you can then ask the person who asked the question to present their own answer.
3. Subsequently the other members can bring their point of view too.
4. There you are, you have started to interact deeply in a group.

3.5 Stimulating listening

1. Give everyone a piece of paper on which they write their name. Demonstrate how you want them to fold the notes so that they are all folded in the same way with the names inside.
2. Collect the papers in a bowl. Mix them up and let each participant draw one. If someone has their own name, collect the notes and distribute them out again.
3. Explain the rules: "The person whose name you have received is the person you are going to give extra attention to during our conversations. Listen to this person extra closely, try to understand what they are saying, and ask them more questions. It is important to listen to everyone closely, but go the extra mile with this person."
4. Later in the session, you can remind members of this activity and encourage them to keep listening intently to and trying to understand the person whose name they received.

TO PREPARE
– Paper & pens
– Bowl

3.6 Written Reflection

1. List the following questions on a sheet of paper, leaving enough space for people to write their answers.
   a. What was new for me?
   b. What touched me? How did I feel? Happy, angry, afraid, sad? Why?
   c. What do I want to learn more about?
2. Give everyone a sheet and a pen.
3. Explain: Take five minutes to think about the answer to these three questions. Jot down a few words as an answer.
4. Invite the participants to work in silence. Optionally play some background music.
5. When the time is up, encourage participants to take their answers home with them for further reflection and study. Tell them that they can find answers to many of their questions in the *Tweeting with GOD* book, or ask their questions during the course.

> **TO PREPARE**
> – Sheet with 3 questions (DL)
> – Pens
> – (Speaker for playing music)

3.7 Interactive activities in this book

Names & statements (SEE WORKSHEET 1.1)
Participants get to know each other better by using statements that regard them.

Walk the line (SEE WORKSHEET 1.2 & 3.2)
Participants are helped in expressing their thoughts by responding to statements.

Sit & share (SEE WORKSHEET 2.1)
Participants get to know each other better in a playful environment

Scripture charades OT (SEE WORKSHEET 3.1)
Participants get acquainted with Old Testament episodes

Find your prayer (SEE WORKSHEET 4.2)
Participants are exposed to the wealth of Catholic prayers in the #TwGOD app.

Quick thinking (SEE WORKSHEET 6.1)
Participants think and speak quickly off the top of their heads about the topic.

Human knot (SEE WORKSHEET 8.1)
Breaking the ice, helping participants to relate to each other.

Jesus & me (SEE WORKSHEET 8.4)
Participants reflect on where they stand in relation to Jesus.

Throwing balls (SEE WORKSHEET 9.1)
Participants learn to know each other better, relate in a playful environment.

Sacraments Memory (SEE WORKSHEET 12.1)
Participants get to know the seven sacraments and their principal effect.

Jesus' story (SEE WORKSHEET 13A.3)
Participants tell a story about Jesus' view on the theme, one word at the time.

Sanitary Bible sharing (SEE WORKSHEET 13B.2)
Participants learn to know each other better, relate in a playful environment.

Rolling balls (SEE WORKSHEET 13C.2)
Participants relate in a playful environment.

Two truths and a lie (SEE WORKSHEET 13D.2)
Participants get to realize how easy it is to lie.

Unfortunately ... fortunately (SEE WORKSHEET 13E.3)
Participants tell a story together, thinking about the subject.

Raise your card (SEE WORKSHEET 13F.3)
Participants think quickly and learn to express their opinion.

Selfie with a saint (SEE WORKSHEET 16.1)
Participants get to know the profiles of saints in the *Online with Saints* app.

Scripture charades NT (SEE WORKSHEET 17.1)
Participants get acquainted with New Testament episodes

Scissors, Paper, Rock (SEE WORKSHEET 18.1)
Participants are helped to relate and have fun.

PARTLY CF. *TWEETING WITH GOD MANUAL*, APPENDIX 3. MANY THANKS TO H. WARMERHOVEN FOR HIS ADVICE.

Appendix 4: Praying with a text from the Bible

According to the method of Saint Ignatius of Loyola (SEE #TwGOD 4.5).

1) Preparing to pray

- Decide which text you will use (SEE #TwGOD 3.4) and how long you will pray.
- Choose a place and a body posture – sitting, standing or kneeling – and read the text.
- Focus on a few passages and imagine what is happening. What do you see and what do you hear? How would you show that in a film? Use your other senses too: What do you feel, smell, or taste?
- Ask for the grace (SEE #TwGOD 4.12) you desire to receive from God at that particular moment.

2) Beginning to pray

- Start your prayer by making the Sign of the Cross. Tell God: "Lord, I am here; I seek you."
- Thank God for the gift of your life and offer it back as your gift to him. Say that you want to listen to him and to be changed by him.
- This opening of your prayer may be the same every day, using your own words or an existing prayer.

3) Listening to God

- Now pray with the text you have chosen. Receive with joy what happens in your prayer, as a gift from God, knowing that you cannot really determine what happens to you during prayer.
- Meditate on the passages that move you. Try to understand what they mean for your life.
- You are not the one talking at this point. Try to be quiet with God. This is the longest part of your prayer.

4) Speaking with God

- While before you tried to listen, now it is your chance to talk. You can talk to Jesus about anything, as if you're talking to a friend. Sometimes you can ask for mercy, sometimes you can accuse yourself of something you did wrong, sometimes you entrust him with your problems and ask for his help.
- Finish with a vocal prayer, such as the Our Father, followed by the Sign of the Cross.
- Be loyal and stick to the time you had reserved for prayer, even if it's hard. After all, you seek God for who he is and not for what he can give you.

5) Looking back

- Take a few minutes to look back on your prayer and to write down, if possible, any possible conclusions you can draw from what you experienced during your prayer. By making a prayer diary, or journal, you can learn to recognize the thread of your life with God. Ask yourself about two things:
  a) *That which depends on you:* the form of your prayer. Did the place where you chose to pray and your chosen body posture help you to pray? Were you fully dedicated to your prayers? How did you deal with distractions and dry periods? How long did you pray?
  b) *That which happened during your prayer:* What were your feelings? Did you experience joy or sadness after reading passages from the Bible? Did a thought or an image come to you? Do not be afraid to listen to your feelings, reactions, and desires, because it is precisely through your deepest longings that God's Will for your life is manifested.

(FROM: M. REMERY, *TWEETING WITH GOD. BIG BANG, PRAYER, BIBLE, SEX, CRUSADES, SIN...*, FREEDOM PUBLISHING BOOKS 2017, APPENDIX 4).

Appendix 5: Prayers for the beginning and end of the meeting

The best way to communicate with God is through prayer. Praying in a group can be quite a challenge in the beginning. It is good to encourage the group members to pray from their heart. Especially in the beginning, you and they may need some help. Fortunately, the Church has a great tradition of beautiful prayers that can be used (SEE #TWGOD APP > 🙏 > ⛪). A short introduction may help to integrate these into your sessions. Always start and conclude your prayer with the sign of the cross. A repetitive meditative song can help the participants to enter in an atmosphere of prayer. Or you can calmly pray (part of) the Rosary. This also helps when you do not know what to say.

Opening Prayers

To begin ...
Lord, I come here before you and I do not know what to say. In fact, I know you very little. Help me to understand better who you want to be for me. Help me to overcome my doubts. Teach me to pray as you please and to listen to what you want to tell me.

My Lord and my God ...
Jesus, you know everything I experience in my heart, even when I am not aware of it. I have a great desire to come near to you, although I do not know how to find you. I want to spend more time with you, but I do not know how to pray. Yet I want to say with all my heart:

All: *My Lord and my God, take from me everything that distances me from you. My Lord and my God, give me everything that brings me closer to you. My Lord and my God, detach me from myself to give my all to you. Amen.*

[PRAYER OF SAINT NICOLAS OF FLÜE]

Take, Lord ...
Dear Lord, we come into your presence to thank you for this moment in which we may consider the greatness of your presence among us and the reasons why it is good to believe. We ask you to help us to think honestly about the faith and to recognize how everything comes together in your love. We want you, not us, to be the center of our lives and thoughts, and therefore we pray:

All: *Take, Lord, and receive all my liberty, my memory, my understanding, and my entire will, all I have and call my own. You have given all to me. To you, Lord, I return it. Everything is yours; do with it what you will. Give me only your love and your grace. That is enough for me. Amen.*

[PRAYER OF SURRENDER OF SAINT IGNATIUS OF LOYOLA]

Come, Holy Spirit ...
Dear Lord, as we gather to think about you and your great gifts during this session, we ask you to be with us with your Holy Spirit. Together we pray:

All: *Come, Holy Spirit, Divine Creator, true source of light and fountain of wisdom! Pour forth your brilliance upon my dense intellect, dissipate the darkness which covers me, that of sin and of ignorance. Grant me a penetrating mind to understand, a retentive memory, method and ease in learning, the lucidity to comprehend, and abundant grace in expressing myself. Guide the beginning of my work, direct its progress, and bring it to successful completion. This I ask through Jesus Christ, true God and true man, living and reigning with you and the Father, forever and ever. Amen.*

[STUDENT'S PRAYER OF ST. THOMAS AQUINAS]

Concluding Prayers

Thank you Lord ...

Dear Lord, we thank you for our conversations, for what we learned about you and ourselves. Help us to make it part of our daily lives. Teach us to open ourselves to you. Holy Mary, Mother of Jesus, pray for us.

All: *Hail Mary ...* (SEE QUESTION 3.9).

Into your hands ...

Thanking you for all we learned, we pray:

V /. Into your hands, Lord, I commend my spirit.

R /. *Into your hands, Lord, I commend my spirit.*

V /. You have redeemed me, Lord God of truth.

R /. *Into your hands, Lord, I commend my spirit.*

V /. Glory be to the Father, and the Son, and the Holy Spirit.

R /. *Into your hands, Lord, I commend my spirit.*

[PSALM 31:5; NIGHT PRAYER]

Tips

- **Intercession.** Formulate written prayer intentions with the participants. Divide the intentions among the participants so that they can pray specifically for this intention during the time of prayer. Also invite the participants to think about a specific person during the prayer and to say their name aloud.
- **Review.** You can animate a brief review of the day and especially of the meeting (SEE APPENDIX 5 IN THE *TWEETING WITH GOD* BOOK). Sing a meditative song and then invite silence. Ask: "What was the strongest moment of my day? What affected me most during today's meeting? For which moments am I particularly grateful? What do I regret?" Finish with an Our Father and a Hail Mary.
- **Praying with the Church.** Always try to end your meeting in a church or chapel, possibly by praying the prayer of the Church, Prayer during the Day, Vespers, Compline (SEE #TwGOD 3.13), or by a moment of adoration of the Blessed Sacrament (SEE #TwGOD 3.14). See the app for many examples or prayers (SEE #TwGOD APP > >).

PARTLY CF. *TWEETING WITH GOD MANUAL*, APPENDIX 5.

Appendix 6: Sample content for extra meetings
Sample Meeting 6.1: What is the Christian view of life?

On these pages we give you an example of how you could speak about the Christian vision of life. You may even decide to dedicate several meetings to this extensive topic. What follows is just a proposal, which you can adapt in accordance with the needs of your group. The procedure for the meeting can correspond to that of other meetings.

The meeting

- *Introduction.* Before he died, Moses urged the people of Israel to "choose life" (DEUT 30:19). This summarizes the Catholic view of life: we always want to choose, protect and promote life in every way because it is a gift from God. This is a very positive view (SEE #TwGOD 4.26)! It comes from the realization that our God is a living God of life, who wants us to have life to the full: that is why Jesus came to us in the first place (JOHN 10:10).
- *Round Table 1.* The painful situation of many refugees, migrants, poor, and homeless people is very much a current issue. Do they not all have a right to a dignified life and to be respected? We know that there is no need to be rich to live in happiness, but everyone needs a minimum to live. These people do not even have that. This is where Christian solidarity and our calling to promote a dignified life for all becomes concrete (SEE #TwGOD 4.45). It is our task to help others live their life in dignity and joy.
- *Round Table 2.* Every life is a gift from God (SEE #TwGOD 4.27 & 4.30). Who are we to decide who has the right to live or not? Even our own life is not ours, because it is entrusted to us by the Lord (SEE #TwGOD 4.31 & 4.41). The protection of life is an important Christian duty. The absolute choice of Christians for life seems to be diametrically opposed to contemporary views on abortion, euthanasia, or the death penalty, for example (SEE #TwGOD 4.28, 4.38 & 4.42). The small and the weak are the first to have a right to be protected and aided in every possible way, from their conception until natural death. It is important to try to understand the reasons why Christians make an absolute choice for human life.
- *Round Table 3.* Ecology, the life of nature given to us in God's creation, is also very precious. Like all life, it is created by God and given in stewardship to humans (GEN 1:28). Therefore, it is our task to protect the environment, our common home, while we can also use it to live – provided this is done in a way that respects God's creation (SEE #TwGOD 1.1, 4.36 & 4.48). The theme of this meeting is above all the principle of choosing life in every circumstance, and the call to every Christian to help their neighbor.

Choosing life

Objective of this meeting:
Recognize the value of life created by God and encountered in daily life, together with the importance of sharing your property and time in defence of the small and weak.

Related Questions:
4.26, 4.28, 4.37, 4.38, 4.41, 4.42, 4.43, 4.44, 4.45, 4.48

Prayer

You could pray for all people in danger of death and for those who cannot live a dignified and joyful life. You can light a small candle for each individual or category of person mentioned, and place these cross-shaped before the altar: at this moment these people participate in the suffering of Jesus; we pray that the Lord will helps them. More specifically, we can also pray for inspiration to personally help someone. And there may be others who will do the same.

Suggestions

- You may wish to remind participants of the importance of not divulging to others what is being said in the group (SEE GS2).
- Address these themes in a peaceful and attentive climate, for they are easily politicised. Strong or closed positions do not help an open and respectful dialogue.
- Note that this theme may indeed generate debate with very strong positions. For example, when talking about abortion or euthanasia, it is necessary to pay attention to all the feelings and possible painful experiences in the group. These are very important issues, but also very delicate ones. Here the role of the moderator is essential.
- Today's hero could be Saint Gianna Beretta Molla, the young mother who was willing to sacrifice her own life so that her child could live. Or Saint Kateri Tekakwitha, who lived very close to nature and found her relationship with Jesus there.

TO PREPARE
- Bibles
- Video equipment (internet)
- *Tweeting with GOD* book & app
- *Online with Saints* app

Sample Meeting 6.2: How should I treat myself?

Here we give you an example of how to talk about the Christian way of seeing and treating your own body. This theme is important for every age in a different way. What follows is just a proposal, which you can adapt in accordance with the needs of your group. The procedure for the meeting can correspond to that of other meetings.

The meeting

- *Introduction.* The Bible invites us to see our own body as a "temple" that is not ours (1 Cor 3:16-17; 6:19-20). Our body is sanctified by the presence of God himself in his creation. On the one hand we are therefore called to take care of our body and not to neglect it. On the other hand, vanity and glorification of our bodies is to be avoided (Rom 12:1 2). We are called to make conscious choices about the correct way to treat our bodies (see #TwGOD 4.31).

- *Round Table 1.* If our body does not belong to us – we have it on loan from God – we have a special duty to take care of it. In terms of daily choices that means among other things: having a healthy lifestyle, playing sports, getting enough sleep, protecting our body from cold or heat, seeking medical treatment if necessary ... (see #TwGOD 4.39). It is also important to realize the negative effect of certain behaviors: taking drugs, smoking, drinking too much alcohol, self-harm or an excess of tattoos and piercings, for example (see #TwGOD 4.31 & 4.46).

- *Round Table 2.* We sometimes hear that it is right and natural to "take care of oneself" through masturbation or occasional sexual relations. But if we look at our body in the light of God, we will see that "taking care of oneself" does not automatically mean sexual activities (see #TwGOD 4.21 & 4.22). The Catholic view of sexuality is very positive and profound; it is based on the total and irrevocable gift of self to another in marriage, which is expressed particularly in the sexual relationship (see #TwGOD 4.19 & 4.20). This gift is always open to life, to children, while also taking a responsible stance (see Meeting 13D).

- *Round Table 3.* In the various stages of life, our awareness of our body develops: teenagers can focus on their physical appearance, in the summer of life people may forget their limits and end up with burnout, while elderly people perceive their physical ailments and limitations. In all these cases, we must learn to accept our body as it is and, if necessary, to reconcile ourselves with it (see #TwGOD 4.31, 4.35 & 4.40). Each of us experiences different physical limits: avoid stopping at what you do not have in order to let grow what you have received from God!

My own body

Objective of this meeting:
See your body as God's precious gift to protect and treat well in accordance with God's view of life.

Related Questions:
4.20, 4.21, 4.22, 4.23, 4.31, 4.32, 4.33, 4.34, 4.35, 4.40, 4.46

Prayer

Psalm 139 (138) may be useful to give thanks for our body created by God and for the fact that he knows us in the very depths of our being. Read a verse from the Psalm and give the participants time to contemplate on the essential message. You may conclude with a text from Saint Paul, who invites us to offer our bodies as a living sacrifice to God as a true and proper worship (ROM 12:1-2).

Suggestions

- You might be tempted to list the dos and don'ts of the Commandments (SEE #TWGOD 4.7, 4.8 & 4.9), but the purpose of this meeting is rather to discover the beauty of the body that God gives us and, from there, to make good conscious decisions on the way to treat it. Leave the participants free to discover the real value of the Christian vision at their own time and manner.
- Today's hero could be, for example, Saint Francis of Assisi who called his body "Brother Ass," Saint Augustine, who learned how to live with his sexual desires, or Mother Teresa who treated the bodies of the dying.
- Be aware that it is always possible that there is someone who practices self-injury or has a very negative view of their body. Therefore, pay special attention to keep the dialogue in a positive light and in gratitude towards God.

TO PREPARE
- Bibles
- Video equipment (internet)
- *Tweeting with GOD* book & app
- *Online with Saints* app

Sample Meeting 6.3: How can I speak of my faith to others? How to evangelize?

Below we give you an example of how to reply when faced with (critical) questions about the faith. Every Christian is invited to share the good news of God's love for them with everyone who wishes to listen. We will look at some concrete ways to do this. The procedure for the meeting can correspond to that of other meetings.

The meeting

- *Introduction.* Jesus appeared to the Apostles and said: "Go into all the world and proclaim the Gospel to the whole creation" (Mk 16:15). Speaking about the faith is a task for every Christian. We are all expected to be ready to give witness of our faith whenever we are asked to account for our hope! (1 Pet 3:15). You may wish to let yourself be inspired by some of the tips for sharing your testimony (see Appendix 2).
- *Round Table 1.* The foundation of all evangelization is your personal relationship with the Lord. You cannot share with others what you do not have, so your first task is to grow in faith. It all starts with your personal life with God: praying, working, learning, and helping. How can you grow in faith? What is needed for this? Your faith is the basis for helping others to grow in faith. Note that evangelization does not mean that we all should start preaching on the market place. Often, a quiet testimony of life can be a much more effective way to show how you are living for and with Jesus in great joy – accepting that not everything in life is easy, even with God at your side.
- *Round Table 2.* Every missionary may ask the question: What if I doubt? Also Abraham (Gen 17:17) and Thomas the Apostle (Jn 20:25) doubted, for example. So, do not be afraid to ask questions, and continue to search for answers. Your questions show your desire to know God! When Saint Peter doubted, Jesus told him: "You of little faith, why did you doubt?" (Mt 14:31). Your doubts can help you relate better to the people you are speaking to, and reveal that you are human after all. Be careful, however, not to confuse them by expounding too much about your doubts. Rather, share the good news of the love of God for them, with a focus on the presence of God in their livesz- right now.
- *Round Table 3.* A few key elements are important whenever you want to speak about the faith. First of all, be yourself: an authentic witness can have a great impact, but when an imposter is exposed, what they said and did is mostly lost. Secondly, start with listening to the persons you wish to talk to: this is about *their* lives, and you wish to help them grow in *their* relationship with God. Thirdly, start where they are at: too often we start preaching without considering the current situation of the people before us,

Evangelization

Objective of this meeting:
Recognizing that every Christian is called to share the good news of God's love with others, and gaining confidence in doing so.

Related Questions:
1.26, 2.18, 3.37, 3.50, 4.45, 4.47, 4.49, 4.50

their needs, their concerns, their questions. Fourthly, recognize that only God can change hearts, and that the decision to accept his love pertains to the other, not to you. Finally, do not be afraid, you are not alone. Jesus promised that especially at the most difficult moment, when you are called to defend yourselves, the Holy Spirit will help (Lk 12:11-12).

Prayer
You could start with a prayer to the Holy Spirit (SEE MEETING 13B). Jesus said: "You will receive power when the Holy Spirit has come upon you, and you will be my witnesses" (ACTS 1:8). And then read a text about the commissioning of the Apostles (MT 10:7-14). You could conclude with Jesus' admonition not to place our light under a bushel, but to let it shine (MT 5:14-16).

Suggestions
- People will especially ask the question: "What's in it for me?" Be ready to share why your faith is useful and important for you personally: what does it bring you?
- Try to avoid too much focus on the Commandments in the beginning: a relationship does not start with rules, but with love! Once someone has entered into a relationship, they will automatically start wondering: How can I please the other best? That's when the Commandments come into play.
- The sacraments are a great help to you, also when you want to speak about the faith, in particular the Sacraments of Confirmation, Eucharist, and Reconciliation (SEE MEETING 13B, 13C & 13F).
- Today's hero can be Saint Peter or Saint Joselito Sanchez, the young boy who stood up for his faith against government troops and was forced to choose between denying Jesus or suffering a terrible death. He chose the latter, without thinking, and is therefore a strong witness (martyr) of the faith.

TO PREPARE
- Bibles
- Video equipment (internet)
- *Tweeting with GOD* book & app
- *Online with Saints* app

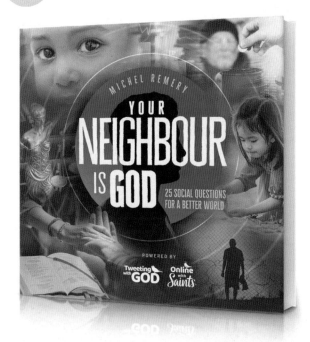

YOUR NEIGHBOUR IS GOD

25 social questions for a better world

"Love your neighbour as yourself", Jesus said (*Mt 22:39*). When you try to put these powerful words into practice you will face many different questions. Should I give money to a beggar? What if I cannot afford an eco-friendly lifestyle? What does the Bible say about discrimination? Can I contribute to world peace? Do I have a right to work? Can the state punish people? Should I pay taxes and vote? Is artificial intelligence okay?

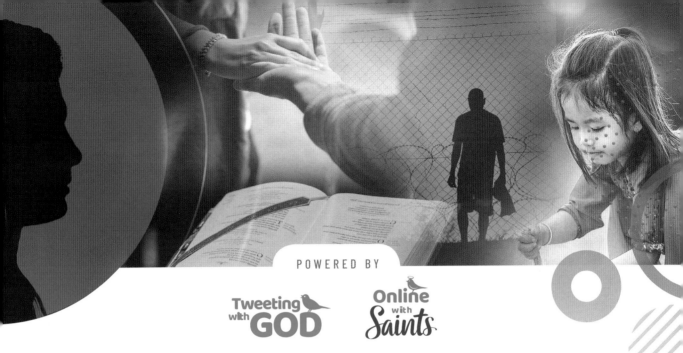

Tweeting with GOD

Online with Saints

The unique book *Your neighbour is GOD* answers many concrete questions on the basis of the social teaching of the Church. There is no need to start on page 1: you can go directly to the question that interests you most. The answer provokes you in an interactive way to continue thinking about the theme you are reading. Apps using augmented reality turn the contents of this book into a multimedia experience. The book can be read by individuals, or used in a group discussion.

www.yourneighbourisgod.com

"To find a comprehensive answer we need to look at Jesus and see how he deals with people and situations. He does so always with love, always with care, and always with justice. He invites you to do the same.

Father Michel Remery - Author

 # Follow us: #OnlineSaints

 /OnlinewithSaints

 Online With Saints

The author expresses his thanks to

H. Warmerhoven, Youth Ministers Coordinator for the Archdiocese of Canberra and Goulburn, and J. Doolan, Theology Writer for Religious Education Texts for the Archdiocese of Melbourne, Australia. Similarly to U. Franzen, P. de Rond, and C. Medrano Dozzetti of the departments for youth pastoral care and catechesis of the Archdiocese of Luxembourg, to the professionals working in these fields in Luxembourg who contributed with their feedback, as well as to Sister My-Lan Nguyen from school pastoral care in Switzerland. Also thanks to S. Alexander-Barnes (UK), A. & A. Andrew (Malaysia), L. & L. Amaro (USA), W. de Brie (Netherlands), J. Bullat (Sweden), B. Carpenter (USA), R. Cocuţ (Romania), J. Klimurczyk (Poland), M. Król (Poland), K. Leiva Avila (Canada), L. Miranda (Brazil), L. Schäfer (Switzerland), B. Schoo (Netherlands), M. Svobodová (Czech Republic), R. Tolmik (Estonia).

Credits for photos

All photo credits to Shutterstock.com, except the following: P. Brijeja: GS1, GS3, GS6, GS7, GS10, GS11; P. van Mulken: GS9; Archdiocese of Sydney / G. Portelly Photography 2019: GS2; Museum Catharijneconvent Utrecht / R. de Heer: Meeting 17; J. Peters: GS4, GS5; Saigon Youth: GS8. Cover photos: Adobestock, cathopic.com, unsplash.com, I. Spruit.

www.tweetingwithgod.com

www.onlinewithsaints.com